WHO LIES WHERE
A Guide to Famous Graves

Michael Kerrigan is a freelance writer and editor. He is the author of *Bluff Your Way in Literature* (1987) and has also contributed articles and reviews to the *Independent, Times Literary Supplement, Scotsman* and *Scotland on Sunday*. He lives in Edinburgh.

WHO LIES WHERE

A Guide to Famous Graves

Michael Kerrigan

FOURTH ESTATE • *London*

This paperback edition published in 1998

First published in Great Britain in 1995 by
Fourth Estate Limited
6 Salem Road
London W2 4BU

10 9 8 7 6 5 4 3 2 1

A catalogue record for this book is available
from the British Library.

ISBN 1–85702–258–0

Typeset by Type Technique, London W1
Printed in Great Britain by
Cox & Wyman Ltd, Reading, Berkshire

CONTENTS

ACKNOWLEDGEMENTS

Gerald Knight of the *Guardian* had the first, macabre vision for this book, while Clive Priddle of Fourth Estate Funeral Directors ('Service with Caring') proved a model undertaker, presiding over the interment of a good idea with sympathy, tact and decorous efficiency. Mari Roberts laid out the corpse with admirable sensitivity and skill. A lengthy cortège of librarians and scholars, clerics and church officials, janitors, council workers and passers-by turned out with tributes of help and advice. Though far too numerous to be acknowledged individually, the generosity of these well-wishers gave considerable comfort at a difficult time.

For the most part I have dug my own grave here, and any errors of fact and taste are entirely my own. Having said which, I do want to thank all the many friends and relations who at one point or another rolled up their sleeves and took their turns with the spade. Especial thanks are due to the many alert readers who have written to point out, gently yet firmly, gaps, errors or other shortcomings in the first, hardback edition of this guide. It has not been possible to incorporate all their suggestions, but the guide is certainly the better for their kind attentions.

INTRODUCTION

Just what is it about the British and their graveyards? It goes beyond our taste for comic epitaphs – every culture has to joke about something as fearful as death – or for the high camp of Victorian monumental sculptuary. There's more to it, too, than the serious insights graveyards can offer into our social history, real as they undoubtedly are. Many cultures prefer to banish death, to keep it at arm's length, and in continental countries cemeteries are often placed well outside towns and villages, screened off from the view of the living by high walls. Churchyards and cemeteries are a part of our everyday life, however, and an essential feature of the British scene. The clichéd English idyll with its village green, slap of leather on willow and pub selling warm beer would be incomplete without its little church, and the lychgate and rambling wall enclosing the verdant sward where the rude forefathers of the hamlet sleep out the centuries. The sward may be less verdant (and the sound of cricket absent) in the farther-flung Celtic fringes, the kirks and chapels dourer and more windswept, but the same broad stereotype holds. Inscriptions can thunder out the dread solemnity of the grave and grinning death's heads deride our fragile mortality, but nothing, it seems, can shake our feeling that, far from being unsettling or alarming, graveyards are essentially agreeable, even welcoming places. The country churchyard has its place in the British consciousness not so much because it tells us that we all must come to dust but because, with all its ivy-grown tombs, its headstones leaning at crazy angles and its mysterious mossy hummocks, it affirms the presence of the past and the continuance of life through untold generations. Though of far more recent provenance, the big urban cemetery provides something of the same reassurance, along with a haven of peace and quiet amid the city's noise. The peace may be merely geographical in origin – we are after all removed from the traffic, and screened from its noise by buildings and walls. To the stroller, however, it feels like more than that; it feels like the companionable quiet of the dead.

Nobody ever seriously believed that death was 'the mighty leveller'. A glance around any graveyard, with its wide range of monuments and headstones, is enough to confirm that differences of rank and class, at any rate, certainly endure beyond the end of life, while a closer study reveals more interesting differences behind the appearance of uniformity which the conventional pieties of the inscriptions and the period styles of the monuments seem at first to confer. All human life is here, albeit set in stone, and one of the bittersweet pleasures of the search for the graves of the famous is the opportunity it provides to consider the obscurer destinies of those who have come to surround them in death: the pious local benefactor or the idle, tyrannical squire; the incorrigible ne'er-do-well who let everyone down or the scholarship boy who did the place proud; the quixotic entrepreneur or the stolid businessman; the village girl who made a smart match and rode around in a carriage or the woman who bore eleven children then died giving birth to the twelfth; the inventor of a long-forgotten system of bookkeeping or the stoker who went down with the *Lusitania* and has his humble memorial ashore. There are a million stories in the naked cemetery.

The graves of the famous are themselves interesting too: their monuments and inscriptions frequently offer hints to the personalities of the personages lying beneath, and the significance their lives had for those around them. Often, too, a visit to the person's grave is a visit to their world. Interred beside his first wife in the churchyard at Stinsford, Dorset, Thomas Hardy's heart is thus buried in the heart of Thomas Hardy Country. Stand by his riverside grave at Llanystumdwy, Gwynedd, and you're at a spot Lloyd George must have passed daily in boyhood, long before anyone ever dreamed he would one day be a great prime minister. Sometimes, on the other hand, the reverse is true, and it's the incongruity of the resting place which is of interest. What is Russian statesman Alexander Kerensky doing in Putney, of all places? (Compiling a list of gramophone choices for neighbour-in-death Roy Plomley, perhaps, or discussing Eisenstein movies with Joseph Losey?) And how on earth did the French mystic Simone Weil end up in Ashford, Kent? It seems unlikely that the poet Gerard Manley Hopkins would have been seen dead (as it were) in Dublin's Glasnevin Cemetery had the Society of Jesus left him any choice in the matter, while the thinking behind composer Frederick Delius's interment at Limpsfield, Surrey, was so tortuous and improbable it amounts to a story in itself.

It's impossible, then, to make any grand overarching claims for the importance of grave studies, or indeed for the present guide. Without even the merit of describing (except, for it is nothing if not inconsistent, very occasionally in passing) the rich architectural heritage of our churchyards and cemeteries, the design and iconography of our tombstones and all the no doubt very interesting masons' marks, mantlings, lesenes and other features that await the dedicated funerary scholar, this book contents itself with the altogether less demanding project of gawping at the graves of (more or less) famous people. Why gawp at the graves of famous people? Well, why not? Such graves permit a thousand reflections – as sombre or as frivolous as you like – on the lives of the famous, on the nature of their fame and on the mortality that would eventually claim them. More than that, though, they offer a way into the wonderful world of the dead. Graveyards are far too interesting to be left to the figurework-fancier and the spandrel-spotter; too hauntingly atmospheric, too full of variety, character, quirkiness, humour and pathos – too full, in short, of life.

A short history of the grave

The history of the grave is shorter than you might think. Human societies have had to dispose of their dead for as long as there have been human societies, but the grave as we know it – with inscribed commemorative slab or headstone, epitaph, etc – is a comparatively modern invention. Before around 1400 the resting places of even quite substantial citizens routinely went unmarked. Whatever their vanity in life, it doesn't seem to have occurred to them to exercise that vanity in the matter of their burial. Those lavish tombs that were constructed clearly served not individuals but institutions – whether those prestigious royal and noble families for whom dynastic continuity was all, or the Church, for which saintly shrines like that of St Thomas at Canterbury or St William at Rochester helped mark out the apostolic tradition that was its central justification.

Even in the fifteenth century, graves were the exception rather than the rule, and few have survived down into the present. In many parts of the country the mood of Cultural Revolution which took hold at the time of the Reformation saw the wholesale smashing of gravestones as idolatrous 'graven images', and those graves were thus lost. Others were simply displaced by later burials. Churchyards couldn't be extended indefinitely, and were usually pretty compact. As one generation followed another into the hallowed ground, God's Acre had no way to go but up, hence the swelling earth of churchyards like the one at Ware, Hertfordshire, for instance, built up by centuries of burial, or those the seventeenth-century diarist John Evelyn noticed on a visit to Norwich:

> most of the Church-yards (though some of them large enough) were filled up with earth, or rather the congestion of dead bodys one upon another, for want of Earth etc to the very top of the Walls, and many above the walls, so as the Churches seem'd to be built in pitts.

The ground in churchyards like this may have been holy, but it was also so much dug over that those buried there could have little confidence that they would be allowed to rest in peace. Increasingly, therefore, those who wanted a more exclusive, permanent place away from the common decay of the churchyard began to express the wish to be buried inside, beneath the church floor. Major dignitaries – monarchs and senior churchmen – had always been buried in this way. By the seventeenth century, however, any Tom, Dick or Harry who could afford the fee was having himself placed inside the church. There was opposition to the practice from those who felt that it smacked of vanity and carried worldly class distinctions over into eternity, but by the time Evelyn's father-in-law Sir Richard Browne was buried at Deptford, it seemed worthy of note that:

> By an especial Clause in his last Will, he ordered to be buried in the Church-Yard under the South-East Window of the Chancel . . . being much offended at the novel

*Custome of burying every body within the body of the
Church and Chancel, as a favour hertofore granted onely
to Martyrs, and greate Princes, this excesse of making
Churches Charnel-houses being of ill and irreverent
example, and prejudicial to the health of the living: besides
the continual disturbance of the Pavement, and seates, the
ground sinking as the Carcases consume, and severall other
undecencies.*

With the practice so widespread, the pressure on space
was growing within the churches too. Diarist Samuel Pepys
was shocked when he went to organize the burial of his late
brother in 1664:

*To church, and with the gravemaker chose a place for my
brother to lie in, just under my mother's pew. But to see
how a man's tombs are at the mercy of such a fellow, that
for sixpence he would (as his own words were), 'I will
jostle them together but I will make room for him:'
speaking of the fullness of the middle aisle, where he was
to lie.*

Church burial was thus losing all its old exclusivity, but
that was not all. 'It is a very serious matter,' said the physician
Sir John Simon in 1842, 'that beneath the feet of those who
attend the services of their church, there often lies an almost
solid pile of decomposing human remains heaped as high as
the vaulting will permit, and generally but very partially
confined.' This was damning condemnation for an age
which considered the exhalations of dead bodies to be
not merely unhealthy but downright poisonous. The
Parliamentary Committee before which Simon was
testifying had been formed to address what had by now

become a burial crisis. If the churches were crowded, the situation in the churchyards outside had gone completely mad, especially in the cities. The coffins of the poor were lowered together into vast pits to save space – seventeen or eighteen would be buried together, without intervening earth – while many bodies were passed on to anatomists by unscrupulous clergy and parish officials, their coffins being chopped up and sold for firewood. Yet despite such measures, churches and churchyards alike were full to bursting. The burial ground of St Martin-in-the-Fields, in London, covered only some 200 square feet, but it was estimated to contain sixty to seventy thousand bodies, while up the road in Islington, Bunhill Fields was packing them in at 2,323 to the acre.

Hence the rise of the cemetery. The cemetery business – and it was from the first a business run along strictly commercial lines – gained considerable impetus when the Parliamentary Committee of 1843 recommended cemeteries on health grounds (the author of the committee's report, Sir Edwin Chadwick, would ultimately put his body where his mouth was, being buried in the Old Cemetery at Mortlake, London). But entrepreneurs had already recognized the demand for a more spacious, socially exclusive burial ground where those with the means could spread themselves as regards their commemorative statuary and where their grieving families could be spared the embarrassment (or worse, in an age when cholera, typhus and other diseases were tearing through the slums) of brushing up against less respectable mourners. Where the rich led, the less affluent middle classes were soon following as best they could, and soon city churchyards were left to the poor. The clergy naturally condemned the cemeteries for their godlessness and commercialism. They did indeed make a point of being non-denominational, and this doesn't seem to have worried their prospective clients. The naked commercialism of the cemeteries may indeed have seemed a little disagreeable, yet the Victorian public could see that, beneath all the pomp and sanctimoniousness, the Church also regarded burial as a business. (The opening of London's Kensal Green Cemetery was estimated to have cost the parish of Paddington around £200 per year in lost burial fees.) The Victorian middle classes were accustomed to buying services and to paying to have things done just as they wanted: why not in death as well as in life? Better the kind of openly commercial relationship they had with the cemetery company than the deferential one they were supposed to have with the Church. The great Victorian cemeteries of our industrial cities – outstandingly, perhaps, the Glasgow Necropolis – are splendid sights. It's one of the ironies of our history that the merchants and industrialists who built their magnificent tombs and monuments (having first effectively built the cities round about) are now for the most part no longer remembered by name, forgotten by a snobbish posterity which, despite all the advantages of a decade of Thatcherism, still remembers a minor aristocratic versifier longer than it does a builder of business empires.

Cremation could of course offer the customer still more freedom and control, since you could have your ashes placed or scattered wherever you liked, provided that you could first overcome the (western) taboos of centuries. These would prove difficult to shift, however, for the mass of the people. Cremation-pioneer Dr Price (of whom more later) was by any standards a crank, and he rather set the tone. Despite the manifest problems caused by the burial system, the first crematorium, at Brookwood (see Woking, Surrey), would not be up and running until the 1880s, and for a long time after that cremation would be the preserve of the freethinker, the self-consciously 'modern' and the simply weird. Brookwood boasted among its early clients Friedrich Engels and theosophist queen Madame Blavatsky, for instance, while London's Golders Green had the honour of reducing to ashes the psychoanalyst Sigmund Freud and the sexologist Havelock Ellis. None of these luminaries, let's face it, was going to set the seal of respectability on cremation for the wider public. Even now the practice of burial has by no means been entirely displaced, especially among the elderly. And with a new sense of 'Green', Whole-Earth modernism taking hold among the young and educated, it could be that decay may soon be back in fashion, and a new lease of life be given to the grave.

1

England

Avon

BATH

THE ABBEY: Beneath an impressive memorial lies the great Falstaff JAMES QUIN (1693–1766). One of the stars of the eighteenth-century stage, until David Garrick came along to eclipse everybody Quin was the acknowledged master. It was to be Garrick who wrote his epitaph, gloomy lines on the passing of a clown:

> That tongue which set the table on a roar,
> And charm'd the public ear, is heard no more:
> Clos'd are those eyes, the harbingers of wit,
> Which spake before the tongue what Shakespeare writ:
> Cold is that hand, which living was stretch'd forth,
> At friendship's call, to succour modest worth:
> Here lies JAMES QUIN: deign, reader, to be taught,
> Whate'er thy strength of body, force of thought,
> In nature's happiest mould however cast
> To this complexion thou must come at last.

Also in the abbey is the king – arguably, indeed, the creator – of Regency Bath, RICHARD 'BEAU' NASH (1674–1762), a flamboyant figure, the son of a Welsh glassmaker, who arrived in the town in 1705 after unsuccessful stabs at being student, army officer and lawyer and finally found his vocation in presiding over the city's social life. Though himself a gambler and seducer, he took his duties as the city's official master of ceremonies with the utmost seriousness, clamping down on all forms of violence and vulgarity, protecting youthful innocence (when he wasn't corrupting it), and generally creating that supreme gentility of tone that made Georgian Bath the glamorous social capital of a glamorous age. He died in poverty, ruined by lawsuits and restrictive legislation on gambling, but his epitaph, written by Dr Harington of the Bath Hospital, recalls him as he was in his glory days:

> If social Virtues make rememb'rance dear,
> Or Manners pure on decent rule depend;
> To His remains consign one grateful Tear,
> Of Youth the Guardian, and of All the Friend...

Beau Nash should not be confused with George Bryan 'Beau' Brummell (1778–1840), whose reign came later, at the end of the eighteenth century, and whose centre of operations was London, where he was the friend of the Prince Regent and the undisputed ruler of the social scene. Like his predecessor, however, he ended up in poverty. He had to flee to Calais to escape his creditors in 1816; he later moved to Caen, where he died in the poor-house and received a pauper's burial.

In his 1798 'Essay on Population', the political economist and priest THOMAS MALTHUS (1766–1834) pointed out that, since population increased geometrically and subsistence only arithmetically, we were headed for trouble. Here it was that, having done his bit to prevent world overpopulation by passing away, Malthus was laid to rest.

LANSDOWN CRESCENT: To the north of the city, in Lansdown Crescent, lived WILLIAM BECKFORD (1759–1844). The author of the curious oriental-cum-gothic romance *Vathek* as well as some memorably idiosyncratic travel literature, Beckford is as famous for his eccentric lifestyle as for his writing. Having inherited the West Indian fortune of his father, a Lord Mayor of London, he was in a position to indulge the most extravagant fantasies to the full. Not content with building himself his own gothic abbey at Fonthill, he also got to work on the hill behind the Lansdown Crescent home where he lived with his dogs and his dwarf servant, erecting an imposing tower at the top. After he died, his daughter gave the hill to the city; it was consecrated as a cemetery, and Beckford's remains were removed from their original grave in Bath Abbey to a new position at the foot of the tower, where he's buried (along with his favourite dog) in a granite tomb inscribed:

Eternal Power,
Grant me through obvious clouds one transient gleam
Of thy bright essence in my dying hour.

The tower is now a Beckford museum.

Madame D'Arblay, better known as the novelist and diarist FANNY BURNEY (1752–1840), is buried in Walcot parish churchyard on Walcot Street with her husband, the *émigré* General Alexandre D'Arblay, and their son. The tombstone you can see now was only placed by the family's descendants in 1906, and was in any case moved in 1955, so it's impossible to pinpoint the grave exactly.

Just to the north of the town, at the church in Charlcombe, SARAH FIELDING (1710–68) lies buried. The younger sister of Henry (who's buried in Lisbon), Sarah Fielding wrote books for children and produced a distinguished translation of *Xenophon* as well as the novels which, though now much read only by scholars of women's writing, were in their day as highly regarded as those of her brother.

The churchyard at Widcombe, south of Bath, came close to making burial history as the last home for Romantic poet WALTER SAVAGE LANDOR (1775–1864) who liked to come here to brood. He wrote:

> Widcombe! few seek in thee their resting place,
> Yet I, when I have run my weary race,
> Will throw my bones upon thy churchyard turf.

In the event, whether because he'd changed his mind in the meantime or because he wasn't consulted about it when he finally breasted the tape, his bones were thrown on the turf of a Florence hilltop, and Widcombe had to continue in its funerary obscurity.

BRISTOL

ST MARY REDCLIFFE CHURCH: Admiral SIR WILLIAM PENN (1621–70) was buried here. A squadron commander in Cromwell's Navy, Penn served with distinction in the First Dutch War. He was for a time in the doghouse (for a few weeks, indeed, he was in the Tower) after he was sent in 1664–5 to conquer Hispaniola but had to make do with Jamaica. He came bouncing back after the Restoration to give sterling service in the Second Dutch War. It was a grant of North American land given him by Charles II that he would pass on to his son (see Jordans, Buckinghamshire) and that would become Pennsylvania.

The 'marvellous boy', poet THOMAS CHATTERTON (1752–70), was buried in a workhouse burial ground in London's Shoe Lane, Holborn (see St Andrew's, Holborn Circus, City of London) but St Mary Redcliffe was practically the family business for the lad, several generations of his ancestors having served as sextons, and its churchyard statuary had a profound influence on his young mind. He grew up among the parish records and was inspired by the tombs here in his creation of the imaginary poet, Thomas Rowley, and the imaginary fifteenth-century Bristol he wove around him. He produced for 'Rowley' a voluminous set of poetic works, written in an inexpertly pastiched, but none the less strongly expressive, pseudo-medieval language. Attempting a literary career *in propria persona*, Chatterton found the going tough, some moralists considering that his experiments with Rowley amounted to malicious, calculated forgery. So discouraged was he that he took arsenic and killed himself, at the age of only seventeen, thus making himself an important icon for the generation of Romantic poets who came after him. Today's more cynical readers often prefer the alternative theory, that he died after taking an accidental overdose of a quack remedy for venereal disease.

In the burial ground of St Peter's Church, now just a gutted shell in Castle Park, was interred RICHARD SAVAGE (c. 1696–1742), who if not English Literature's most distinguished figure was certainly one of its most colourful. Firmly convinced that he was the illegitimate son of Richard Savage, Earl Rivers, and the Countess of Macclesfield, when these personages refused to acknowledge his (entirely imaginary) claims, Savage railed against them bitterly, and extremely publicly. As if that hadn't got him into enough trouble, Savage proceeded to kill a man in a tavern brawl, after which he was very lucky indeed to escape the gallows. Rather surprisingly, perhaps, Savage made it into his late forties – though he did die in jail, in the nearby Newgate Prison where he'd been incarcerated for debt.

In Henbury parish churchyard is the novelist, traveller and Egyptologist AMELIA BLANDFORD EDWARDS (1831–92), her monument an obelisk in Egyptian style.

CLEVEDON

In the churchyard at St Andrew's Church, Clevedon, lies the man in whose memoriam *In Memoriam* was written. ARTHUR HENRY HALLAM (1811–33) of Clevedon Court had become Tennyson's friend at Cambridge but died a couple of years later. Though a scribbler of sorts himself, it would be his friend's great poem that would immortalize him.

WRINGTON

The moralist, educationalist, playwright and poet HANNAH MORE (1745–1833), who spent most of her last twenty years at nearby Barley Wood, is buried in the churchyard.

Bedfordshire

CARDINGTON

In a family vault in the church sleep various members of the Whitbread brewing family, including, notably, the founder's son, politician SAMUEL WHITBREAD (1758–1815), Whig reformer. By rights he shouldn't be here, having committed suicide. By tradition – and indeed by law – he should have been buried at a crossroads, with a stake through his heart.

SUICIDE

The macabre custom of burying a suicide at a crossroads with a stake through the heart dated from medieval times. Suicide then was held by the Church to represent the mortal sin of despairing in God's mercy and grace. It was the ultimate sin since it could not, by definition, be repented. By the early nineteenth century, however, suicides were being regarded with increasing sympathy and coroners and clergymen were finding ways round the traditional punishments, especially, of course, where those concerned were well-born and wealthy. High-profile deaths like Castlereagh's suicide in 1822 (see Westminster Abbey, London) opened the whole question of suicide and its penalties for public debate. Though notoriously moralistic, the Victorians were sentimentalists too. They were also self-consciously progressive, and the grotesque appurtenances of stake, mallet and crossroads really didn't tie in with their image of themselves as forward-looking moderns. As early as 1823, the highway rule was dropped, and although religious rites would strictly speaking be forbidden for suicides until the Burial Act of 1880, in practice the rules were being relaxed more and more. The move in mid-century towards municipal cemeteries made death a lot easier – not only did lay public officials look more kindly upon suicides than professional men of God, but given the size of the big urban cemeteries and the scores of burials taking place every week, it was easier for a suicide to be 'smuggled' in without attracting attention.

COCKAYNE HATLEY

Jingoistic journalist and poet W. E. HENLEY (1849–1903) was buried at the church here. A sort of poor man's Kipling, now that volumes like *The Song of the Sword* and *For England's Sake* are pretty much forgotten he is of interest chiefly because his daughter, Wendy, gave her name to the character in Barrie's *Peter Pan*.

SOUTHILL

In a family vault in the church lies Admiral JOHN BYNG (1704–57), shot on the quarterdeck of the *Monarque* in Portsmouth Harbour for 'cowardice in the face of the enemy'. Actually, all the evidence is that his conduct could at worst be described as indecision or hesitation in a minor altercation with a couple of formidably armed French warships in the Bay of Biscay. The decision to execute an otherwise admirable admiral, the scion of a distinguished naval family, tends to confirm Voltaire's contemptuous view that in England they like to shoot an admiral from time to time, 'to encourage the others'.

Berkshire

ALDWORTH

In the churchyard is LAURENCE BINYON (1869–1943), who did much to interpret Far Eastern art for the West, and produced a distinguished translation of Dante, but who lives on in the popular imagination in his lines 'For the Fallen', which appear on war memorials throughout Britain:

> They shall grow not old, as we that are left grow old:
> Age shall not weary them, nor the years condemn.
> At the going down of the sun and in the morning
> We will remember them.

BISHAM

The church here boasts some splendid Elizabethan tombs for various members of the local Hoby family, including SIR THOMAS HOBY (1530–66), famous for translating Castiglione's classic *Book of the Courtier*; he picked up sufficient skills in the process to get himself appointed Elizabeth's ambassador to France, where he died. The sometime family home at nearby Bisham Abbey (now owned by the Sports Council) is said to be haunted by a Lady Hoby who went away on business forgetting that she'd left her son locked in a cupboard in punishment for making a mess of his schoolwork. He starved to death, but it's not reported where he was buried.

COOKHAM

Cookham church provided the last resting place for the artist and illustrator FRED WALKER (1840–75), but the town was really put on the gothic map by another painter SIR STANLEY SPENCER (1891–1959), who was born in the town and lived and worked here until his death, after which he was buried in the churchyard – the same churchyard in which, in his scandalous 1930s painting *Resurrection*, the town's dead can be seen rising from their graves. Spencer's first wife HILDA CARLINE (1889–1950), another artist, lived with him here, but she was mentally unstable and the marriage eventually foundered. She gets a mention on his tombstone but is actually buried in the town cemetery.

ETON

The Scottish novelist, historian and essayist MRS MARGARET OLIPHANT (1828–97) was buried here, in the town cemetery. The two sons she'd worked so hard to put through the nearby school with her writing ended up dying before she did, and she was buried here with them.

HURLEY

In the churchyard here is actress DAME IRENE VANBRUGH (christened, less elegantly, Irene Barnes, 1872–1949), who was a star of the London stage in the early years of the present century but who managed to make the transition to screen and so go on enthralling audiences well into the film era.

MEDMENHAM, NEAR HENLEY-ON-THAMES

In the churchyard lies SIR BASIL LIDDELL HART (1895–1970), the military historian and strategist. He was radical in his advocacy of mechanization and air power to gain advantage through surprise and mobility. Though an official adviser to the British government during the 1930s, he had more influence, ironically, upon the Germans and their policy of *Blitzkrieg*.

NEWBURY

Wash Common, on the Andover Road, was the scene in 1643 of a pyrrhic victory for a Royalist army commanded by

Charles I himself. The King succeeded in repelling a force of Parliamentarians led by Lord Essex, but Cavalier casualties were so high that they had to retire, and Essex was left with a clear run to London. You can still see the mounds where the dead were buried. A return fixture was fought a year later, over possession of the bridge at Donnington.

READING

Among the ruins of the Royal Abbey he founded here in 1121 is the grave of HENRY I (1068–1135, reigned 1100–35) with his queen Matilda. William, son of Henry II, is also here.

SLOUGH

St Lawrence's Church, Upton, whose graveyard is a rival claimant to Stoke Poges as setting and inspiration for Gray's *Elegy*, has a rather firmer title to fame as the burial place of the German-born royal astronomer SIR WILLIAM HERSCHEL (1738–1822). A stone tablet under the tower marks the spot. It's inscribed *Coelorum percipit claustra* (He broke through the barriers of the heavens). Since he was the founder of stellar astronomy and the discoverer, in 1781, of the planet Uranus, this is no empty vaunt. Herschel's son, John Frederick William, succeeded him in profession and post, and is buried in Westminster Abbey.

SUNNINGDALE

Now resting for the duration, the actress DIANA DORS (1931–84) is in the Sunningdale town cemetery, beside her husband ALAN LAKE (1940–84).

SWALLOWFIELD

The poet and novelist MARY RUSSELL MITFORD (1787–1855), who spent her last years in the village, is buried in the churchyard here. Her wry, humorous and frankly rather twee *Our Village: Sketches of Rural Life, Character and Scenery* (1824–32) was much mocked by sophisticates, but loved by the general readers of its time and – for all the sneers – much imitated.

WINDSOR CASTLE

The first of a series of royal inmates, the Holy King HENRY VI (1421–71) ended up here in St George's Chapel. Henry's father had died a year after his birth and he'd reigned from the time he reached his legal majority in 1442 (at least he'd attempted to: his unruly nobles had other ideas, and eventually murdered him in the Tower). Miracles worked at his Chertsey Abbey shrine were bringing pilgrims flocking in, and in 1484 Richard III had the tomb brought here so he could have a share in the profits. The shrine disappeared during the Reformation, but its site is now marked by a slab. Altogether less pious was 'Defender of the Faith' HENRY VIII (1491–1547, reigned 1509–47), buried here in a vault under the floor with JANE SEYMOUR (c. 1509–37), his third and favourite queen, who died of

puerperal fever after giving birth to Henry's long-awaited son Edward. Thomas Wolsey having died in disgrace in Leicester, Henry had planned to hijack the grand mausoleum Wolsey had had commissioned from Italian craftsmen, but in the event the monument went uncompleted, so Henry didn't get it either. The tomb went begging for over two centuries before being adapted for Nelson's burial in St Paul's. CHARLES I (1600–49), who was to have been buried in Westminster Abbey, in the Henry VII Chapel, but was rather spitefully refused a place there by his Roundhead executioners, was brought here after his execution and placed, given the haste and improvisatory nature of his obsequies, in the same vault with Henry and Jane. It was all an emotive affair, of course, and some diehard conspiracy theorists disputed that Charles was here at all: according to John Aubrey,

> I well remember it was frequently and soberly affirmed by officers of the army, &c. Grandees, that the body of King Charles the First was privately putt into the Sand about White-hall; and the coffin that was carried to Windsor and layd in King Henry 8th's vault was filled with rubbish, or brick-batts. Mr Fabian Philips, who adventured his life before the King's Tryall, by printing, assures me, that the Kings Coffin did cost but six shillings: a plaine deale coffin.

Despite its Victorian name, the Albert Memorial Chapel is ancient in origin. It was rebuilt by Henry VII but not completed till the time of Wolsey. Victoria had it fitted out as a memorial to her husband Albert after his death in 1861. It contains the tombs of the DUKE OF CLARENCE (d. 1892), elder son of Edward VII, and the DUKE OF ALBANY

(d. 1884), Victoria's youngest son. Beneath the chapel are
GEORGE III (1738–1820, reigned 1760–1820), the King who
lost the American colonies and went mad, together with his
queen, CHARLOTTE, and six of their sons, including GEORGE
IV (1762–1830, reigned 1820–30). One lady who went to see
his lying in state, Mrs Arbuthnot, was much impressed by the
size and splendour of his coffin, but reported that:

> They were very near having a frightful accident for, when
> the body was in the leaden coffin, the lead was observed to
> have bulged considerably & in fact was in great danger of
> bursting. They were obliged to puncture the lead to let out
> the air & then to fresh cover it with lead. Rather an
> unpleasant operation, I should think, but the embalming
> must have been very ill done.

George's younger brother and successor WILLIAM IV
(1765–1837, reigned 1830–7) is also here. On the south side of
the chapel's high altar lies EDWARD VII (1841–1910, reigned
1901–10), while GEORGE V (1865–1936, reigned 1910–36) has
a grand Lutyens tomb on the north side of the nave.

Frogmore Mausoleum, at Frogmore, in the Home Park,
houses the mortal remains of VICTORIA (1819–1901) and
ALBERT (1819–61) themselves, as well as the man who would
have been Hitler's King, EDWARD VIII (1894–1972), who
reigned briefly during 1936 then had to abdicate over his
marriage to American divorcée MRS WALLIS SIMPSON
(1896–1986). She was later interred here beside her husband.

YATTENDON

ROBERT BRIDGES (1844–1930), poet laureate, was buried in
the churchyard here. Bridges' own verse seems pallidly

academic now, and he has his little place in literary history largely on account of the friendship and encouragement he gave to Gerard Manley Hopkins, whose verse he seems not to have understood but which he determinedly promoted over many years until, in 1918, thirty years after Hopkins' death, he succeeded in getting a selection published. The composer SIR LENNOX BERKELEY (1903–89) is also here.

Buckinghamshire

AMERSHAM

After lying some fifteen years in a yard at London's Holloway Prison, the remains of RUTH ELLIS (1926–55) were brought to Amersham for reburial at St Mary's Church. Convicted of murdering her lover, David Blakely (see the film *Dance With a Stranger* for details), Ellis became the last woman to be hanged in Britain.

BEACONSFIELD

In the churchyard is the poet EDMUND 'Goe, Lovely Rose' WALLER (1606–87), a staunch royalist who befriended Cromwell during the Protectorate and then, with the Restoration, made himself a royalist again. Waller seems to have had more talent than integrity, though from what Aubrey says his spelling was as shaky as his loyalty, and he wrote 'a lamentably poor hand, as bad as the scratching of a hen'. Another Edmund, conservative thinker EDMUND BURKE (1729–97) is also buried here. In 1750 he had remarked in a letter to Matthew Smith: 'I would rather sleep in the southern corner of a little country church-yard, than in the tomb of the Capulets. I should like, however, that my dust should mingle with kindred dust.' In the event he got the first but not the second. His kindred dust lay in Ireland, where Burke himself was born and brought up. He had bought his Beaconsfield estate in 1768, before the stock-market disaster which would see him strapped for the rest of his life. The Catholic cemetery in Candlemas Lane is the last resting place of G.K. CHESTERTON (1874–1936), creator of the clerical detective Father Brown (and of radical-conservative journalism by the ton).

CLIVEDEN, NEAR COOKHAM

In the eighteenth-century Octagon Temple in the grounds of Cliveden, the ashes of NANCY ASTOR (1879–1964) are buried with those of her husband. Nancy was the first woman to take a seat in the House of Commons, serving as member for Plymouth from 1919 to 1945; but her political influence, as hostess to the 'Cliveden Set', was far greater than the average MP's, and rather unfortunate, given her advocacy during the 1930s of the policy of appeasement towards Hitler, who was then arming Germany for war. Though a British citizen on account of her marriage, she never forgot her American, Southern background, and she had herself buried with a Confederate Flag she'd been given in Danville, Georgia, in 1922.

GERRARDS CROSS

In the churchyard extension, behind the parish church, lies the actress DAME MARGARET RUTHERFORD (1892–1972). Her tombstone bears the words 'A Blithe Spirit' in reference to Noël Coward's play of that name, in which she'd first made her mark. Coward himself (1899–1973) is buried in Jamaica, where he lived during his last years.

GREAT HAMPDEN

The rebellious JOHN HAMPDEN (1594–1643) is in the churchyard here. His defiant opposition to the ship tax of Charles I helped galvanize a more general resistance to that monarch's absolutism. When civil war resulted, Hampden fought for the parliamentarians; he died at Thame from wounds sustained at the Battle of Chalgrove Field.

GREAT MISSENDEN

Unrivalled master of the grotesque and ghoulish in modern children's fiction, the author ROALD DAHL (1916–90) is buried in St Peter and Paul's churchyard.

HUGHENDEN, NEAR HIGH WYCOMBE

Just down the hill from his Hughenden Manor home, in the graveyard of St Michael's Church, is BENJAMIN DISRAELI, Earl of Beaconsfield (1804–81). One of British political history's more dashing figures, an upstart from a family of converted Jews, Disraeli led the Young England movement of conservatives against laissez-faire economics, and ultimately became prime minister. He was also a novelist of note, and it was his 1845 social novel *Sybil*, with its suggestion that Britain had disintegrated into 'two nations, the rich and the poor', which gave rise to the notion of 'One Nation Toryism' that still inspires left-wingers in the Conservative Party. There's a memorial tablet in the church, placed there by Disraeli's 'grateful and affectionate sovereign and friend, Victoria R.I.' It was Dizzie's own choice, apparently, that he should be buried here rather than in Westminster Abbey, though some suggested there was something distinctly ostentatious about this excess of modesty, especially since the funeral seems to have taken place anything but quietly, with hordes of princes, ambassadors and aristocrats descending on the village and cascades of flowers and wreaths. And then, says the Portuguese novelist Eça de Queiroz, on diplomatic service in England at the time and looking on with cynical bemusement:

> the following day, in all the cathedrals throughout
> England, in every rustic chapel, the clergy extolled Lord
> Beaconsfield from the pulpit; in the universities and
> institutes and academies the professors commemorated that
> splendid career; on the platform at public meetings, at
> business conferences, wherever men were assembled together,
> voices were raised to honour his services and his brilliance
> ... And so Lord Beaconsfield disappeared – as had been
> his desire all his lifetime – amid a murmur of apotheosis.

JORDANS, NEAR CHALFONT ST GILES

A purpose-built Quaker village, Jordans was founded in the late seventeenth century when the Society of Friends bought a quarter-acre plot from a local farmer for £4. It became the site for the oldest (1688) Friends' Meeting House and burial ground, where WILLIAM PENN (1644–1718) and various family members and followers are to be found. Expelled from Oxford and twice imprisoned for preaching the doctrines of the Society, Penn was given what was to become Pennsylvania by his father, an admiral and general pillar of the Restoration establishment (see Bristol), who had in turn been given the territory by Charles II in payment of a debt. In 1682 William set out to establish his community in the New World, though his utopian dreams ended in tears and he ended up ruined by the dishonesty of one of his agents. Jordans is still run by the Quakers, for whom it is a place of pilgrimage.

LITTLE MARLOW

In the churchyard here the writer EDGAR WALLACE (1875–1932), who lived nearby at Bourne End, lies buried. He was brought to this improbably quiet, bucolic English setting after his death in Hollywood, where he had been spending money hand over fist and, in between, working on the script for *King Kong*. He'd lived fast but written even faster – producing 170 novels, fifteen plays and countless magazine articles – and though he left enormous debts on his death, within a couple of years royalties had paid them all off.

MARLOW

The Caribbean-born fairground freak, the 'Spotted Boy', was buried here after his death in 1811. William Richardson, the man who exhibited him, was later buried alongside him, at his own request.

OLNEY

In St Peter and St Paul's Church is the tomb of JOHN NEWTON (1725–1807), the reformed slave-trader turned cleric who, as curate here, got to know the troubled poet William Cowper, saw him through a bout of mental illness, and collaborated with him on the *Olney Hymns*. Newton himself was author of, among other classics, 'Amazing Grace', while the anti-slavery sermons he gave in the City of London, where he went to serve as a priest in 1779, inspired Wilberforce in his campaign to outlaw slavery.

PENN

Having been born in Australia, married in Germany to a Pomeranian *Junker*, spent much of her later life in France and died in Charleston, South Carolina, it was fitting that the novelist ELIZABETH VON ARNIM (1866–1941) should have made one last voyage in death to be buried in the churchyard here. A similar, albeit more furtive, journey was made by DONALD MACLEAN (1913–83), one of the Cambridge ring of traitors, who learned of his eventual exposure in time to escape to the Soviet Union. While the ashes of his friend Guy Burgess remained in Moscow after his 1963 death, Maclean's were brought back to England and buried here by torchlight in his parents' grave. In the graveyard extension lies a somewhat less sinister figure: ALISON UTTLEY (1884–1976), creator of the *Little Grey Rabbit*, her headstone marked 'Alison Uttley, Writer, a Spinner of Tales'.

QUAINTON

Along the old Roman road known as Gypsy Lane, a stone dated 1641 marks the grave of a King of the Gypsies.

SPEEN

In the Baptist churchyard here is the unlikely resting place of the controversial Catholic sculptor and writer ERIC GILL

(1882–1940), who had lived nearby at Piggotts. The authorities at Westminster Cathedral allowed his initials to be sunk into the floor beneath the fourteenth of the Stations of the Cross he'd created for them, but drew the line at his request to have his severed right hand buried there.

STOKE POGES

The *Elegy, Written in a Country Churchyard* is one of the few poems for which THOMAS GRAY (1716–71) is now remembered, but it's obviously a classic work for the graveyard buff, and it was written right here in Stoke Poges (though St Lawrence's, Upton, Slough makes its own rather unconvincing claim to be the setting). Gray was buried here next to his mother in a brick tomb just outside the east end of St Giles' Church. The setting remains as atmospheric as ever, though the graveyard seems to have been tidied up a little since Gray's time, and the tower of the flint and brick church has been relieved of its ivy mantle.

WEST WYCOMBE

In a family vault at the east end of St Lawrence's Church lies a shameless SIR FRANCIS DASHWOOD (1708–81). The builder of the present church, he's famous for his less pious moments. How far his notoriety was merited is hard to say: all agree he was a genial host, but while his friends and political allies seem to think it was a matter of having a few friends over for a quiet drink, his enemies (and a posterity eager for lurid gossip) talk of a 'Hellfire Club' meeting at dead of night in his Medmenham Abbey house, and later in some caves on his nearby West Wycombe estate, where naked striplings plied whips, local virgins were ravished and the arched bodies of naked women formed the altars upon which black masses were celebrated.

GRAY'S ELEGY, WRITTEN IN A COUNTRY CHURCHYARD

The Curfew tolls the knell of parting day,
The lowing herd wind slowly o'er the lea,
The plowman homeward plods his weary way
And leaves the world to darkness and to me.

Now fades the glimmering landscape on the sight,
And all the air a solemn stillness holds,
Save where the beetle wheels its droning flight,
And drowsy tinklings lull the distant folds;

Save that from yonder ivy-mantled tow'r
The mopeing owl does to the moon complain
Of such, as wand'ring near her secret bow'r
Molest her ancient solitary reign.

Beneath those rugged elms, that yew-tree's shade,
Where heaves the turf in many a mould'ring heap,
Each in his narrow cell forever laid,
The rude Forefathers of the hamlet sleep.

. . .

Let not Ambition mock their useful toil,
Their homely joys, and destiny obscure;
Nor Grandeur hear with a disdainful smile,
The short and simple annals of the poor.

The boast of heraldry, the pomp of pow'r
And all that beauty, all that wealth e'er gave
Awaits alike th'inevitable hour.
The paths of glory lead but to the grave...

Cambridgeshire

CAMBRIDGE

CHRIST'S COLLEGE: In a classical urn by the pool in the (private) Fellow's Garden are the ashes of one of Christ's most famous alumni, the scientist, committee-man and novelist C.P. SNOW (1905–80), author of the middlebrow-classic novel sequence *Strangers and Brothers*.

SIDNEY SUSSEX COLLEGE The head of OLIVER CROMWELL (1599–1658), Lord Protector (though decidedly not king protector), ended up here. Dying as the head of a loyal Commonwealth, he was given a grand state funeral – the elaborate ceremonial modelled, ironically enough, on the interment of the Stuart king James I, with a few refinements thrown in from that of Philip II of Spain. Joe Public wasn't quite so moved by his death, though – if, that is, we can believe diarist (and royalist) John Evelyn, who said it had been:

> *the joyfullest funeral that I ever saw; for there was none that cried but dogs, which the soldiers hooted away with a barbarous noise, drinking and taking tobacco in the streets as they went.*

After the Restoration, Cromwell was dug up from his resting place in Westminster Abbey's Henry VII Chapel, along with his henchmen, his son-in-law Henry Ireton (1611–51), and John Bradshaw (1602–59), president of the court which had condemned Charles I to death. The partly decayed regicides were given a posthumous execution at

Tyburn (talk about hanging them high), then cut down and decapitated, their bodies being placed in a pit at the foot of the gallows, which stood by what is now the corner of Edgware Road and Connaught Place, and their heads mounted on spikes on the front of Westminster Hall. There they would remain for more than twenty years, Cromwell's eventually being blown down in a storm. Realizing he was on to a good thing, its finder sold it, and for the next century or so the head would pass through the hands of a number of owners – romantic sympathizers who prized it as a symbol, antiquarians who were simply curious, and freakshow exhibitors who saw it as a way of making an honest bob. It was only in 1960 that it would be given a decent burial. Thanks to the Last Will and Testament of one Canon Wilkinson, Cromwell's *alma mater* found itself in receipt of one Protector's head, more than slightly soiled. The fellows of Sidney Sussex decided to bury it near the entrance to the college chapel. The exact site has been left unmarked to discourage student pranksters and royalist vandals.

One way and another, the fate of Cromwell's body has given rise to the sort of mythology usually only associated with medieval saints. Inevitably it has been claimed that the body strung up at Tyburn never belonged to the Protector in the first place, his body having been substituted after the exhumation (or even earlier, after its first burial, Cromwell having feared some such interference later). And then there are the claims that Cromwell's daughter Mary bribed the Tyburn hangman and was able to save his body from the common pit, spiriting it away to a resting place under the floor at St Nicholas', Chiswick, where she herself was later buried, or at Newburgh, her husband's North Yorkshire home.

ST GILES': A good half-mile from St Giles' Church, down a little track leading off to the left from the Huntingdon Road, is St Giles' churchyard. Those buried here include the classicist and anthropologist SIR JAMES GEORGE FRAZER (1854–1941), author of *The Golden Bough* (published in stages from 1890 to 1915), which proved a sort of weirdo's charter for modernist writers, notably Eliot. G.E. MOORE (1873–1958), the anti-idealist, pro-'common sense' philosopher, is here too, lying right next to the literary and theatre critic DESMOND MCCARTHY (1877–1952). 'Whereof one cannot speak, thereof one must be silent,' sagely remarked LUDWIG WITTGENSTEIN (1889–1951), who rests, duly quiet, not far away. The Nobel prizewinning atomic physicist SIR JOHN COCKCROFT (1897–1967) is also buried here.

CARLTON

SIR THOMAS ELYOT (C. 1490–1546), diplomat and writer on education and politics, was buried at the church here. A pupil of Thomas More, he held the same humanist principles. At a time when Latin was still the international language of learning, the Latin–English *Dictionary of Sir Thomas Elyot* (1538) helped establish English as an appropriate language for serious scholarly discussion.

ELY

In the cathedral is what is left of the tomb of ST ETHELDREDA (C. 630–79), Queen of Northumbria and Abbess of Ely. Only a few fragments of her shrine survive: they are kept here in the retrochoir.

FENSTANTON

Here, in the church with his wife and son, is landscape gardener Lancelot 'CAPABILITY' BROWN (1716–83). Radical in his rejection of the old ways, he preferred to work round the natural features, or 'capabilities' as he called them, of the scene before him, rather than simply impose a rigid, formal order as previous gardeners had done.

VILLAGE RHYME

On the outside wall of St Andrew's Church at Chesterton in Cambridge, by the porch, a tablet indicates that 'Near this place lies interred Anna Maria Vassa, daughter of Gustavus Vassa, the African. She died July 21st, 1797, aged 4 years.' It continues:

> *Should simple village rhymes attract thine eye,*
> *Stranger, as thoughtfully thou passest by,*
> *Know that there lies beside this humble stone*
> *A child of colour haply not thine own.*
> *Her father born of Afric's sun-burnt race,*
> *Torn from his native fields, ah foul disgrace;*
> *Through various toils at length to Britain came*
> *Espoused, so Heaven ordain'd, an English dame,*
> *And follow'd Christ; their hope two infants dear.*
> *But one, a hapless orphan, slumbers here.*
> *To bury her the village children came,*
> *And dropp'd choice flowers, and lisp'd her early fame;*
> *And some that lov'd her most, as if unblest,*
> *Bedew'd with tears the white wreath on this breast;*
> *But she is gone and dwells in that abode,*
> *Where some of every clime shall joy in God.*

GLATTON

The ashes of writer BEVERLEY NICHOLS (1898–1983) were scattered here, on the village green. He'd immortalized

Glatton in his enormously popular book *Down the Garden Path* (1932), which chronicled his attempts to impose some kind of order on the garden of his weekend cottage in the village.

HELPSTON

The poet JOHN CLARE (1793–1864) was born and brought up here. The acclaim that greeted his *Poems Descriptive of Rural Life and Scenery. By John Clare a Northamptonshire Peasant*, published in 1820, was by no means entirely condescending, though he was the victim of rather a lot of good advice from the Lions of Romantic London, who understood neither his true gifts nor the penury in which he and his large family were trying to survive in Helpston. His mental health gave way, and he spent his last twenty-seven years in the Northampton Lunatic Asylum, subject to delusions that he was Byron or Napoleon. He died there, but was brought back to Helpston to be buried in St Botolph's churchyard. A plaque marks the cottage, and a cross has been erected in his memory.

KIRTLING

In the village's flint-walled church lies EDWARD LORD NORTH (c. 1496–1564), Chancellor to Henry VIII. His Majesty's loyal servant, North made himself a pile out of monastic confiscations, before going on to be a loyal servant to the Catholic Queen Mary. For a time he was gaoler to the young Princess Elizabeth, but since she came to stay with him a couple of times of her own accord once she was Queen, he can't have been too harsh a keeper.

LEVERINGTON

Oliver Goldsmith stayed in the village in 1773 while he was

writing *She Stoops to Conquer*. The original for that play's Tony Lumpkin is buried in the village church.

PETERBOROUGH

In the north transept of the cathedral, well away from the high altar, Henry VIII's first cast-off queen CATHERINE OF ARAGON (1485–1536) was buried after her death from what is thought to have been cancer. She was exiled to the provinces because Henry deemed that a St Paul's funeral would cost more than was 'either requisite or needful'. Despite this, she had a rousing send-off from a people not entirely convinced of the correctness of their ruler's conduct, the route from London to Peterborough being crowded by country people gathered to pay their last respects. (A few months later the unlit tapers about her tomb were reported to have flared spontaneously into life during matins, in apparent sympathy with Catherine's successor, Anne Boleyn, who was to be executed at the Tower the following day.) For a while, Mary, Queen of Scots was here too, though her remains were later moved to Westminster Abbey by her son, James I & VI.

Channel Islands

JERSEY

'The Jersey Lily' sleeps off an eventful life as actress and international celebrity in St Saviour's churchyard. LILLIE LANGTRY (1853–1929), née Emilie Charlotte Le Breton, was the prodigal daughter of St Saviour's rather stuffy rector.

In St John's cemetery, St Helier, Holiday Camp King BILLY BUTLIN (1899–1980) was buried, dressed, in accordance with an obscure fairground showman's tradition, in a blue suit with brown shoes. Butlin started out his career in 1921 with a hoop-la stall, then founded his first holiday camp at Skegness in the mid-1930s. By the end of that decade he'd made his fortune. His headstone is engraved with images such as a holiday camp scene, an amusement park and the 'bracing' Skegness fisherman.

Cheshire

CHESTER

So holy was ST WERBURGH (d. c. 700) that she could hang her veil from a sunbeam. The daughter of a Mercian king, her remains were moved westward for safe-keeping from Ely, where she had been abbess, during the Danish raids of the ninth century. They have been in the cathedral here ever since. Also here is the chronicler RANULF HIGDEN (d. 1364), author of the *Polychronicon*, an enormously ambitious history of the world from the Creation down to the fourteenth century, amounting practically to a complete catalogue of available knowledge – not only in history but in geography and science.

HALE

In a (somewhat) elongated grave at the church here lies John Middleton, a famous local giant who lived in the seventeenth century. He is reported to have been over nine feet tall.

KNUTSFORD

Victorian novelist ELIZABETH CLEGHORN GASKELL (1810–65) is buried behind the 1688 United Reform Chapel in Brook Street. The author of industrial social novels such as *Mary Barton* (1848) and *North and South* (1855), as well as quiet comedies of genteel country life such as *Cranford* (1853) – set in a town unmistakably modelled upon the Knutsford in which she'd grown up – 'Mrs Gaskell', as she allowed herself to be called, has been much patronized on account of her extreme well-meaningness, though much enjoyed and, albeit secretly, admired. Fyodor Dostoyevsky was one writer who was prepared to come clean, admitting that *Mary Barton* had provided the inspiration for his *Crime and Punishment*.

WARRINGTON

In the Catholic Cemetery, Manchester Road, lies the singer, ukulele-man and film actor GEORGE FORMBY (1904–61). He was found by Mass Observation to be the greatest single morale-booster in wartime Britain, which shows just what grim times they were. Formby, who went into showbusiness only after an unsuccessful apprenticeship as a jockey in Ireland, is buried beside his father George Formby Senior (originally Jimmy Booth), 'The Wigan Nightingale', who died in 1921.

Cornwall

FOWEY

Rebecca-writer DAPHNE DU MAURIER (1907–89) who wrote about the wild Cornish coast in fiction and memoir alike, lived at Menabilly House. Her ashes were scattered on the cliffs here.

MORWENSTOW

The churchyard here contains over forty victims of shipwreck, including the crew of the *Caledonia*, which ran aground and was destroyed by a storm of 1843. Its figurehead serves as their headstone. They perhaps owe their decent burial to the eccentric nineteenth-century vicar Robert Hawker, author of 'Song of the Western Men', who laboured hard to get his flock to take a less mercenary, more Samaritan view of shipwrecks than had hitherto been customary on this coast.

MYLOR

The Cardiff-born popular novelist HOWARD SPRING (1889–1965) lived here from 1939 to his death. His ashes were buried in St Mylor's churchyard.

PAUL

On the hill above the village lies DOROTHY 'DOLLY' PENTREATH (d. 1777), supposedly the last person to speak only Cornish.

ROCK

In the church of St Enodoc, now marooned in the middle of

a golf course, is SIR JOHN BETJEMAN (1906–84), poet laureate, who'd known the place since childhood holidays:

> *Blessed be St Enodoc, blessed be the wave,*
> *Blessed be the springy turf, we pray, pray to thee,*
> *Ask for our children all the happy days you gave*
> *To Ralph, Vasey, Alastair, Biddy, John and me.*

ST KEVERNE

In the churchyard are buried over four hundred victims of shipwreck.

ST MAWGAN

A wooden headboard in the churchyard here commemorates ten men who froze to death in a lifeboat after their ship went down in 1846. The headboard was reputedly made from the stern of that same lifeboat.

STRATTON

In 1643, the Royalists defeated the Parliamentarians near here; those killed in the Battle of Stratton were buried in the churchyard.

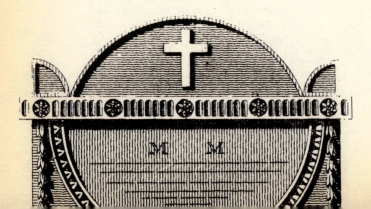

Cumbria

BUTTERMERE

In the church is a memorial for A. WAINWRIGHT (1907–91), the writer and fell-walker who did more to popularize the Lake District than anybody since Wordsworth, and raised large sums for charity in the process. His ashes were scattered above the village on his favourite mountain, Haystacks.

CALDBECK

In the churchyard here lies JOHN PEEL (1776–1854), who died after a fall from his horse (though he always followed his hounds on foot, in the approved local style). Peel, who maintained a pack at his own expense for over fifty years and was by all accounts a consummate huntsman, seems to have been otherwise completely unmemorable, living on in the popular memory thanks to the song written by his friend John Woodcock Graves and set to music by Carlisle Cathedral's organist William Metcalfe.

> *D'ye ken John Peel with his coat so gray?*
> *D'ye ken John Peel at the break of the day?*
> *D'ye ken John Peel when he's far far away*
> *With his hounds and his horn in the morning?*
>
> *'Twas the sound of his horn called me from my bed,*
> *And the cry of his hounds has me oft times led;*
> *For Peel's view-hollo would wake the dead,*
> *Or a fox from his lair in the morning.*

CHAPEL STILE

In the churchyard, just to the east of the church, is the grave of the social historian G.M. TREVELYAN (1876–1962). A lively stylist and a great popularizer, he's best known for his great *English Social History* (1944), which came out in an illustrated edition in 1965, bringing to many thousands of readers the idea that there might be more to history than dynasties and dates.

CONISTON

His grave marked by a stone cross (designed by his secretary and friend W.G. COLLINGWOOD and carved, as he would have wished it, by a local craftsman) JOHN RUSKIN (1819–1900), art critic and social prophet, lies buried in the churchyard here. Having lived on the eastern shore of the lake, at Brantwood, from 1871 to 1900, Ruskin chose to be buried in this beautiful setting, rather than in Westminster Abbey. Yet his love of the place was not untinged with sadness:

> *Morning breaks, as I write, along those Coniston Fells,*
> *and the level mists, motionless, and grey beneath the rose*
> *of the moorlands, veil the lower woods, and the sleeping*
> *village, and the long lawns by the lake-shore.*
> *Oh, that some one had but told me, in my youth,*
> *when all my heart seemed to be set on these colours and*
> *clouds, that appear for a little while and then vanish away,*
> *how little my love of them would serve me, when the*
> *silence of lawn and wood in the dews of morning should be*
> *completed; and all my thoughts should be of those whom,*
> *by neither, I was to meet more.*

Among these were his cousin Joanna and her husband, the artist and devout Ruskinian Joseph Severn (1793–1879).

Collingwood, a painter and antiquarian of note, was himself subsequently buried here with his wife, later to be joined by their son, the distinguished philosopher ROBIN GEORGE COLLINGWOOD (1889–1943). His father's son, R.G. Collingwood did much of his most important work in the philosophies of aesthetics and of history.

There's a memorial here too for DONALD CAMPBELL, who died while attempting a world water-speed record in 1967. His boat, *Bluebird*, span out of control at over 300 miles per hour: Campbell's body was never found.

DALTON-IN-FURNESS

The portrait painter GEORGE ROMNEY (1734–1802) is buried here in St Mary's churchyard. Brought up in Dalton, Romney worked for a time in his father's trade of cabinet making before being articled to a Kendal painter in 1755. Seven years later he abandoned his wife and children, going down to London to launch himself as a fashionable portraitist. Thanks to his brilliant (not to say flashy) technique he was soon all the rage. His health was poor, however, and in 1798, sick and impoverished, he limped back to Dalton-in-Furness and to the bosom of his long-suffering family.

GRASMERE

In the northeast corner of St Oswald's churchyard lies 'Daffodils' poet WILLIAM WORDSWORTH (1770–1850), with his wife Mary, and his sister DOROTHY WORDSWORTH (1771–1855) who was a consistent stimulus to her brother's creativity and, in her *Grasmere Journal*, a significant author in her own right. Two of William and Mary's children – Catharine and Thomas – died in childhood and are buried nearby (Thomas De Quincey was so upset by Kate's death, he said, that for months he spent the night on her grave, sick with grief). She was only three when she died in 1812; and six months afterwards she was joined by Thomas, aged six, for whom Wordsworth wrote an epitaph:

> Six months to six years added, he remained
> Upon this sinful earth, by sin unstained:
> O blessed Lord! whose mercy then removed
> A Child whom every eye that looked on loved;
> Support us, teach us calmly to resign
> What we possessed, and now is wholly thine!

The poet's grandson William lies with Catharine and Thomas: he too died as a young child. Wordsworth's daughter Dora, and her husband Edward Quillinan, are also here. There's a stone too in commemoration of William's younger brother, John, died at sea 1805 and buried in Lyme Regis, Dorset.

Family friend and longtime Grasmere resident HARTLEY COLERIDGE (1796–1849) has a place on the edge of this throng. The son of Samuel Taylor Coleridge, Hartley had failed to live up either to his father's achievement or to his own early promise, but had still written some beautiful poems and some worthwhile literary criticism.

KESWICK

SIR HUGH WALPOLE (1884–1941), who had a house nearby at Brackenburn, is buried in St John's churchyard. A once-popular novelist, he is now read mostly by accident when he's confused with Horace Walpole of Strawberry Hill.

At St Kentigern's churchyard, Great Crosthwaite, the

grave of the poet ROBERT SOUTHEY (1774–1843) is to be found. A friend of Wordsworth and Coleridge, Southey is now comprehensively overshadowed by these associates as a poet; as a historian, though once distinguished, he is now practically forgotten. (Everywhere, that is, except Brazil. Between 1810 and 1819 Southey wrote a major history of that country, and its government recently paid for the restoration of his tomb in gratitude.)

MARDALE

You can't actually visit Mardale without an aqualung, since it now lies some distance beneath the surface of Haweswater, courtesy of Manchester Corporation, who built a dam in the 1930s to extend the natural limits of the lake and improve the city's water supply. If you're feeling energetic enough, however, you can still follow the vertiginous Corpse Road along which the coffins of the dead were carried by packhorse in the days before Mardale's Holy Trinity Church had its own consecrated graveyard, when the deceased had to be taken over the fells to Shap for a Christian burial. From 1729 burial was authorized in the churchyard at Mardale, which saved the dead and their mourners quite a hike. Yet those who were laid to rest here would only be postponing the journey: prior to the inundation, Holy Trinity was demolished, the churchyard dug up and the remains of the dead transferred to a special cemetery at Shap, just to the east of the churchyard where their forebears had been buried. By then, at least, they could expect a more comfortable ride.

PENRITH

In the parish churchyard can be seen the 'Giant's Grave', a monument said to be the tomb of OWAIN CAERANIAS, King of Cumbria 920–937. Daniel Defoe, passing through Penrith in the 1720s on his 'Tour Through the Whole Island of Great Britain', was impressed:

> *Two remarkable pillars fourteen or fifteen foot asunder and twelve foot high the lowest of them, though they seem equal. The people told us, they were the monument of Sir Owen Caesar. This Sir Owen, they tell us, was a champion of mighty strength, and of gigantic stature, and so he was, to be sure, if, as they say, he was as tall as one of the columns, and could touch both pillars with his hand at the same time. They relate nothing but good of him, and that he exerted his mighty strength to kill robbers, such as infested the borders much in those days…*

Some accounts suggest that he actually spent his time hunting wild boar, admits Defoe, but he prefers to find the Caped Crusader Sir Owen 'most probable'.

Having finished his great factional account of the London pestilence in *A Journal of the Plague Year* only a few years earlier in 1722, Defoe also took a professional interest in a monument inside the church recording the deaths of over 8,000 inhabitants of Penrith and environs in an outbreak of 1598. Sir Owen Caesar, meanwhile, would surface again in an improbable literary context after James Joyce was sent a photo of the Giant's Grave by his patron Harriet Weaver, when she holidayed here in 1926. The monument's scale, shape and orientation would suggest to him the form of his hero Earwicker at the opening of *Finnegans Wake*.

RUSLAND

In a corner of this little churchyard among the Furness Fells lies ARTHUR RANSOME (1884–1967), journalist and author of the classic *Swallows and Amazons* children's books. His wife Genia, who died in 1975, is buried beside him. The story of Evgenia Petrovna Shelepina is largely unknown, though it must have been an exciting one. The two met in revolutionary Russia, which he was visiting as a reporter, while she was the secretary to Leon Trotsky.

Derbyshire

AULT HUCKNELL

The church of St John the Baptist contains the tomb of THOMAS HOBBES (1588–1679), whose home was nearby at Hardwick Hall. He lived to the age of ninety one, so while his life may have been nasty and brutish, it wasn't especially short. His last words, reportedly, were: 'I am about to take my last voyage, a great leap in the dark.' A distinguished philosopher and political thinker, Hobbes none the less prized practical experience over high-flown theory. According to his friend John Aubrey,

> *He was wont to say that he had rather have the advice, or take Physique from an experienced old Woman, that had been at many sick people's Bed-sides, than from the learnedst but unexperienced Physitian.*

The same instinct came through strongly in his studiously hard-bitten *Leviathan* (1651), which argued the need for naturally selfish, quarrelsome men to be kept in order by strong, preferably monarchical, government. His funeral, from Aubrey's account, seems to have been an enjoyable affair for those present: 'The company, consisting of the family and neighbours that came to his Funerall, and attended him to his grave, were very handsomely entertained with Wine, burned and raw, cake, biscuit, etc.'

BREADSALL

Charles' grandfather, ERASMUS DARWIN (1731–1802), is buried in the parish church. A distinguished physician and general historian who himself did pioneering work on the evolution of plants, Erasmus Darwin was also a friend of industrial revolutionaries like Matthew Boulton, James Watt, Josiah Wedgwood and Benjamin Franklin. His ingenious scientific verse, if now remembered at all, is held in ridicule. For a brief time, however, it was much admired, Coleridge even awarding Darwin the title of 'The first *literary* character in Europe'.

CHESTERFIELD

Under the communion table of Holy Trinity Church lies Rocket Man GEORGE STEPHENSON (1781–1848), who lived at Tapton House, northeast of the town. An entrepreneur as well as an inventor, it had been he who discovered the seam of coal underneath the town and started a company to work it. His pioneering Liverpool–Manchester Railway inaugurated the Railway Age and made Stephenson the first of a new breed of craggy, hard-bitten heroes. Actress Fanny Kemble, given a ride on the railway before its official opening in 1830, was much taken with the railway but even more so with its inventor:

Now for a word or two about the master of all these
marvels, with whom I am most horribly in love. He is a
man of from fifty to fifty-five years of age; his face is fine,
though careworn, and bears an expression of deep
thoughtfulness; his mode of explaining his ideas is peculiar
and very original, striking, and forcible; and although his
accent indicates strongly his north-country birth, his
language has not the slightest touch of vulgarity or
coarseness. He has certainly turned my head.

CROMFORD

The inventor and entrepreneur SIR RICHARD ARKWRIGHT
(1732–92), who developed the water frame for spinning
cotton, built Derbyshire's first water-powered cotton mill in
Cromford in 1771. His remains lie in the church he built in
1792. Visiting the neighbourhood in 1801, Joseph Farington
was most impressed by the conditions – physical and spiritual
– in which Arkwright's young employees lived, noting in
his diary:

August 22 – In the evening I walked to Cromford & saw
the Children coming from their work out of one of Mr
Arkwrights Manufactories. I was glad to see them look in
general very healthy and many with fine, rosy,
complexions. – These children had been at work from 6 or
7 o'clock this morning, & it was now near or abt. 7 in the
evening. The time allowed them for resting is at 12 o'clock
40 minutes during which time they dine. One of them, a
Boy of 10 or 11 years of age, told me his wages were 3s6d
a week, & a little girl said her wages were 2s3d a week.
 August 23 – We went to Church at Cromford where is
a Chapel built abt. 3 years & H ago by Mr Arkwright.

On each side the Organ a gallery in which about 50 Boys were seated. These children are employed in Mr Arkwrights work in the week-days, and on Sundays attend a school where they receive education...

'The whole plan appears to be such as to do Mr Arkwright great credit,' concludes Farington warmly and – talking of credit – Arkwright's bank manager must have been pretty pleased with him too, given the 100 per cent profit rate his economies of scale were allowing.

DERBY

In the Cathedral of All Saints is the tomb of HENRY CAVENDISH (1731–1810), chemist and physicist, the discoverer of hydrogen. Cambridge University's Cavendish Laboratory is named after him, and contains much of his equipment.

EYAM

In and around the churchyard are buried the victims of the plague of 1665. According to tradition, the plague first reached Eyam in a consignment of clothing sent from London to the local tailor, George Vicars. When he sickened and died panic spread, but Eyam's rector William Mompesson encouraged the villagers to stay put, and thus protect neighbouring communities. So Eyam battened down hatches and cut itself off from the outside world. The plague seemed to die down during the winter but returned with a vengeance during the following summer. In all 257 died out of a total population of only 350. They wouldn't all fit in the churchyard, and many lie round about in unmarked graves as a result. The chest in which the fatal clothing is supposed to have arrived can be seen in the north aisle of St Lawrence's

Church. At Mompesson's well, three-quarters of a mile east of the village, neighbours left supplies, the coins left in payment being washed in vinegar and water to kill the infection.

HATHERSAGE

A mound fourteen foot long in the churchyard here is reputed to cover LITTLE JOHN, Robin Hood's Merrie Man.

OVER HADDON

Spymaster SIR MAURICE OLDFIELD (1915–81), Director General of MI6 from 1973 to 1978, is buried in the churchyard here.

Devon

BICKLEIGH

A local rector's son, BAMFYLDE MOORE CAREW (1693–c. 1770) turned out badly but colourfully, running away from school to join the gypsies (of whom he was eventually elected king). He enjoyed considerable success as swindler, adventurer, and all-round bad lot. Transported to Maryland, he soon escaped, and was back in time to fight with Bonnie Prince Charlie in the 1745 rebellion. He was buried in the churchyard here.

DARTMOUTH

In Long Cross Cemetery lies FLORA THOMPSON (1876–1947), who didn't begin writing until after she'd moved here in 1928. Freshly as it is evoked, the Oxfordshire childhood of her *Lark Rise to Candleford* (1945) was in fact recalled from a considerable distance both in time and place.

DEAN PRIOR

Poet ROBERT HERRICK (1591–1674) is buried in the churchyard. The London-born vicar had his differences with his rustic flock. From the first perhaps regarded as something of a carpet-bagger (he didn't even come to live here until getting on for two years after he'd been granted the living), the Cavalier high-churchman was ejected under the Protectorate, after which he touched upon the limitations of his rustic congregation in a poem addressed to 'Dean-bourn, a rude River in Devon, by which sometimes he lived':

> *A people currish; churlish as the seas;*
> *And rude (almost) as rudest Salvages.*
> *With whom I did, and may re-sojourne when*
> *Rockes turn to Rivers, Rivers turn to Men.*

In the event he was to return rather sooner than that, his own restoration following hard upon the King's, but the tensions seem to have continued, the puritan who had taken his place for the interregnum carrying on his mission in rivalry at great personal risk to himself. How fully Herrick was accepted by his parishioners isn't clear: his grave was unmarked, and its exact whereabouts is unknown, which is perhaps ominous.

GEORGEHAM

At the edge of St George's churchyard, just across the stream from Skirr Cottage, where he lived from 1921 to 1937, lies

HENRY WILLIAMSON (1895–1977), his headstone marked with his personal owl symbol. Returning from the trenches of the Western Front a bitter, cynical man, Williamson took his cottage here as a sort of escape, but his classic animal stories such as *Tarka the Otter* (1927) derive much of their impact from their unsentimental awareness of a nature red in tooth and claw. His feelings of disenchantment having led him into fascism, Williamson set up as a farmer in Norfolk in 1937, convinced that national regeneration depended upon a strong, productive rural economy as opposed to an urban industrial one. The experiment was not a success and, chastened both by this experience and by the increasingly alarming news from Germany, Williamson returned to Georgeham, took another cottage, and lived out the rest of his life here.

OKEHAMPTON

The Cavalier poet SIDNEY GODOLPHIN (1610–43) was killed not far away from here at Chagford, in one of the inglorious little skirmishes of which the Civil War was so largely composed. He was buried in the churchyard here.

PLYMOUTH

In the sanctuary of the Church of St Andrew, the heart and entrails of the Elizabethan explorer SIR MARTIN FROBISHER (1535–94) were laid to rest, the remainder being interred in London at St Giles, Cripplegate.

SALCOMBE

Historian J.A. FROUDE (1818–94) is in the churchyard here. One of the leading exponents of the Great Men school of history, Froude was also a joyous proclaimer of England's imperial mission.

SALCOMBE REGIS, NEAR SIDMOUTH

In St Mary and St Peter's churchyard are two eminent scientists: the electrical engineer SIR AMBROSE FLEMING (1849–1945), who in 1904 invented the wireless valve, and the astronomer SIR NORMAN LOCKYER (1836–1920), who conducted important research into sunspots from the observatory which can still be seen at the top of the nearby hill.

SHEEPSTOR

The churchyard at Sheepstor is the improbable last resting place of Rajah JAMES BROOKE OF SARAWAK (1803–68), a gentleman adventurer given his throne by Rajah Muda Hassim, the heir apparent to the sultanate of Brunei, in return for his help in putting down a threat to his power at home. Hassim had regarded the title as a meaningless sop: he reckoned without the Quixotic Brooke, who took like a duck to water to being an (as he liked to think) enlightened despot with absolute power over 30,000 Malays and Dyaks. His nephew Charles, who succeeded him on the throne, is also buried here.

SHIRWELL

Round-the-world yachtsman SIR FRANCIS CHICHESTER (1901–72) spent his childhood in Shirwell, where his father was the vicar. He pulled off his remarkable solo circumnavigation in 1966–7, when he was sixty-five, and didn't indeed have too many years left to live. He is buried in the churchyard.

SPREYTON

Somewhere in St Michael's churchyard lies the original Uncle Tom Cobley, who died in 1794. His grave is unmarked, however, and its exact whereabouts unknown.

STOKE FLEMING

In the churchyard, by the tower, was buried GEORGE PARKER BIDDER (1806–78), celebrated in childhood for his prodigious feats of mental arithmetic, which gained him the title 'The Calculating Boy'. He subsided into an adulthood as an engineer of rather quieter distinction.

SWIMBRIDGE

Vicar here for almost half a century, from 1833 to 1880, the Reverend JOHN RUSSELL (1795–1883) was buried at the east end of St James' churchyard. Famous in his day as 'The Sporting Parson', he is now known as the original breeder of the Jack Russell Terrier.

Dorset

BOURNEMOUTH

Much of the population of Bournemouth has one foot in the grave. Among those more comprehensively interred are the Godwin–Wollstonecraft–Shelleys. This famous literary clan lies all together in a tomb of white marble in St Peter's churchyard, Hinton Road. After the Shelley family moved to a new country home near here, the remains of pioneer feminist and novelist MARY WOLLSTONECRAFT (1759–97) and WILLIAM GODWIN (1756–1836), radical thinker and novelist, were brought here by their daughter, MARY SHELLEY (1797–1851), who was concerned that their original London resting place, Old St Pancras' churchyard, had been allowed to go to rack and ruin. Famous herself for her influential Gothic shocker *Frankenstein* (1818), Mary was buried here in her turn, along with, for good measure, a silver casket containing the heart (if that's what it is) of her still more famous husband, the poet PERCY BYSSHE SHELLEY (1792–1822). P.B. had drowned tragically (if, some hinted, purposefully, in an overpowering access of Romantic *Weltschmerz*) in the sea at Leghorn (Livorno), Italy in 1822. His body was cremated openly on the beach, but his heart was snatched from the flames by his friend Trelawny. At least Trelawny thought it was his heart: it seems most likely, if less fitting somehow, that it was really his liver. The ashes of the rest of Shelley were buried in Rome, in the Protestant Cemetery with fellow poet John Keats.

CANFORD

In the churchyard here lies the English-born scholar of Welsh language and folklore LADY CHARLOTTE GUEST (1812–75), translator of the myth-cycle *The Mabinogion* (1838–49).

CHRISTCHURCH

The body of local eccentric Mrs Perkins (d. 1783) occupies a mausoleum in the Priory Gardens. Such was her fear of being buried alive that she had her coffin fitted with a lock which she could open from the inside, and had her mausoleum placed within earshot of the boys' school, so her cries would be heard. The mausoleum was moved to its present position after her husband's death in 1803, by which time it must have seemed pretty certain that she wasn't going to wake up.

MAPPOWDER

In the churchyard here lies novelist T.F. POWYS (1875–1953), one of the famous Powys brothers (see Weymouth, below), of whom he's now widely held to have been the most important, thanks to quirky, mythical novels such as *Mr Weston's Good Wine* (1927). Having for many years lived quietly with his family in East Chaldon, near Weymouth, he moved here towards the end of his life, living not so much quietly as reclusively.

MORETON

T.E. LAWRENCE (1888–1935), Lawrence of Arabia, lived nearby at Clouds Hill, in an old gamekeeper's cottage. He was killed in a motorbike accident and buried here.

POOLE

A year after their father's death, half-brothers Gip Wells and Anthony West hired a boat in Poole harbour, rowed it out into the Solent and scattered upon the waters the ashes of H.G. WELLS (1866–1946).

PORTLAND BILL

Contraception campaigner MARIE STOPES (1881–1958), author of the sensational book *Married Love* (1918) (as well as some not insignificant, but far less notorious, work on fossil plants), had her rural retreat nearby in the village of Easton. After her death her ashes were scattered from the headland here, at her own request. Revisionists and Roman Catholics point snidely to the fact that her heroic struggle for women's control of their fertility seems to have been motivated in large part by her desire to keep down the population of undesirable social and racial groups.

SHAFTESBURY

King Edward the Martyr was here at the abbey until quite recently. Now he's at Brookwood, near Woking, Surrey.

SHERBORNE

A memorial slab in the north transept of the abbey church marks the probable burial place of SIR THOMAS WYATT (1503–42), poet, courtier and lover of (before she found herself bigger fish to fry) Anne Boleyn. Somewhat remarkably for one so close to the centre of life – social, sexual and political – in Henry VIII's court, Wyatt managed to escape the block, only to die here of a fever. Other, older inhabitants include a couple of Saxon Kings of Wessex, AETHELBALD (d. 860), and AETHELBERT (d. 866).

STINSFORD, NEAR DORCHESTER

The heart of novelist and poet THOMAS HARDY (1840–1928), creator of 'Wessex', was buried in the churchyard here, in the grave of his first wife, Emma, who had died in 1912; the rest of him was cremated and the ashes placed in Westminster Abbey, in Poets' Corner. This arrangement was the result of a rather grisly compromise. Hardy himself had always intended to be buried with Emma, in the same churchyard in which his parents had earlier been buried. And so shocked and disappointed were Hardy's family and the Stinsford community (not to mention his many freethinking, anti-establishment intellectual friends) when they learned of the grand Abbey funeral that was being planned, that the local vicar suggested the removal of the heart for local burial. That seems to have shocked them as well, but the family agreed in the end and the heart was removed and carried home in a biscuit tin. The story that it had to be rescued from a pet cat has proved persistent but seems to have no basis in fact.

Nearby is C. DAY-LEWIS (1904–72), poet laureate. The epitaph on his headstone reads:

> Shall I be gone long?
> *For ever and a day.*
> To whom there belong?
> *Ask the stone to say.*
> *Ask my song.*

Of Anglo-Irish stock, Day-Lewis was sent to Sherborne school and married a local woman, but was otherwise unconnected with Dorset. He loved the county, and Hardy, however: hence his interment here.

TOLPUDDLE

In the churchyard lies JAMES HAMMETT, one of the Tolpuddle Martyrs, six men (including two lay-preachers) who in 1833 met to agree about resisting a wage reduction and were transported to Australia for their pains. Their sentences were repealed after a public outcry, though it wasn't so easy to repeal a transportation in the back of beyond on the other side of the world: Hammett was four years into what was supposed to be his seven-year exile when he chanced to read about his pardon in an old newspaper. He was the only martyr to return to England; the others went on to Canada. Eric Gill's headstone to the martyrs is inside the church.

WEYMOUTH

Just to the west of the town, Chesil Beach was the scene of a memorable shipwreck in the novel *Weymouth Sands*, by Dorset writer JOHN COWPER POWYS (1872–1963). After his death his ashes were brought here to be scattered on the sea off Abbotsbury. Always a minority taste, John Cowper Powys is considered one of the great neglected masters by his admirers, though some readers find his deep, poetic novels unendurably pretentious. A few miles along the coast to the east, at the top of the cliffs south of Chaldon, the ashes of his brother, the essayist LLEWELYN POWYS (1884–1939) were placed beneath a block of Portland stone inscribed with his name, dates and the words: 'The living the living he shall praise thee'. The other famous Powys boy, T.F. (Theodore Francis) Powys was also buried in Dorset, though well inland of here at Mappowder (above). (There were seven further siblings, including another brother who was a noted architect, and three sisters, of whom one was a novelist, one an artist and the other a world authority on old lace.)

WHITCHURCH CANONICORUM

In a thirteenth-century shrine in the village church is the earlier sarcophagus of the church's patron, the Saxon St Candida, thought to have been murdered by Danish raiders. Three oval holes in the side of the tomb allowed kneeling pilgrims to touch their foreheads against the reliquary itself.

WOOL

At the church here are buried many members of the true-life Turberville family. In Hardy's novel, *Tess of the D'Urbervilles*, the sleepwalking Angel Clare places the frightened Tess in an open tomb among the nearby ruins of Bindon Abbey.

WORTH MATRAVERS

Benjamin Jesty, who in 1774 – some years before Jenner (see Berkeley, Gloucestershire) published his discoveries – inoculated his wife and two sons against smallpox, is buried in the churchyard here. Mrs Jesty, according to her tombstone, died fifty years later, by which time she was eighty-four, so he must have been doing something right. They lived at the nearby Manor Farm of Downshay.

Durham and Cleveland

BOWES

In the churchyard here is the grave of George Ashton Taylor, who died, his gravestone tells us, 'suddenly at Mr William Shaw's Academy, of this place, April 13th, 1822, aged 19 years. Young reader,' it concludes, 'thou must die, but after this the judgement.' A stern judgement indeed must have been awaiting Mr William Shaw. The novelist Charles Dickens thought so, at least, though local magistrates had let the school proprietor off with a slapped wrist when he was prosecuted for allowing several boys in his 'care' to go blind through gross neglect. Dickens had followed events at Bowes Academy for some years before he immortalized it as Dotheboys Hall, and its proprietor as Wackford Squeers, in his 1838 novel *Nicholas Nickleby*. He had even visited the school. In a letter to a friend he described how afterwards, appalled by what he had seen, he had gone into the nearby churchyard:

> *the first grave-stone I stumbled on that dreary winter afternoon was placed above the grave of a boy, eighteen [sic] long years old, who had died – suddenly, the inscription said; I suppose his heart broke – the Camel falls down 'suddenly' when they heap the last load upon his back – died at that wretched place. I think his ghost put Smike into my head upon the spot.*

The consumptive boy Nicholas rescues from the horrors of Dotheboys Hall and attempts to save, Smike stirred public outrage and compassion as no amount of prosecution could have done. Shaw was finished, of course, but it didn't end there. Despite Dickens' insistence that he was describing an exceptional case rather than the general rule, the furore, in the words of one schoolmaster, 'passed like a whirlwind over the schools of the North', closing down good schools, some claimed, as well as bad.

DURHAM

The cathedral contains two saints, both resting after rather peripatetic posthumous careers. ST CUTHBERT (d. 678) was first buried at the priory he'd founded on Lindisfarne. The monks tried to move him eleven years later, when they wanted to place him in a more fittingly impressive tomb; when his body was found to be still undecayed it became a sacred relic, and the monks took it with them wherever they went, which in those days of Viking raids and political turbulence meant pretty well all over northern England. A divine vision urged them, at last, to take the saint to Dunholm, to what would eventually become the city of Durham. Since then he's been allowed to rest in peace, behind the high altar of the cathedral here.

The remains of THE VENERABLE BEDE (673–735), Cuthbert's biographer and author of the *History of the English Church and People*, have led a sedentary existence by comparison, having come only from as far away as Jarrow, whence they were stolen by Durham monks eager to boost their community's standing. Some indication of the lustre possession of Bede's remains might confer can be gained from the testimonial a later chronicler, William of Malmesbury, gives him. Bede was, he says:

> *a man whom it is easier to admire than worthily to extol;*
> *who, though born in a remote corner of the world, was able*
> *to dazzle the whole earth with the brilliancy of his*
> *learning... With this man was buried almost all*
> *knowledge of history down to our times, inasmuch as there*
> *has been no Englishman either emulous of his pursuits, or*
> *a follower of his graces, who could continue the thread of*
> *his discourse, now broken short.*

EBCHESTER

In the churchyard lies ROBERT SMITH SURTEES (1805–64), who lived nearby at Hamsterley Hall. A Justice of the Peace and, eventually, High Sheriff for Durham, Surtees is most famous as the father of the 'sporting novel', satirical stories of fox-hunting folk.

HARTLEPOOL

At All Saint's Church, Stratton, is the grave of the Barnard Castle clockmaker on whom Dickens based his story *Master Humphrey's Clock*.

HURWORTH-ON-TEES

The mathematician and eccentric inventor WILLIAM EMERSON (1701–82) was born here in the Emerson Arms, and buried in All Saints' churchyard with epitaphs in Latin and Hebrew.

Essex

HEMPSTEAD

The church here contains the tomb of WILLIAM HARVEY (1578–1657), who in 1616 published his theory on the circulation of the blood. A revolutionary breakthrough, his discovery didn't do him too much good at the time, according to Aubrey:

> *I have heard him say, that after his Booke of the Circulation of the Blood came-out, that he fell mightily in his Practize, and that 'twas beleeved by the vulgar that he was crack-brained...*

But Aubrey, his friend, who helped carry his coffin, admits to his medical shortcomings: 'All his Profession would allow him to be an excellent Anatomist,' he says, 'but I never heard of any that admired his Therapeutique way. I knew severall practisers in London that would not have given 3d. for one of his Bills; and that a man could hardly tell by one of his Bills what he did aime at.'

HIGH LAVER

In the churchyard is the grave of the great philosopher JOHN LOCKE (1632–1704), who spent his last years nearby at Oates, the house owned by his patrons, the Masham family.

STONDON MASSEY

Somewhere in the churchyard lies the composer WILLIAM BYRD (1543–1623), who spent his last thirty years at nearby Stondon Place, having left the city to escape the plague and then taken root. His grave had to be left unmarked because he was a recusant who refused to give up his Catholicism. That being the case, he could be permitted burial at a push but couldn't be given any memorial.

THEYDON BOIS

Pioneer of girls' education FRANCES BUSS (1827–94), who had often stayed in a nearby country cottage, is buried in St Mary's churchyard, Piercing Hill. In 1850 she founded the North London Collegiate School. Her friend Dorothea Beale is buried in Gloucester (see Gloucestershire).

TOLLESHUNT D'ARCY

Crime novelist MARGERY ALLINGHAM (1904–66), creator of Albert Campion, lived nearby and is buried in the churchyard.

WALTHAM

A slab among the abbey ruins marks what is supposed to be the grave of HAROLD II (c. 1022–66, reigned 1066), whose short rule came to grief on the field of Hastings, where he took a Norman arrow in the eye. His conqueror, William, is buried in France, in Caen, Normandy.

Gloucestershire

BERKELEY

In the chancel of the parish church of St Mary, which has in his honour a commemorative window with pictures of Christ healing the sick, lies EDWARD JENNER (1749–1823), a native of Berkeley who was generally held to have been the first person to use vaccination for smallpox. The title is disputed, however – both Lady Mary Wortley Montagu (see South Audley Street, London West End) and Benjamin Jesty (see Worth Matravers, Dorset) also have a claim. In any case, as Montagu discovered, the practice of inoculation had long been in use in the Near East.

IN MEMORY OF A FISH

At the Dovedale end of the High Street in Blockley, Gloucestershire, in the (private) garden of Fish Cottage, there's a stone inscribed:

IN MEMORY
OF THE
OLD FISH.
UNDER THE SOIL
THE OLD FISH DOE LIE
20 YEARS HE LIEVED
AND THEN DID DIE
HE WAS SO TAME
YOU UNDERSTAND
HE WOULD COME AND
EAT OUT OF OUR HAND
DIED APRIL THE 20TH 1855
AGED 20 YEARS

CHELTENHAM

The poet, dramatist, orientalist and traveller JAMES ELROY FLECKER (1884–1915),who spent most of his childhood here, was buried in the town cemetery. His grave is marked with an Alexandrian laurel and an *Olearia haastii* in allusion to his poem 'Oak and Olive'. Though his sense of Englishness was as romantic and intense as his friend RUPERT BROOKE's, the study of Persian and Arabic, and subsequent diplomatic service in Greece, Turkey and Lebanon gave Flecker something else that he needed, enabling him to escape the drab discipline of English life into a more exotic, sensuous world. Unfortunately, it also exposed him to the TB which he contracted in Constantinople – an impeccably poetic experience but one that was to prove fatal. (Brooke died that same year, at sea off the Greek island of Skyros en route to Gallipoli: his body was rowed ashore and buried in the corner of an olive grove which should, as a result, be forever England but which may in fact be reclaimed by Greece. It is feared that a new naval base currently being built on the site may close off access to the grave.)

COLN ST DENNIS

On the north wall inside the tower is an inscription for an unknown person:

> *Heare lyes my body fast inclosed within this watery*
>   *ground;*
> *but my precious soule it cannot nowe be founde…*

GLOUCESTER

The ashes of DOROTHEA BEALE (1831–1906) are buried in the Cathedral, in the Lady Chapel. The principal of Cheltenham Ladies' College for over fifty years, she was also founder of St Hilda's College, Oxford. Along with her friend and fellow trailblazer Frances Buss (see Theydon Bois, Essex) she inspired the following doggerel which seems to have acquired a certain obstinate immortality:

> *Miss Buss and Miss Beale*
> *Cupid's darts do not feel.*
> *How different from us*
> *Miss Beale and Miss Buss.*

The body of EDWARD II (1284–1327, reigned, at least in theory, 1307–27) was buried here, after his sadistic murder at

Berkeley Castle. Cause of death was, according to tradition, a red hot poker up the rectum, considered fitting punishment for a sodomite. Edward had been deposed and imprisoned by his queen, Isabella, who was supported by leading barons angry at the influence he was allowing favourites like Piers Gaveston, Earl of Cornwall (see Kings Langley, Hertfordshire), and later Hugh Despenser the Younger, 'the King of England's Right Eye', to wield. Despenser, who with his father rose up in support of the King, came to an even nastier end in 1326, as Froissart describes:

> First, he was dragged on a hurdle through all the streets of Hereford, to the sound of horns and trumpets, until he reached the main square of the town, where all the people were assembled. There he was tied to a long ladder, so that everyone could see him. A big fire had been lit in the square. When he had been tied up, his member and his testicles were first cut off, because he was a heretic and a sodomite, even, it was said, with the King, and this was why the King had driven away the Queen on his suggestion. When his private parts had been cut off they were thrown into the fire to burn, and afterwards his heart was torn from his body and thrown into the fire, because he was a false-hearted traitor, who by his treasonable advice and promptings had led the King to bring shame and misfortune upon his kingdom... After Sir Hugh Despenser had been cut up in the way described, his head was struck off and sent to the city of London. His body was divided into four quarters, which were sent to the four principal cities of England after London.

Edward's outing by Isabella and her friends doesn't seem to have bothered the common people too much: the magnificent tomb built for him by his son and heir Edward III would be a place of pilgrimage right up to the Reformation, even though his son's efforts to get him canonized were to prove unavailing.

LECHLADE

Shelley wrote his take on Gray's *Elegy* here in 1815, including the pleasing thought that:

> *The dead are sleeping in their sepulchres:*
> *And, mouldering as they sleep, a thrilling sound,*
> *Half sense, half thought, among the darkness stirs,*
> *Breathed from their wormy beds...*

SAPPERTON, NEAR CIRENCESTER

SIR STAFFORD CRIPPS (1889–1952), Labour MP and Chancellor of the Exchequer 1947–50, is buried in the churchyard here.

SLIMBRIDGE

The ashes of naturalist and artist PETER SCOTT (1909–89), son of Scott of the Antarctic, were scattered here on the Doubles, where his Wildfowl Trust had been born.

STROUD

Southeast of the town on Minchinhampton Common, Tom Long's Post marks the spot where six roads meet – and where executed highwaymen were buried.

TEWKESBURY

In the abbey church of St Mary the Virgin is the tomb of

EDWARD, PRINCE OF WALES (1453–71), the son of Henry VI and the Lancastrian pretender to the throne, killed on the orders of the Yorkist Edward IV.

TWIGWORTH

The poet, songwriter and composer IVOR GURNEY (1890–1937) was buried in the churchyard here. His tendency to mental instability was not helped by service on the Western Front and he spent his last fifteen years in an asylum. The neglect his poetry suffered during his lifetime was another factor in his paranoia, but editors, critics and readers have now begun to make belated amends.

UPLEADON, NEAR NEWENT

In the churchyard is the tombstone of village blacksmith James Broadstock (d. 1768). His epitaph reads:

> *My sledge and hammer He's reclined*
> *My bellows too has lost its wind*
> *My fire extinct, my forge decayed*
> *And in the dust my vice is laid*
> *My coal is burnt, my fire's gone*
> *My nails are drove, my work is done.*

WINCHCOMBE

In the chapel of nearby Sudeley Castle lies CATHERINE PARR (1512–48), Henry VIII's sixth and last queen. Earning the title *eruditissima regina* for her learning and intellectual abilities, Catherine was not only a writer of considerable merit but a patron of other writers and artists. She also went some way towards being a match for her husband as a collector of marriage-partners (though she never resorted to quite the same drastic measures): she had already been twice widowed by the time she married Henry in 1543, and when left a widow a third time on his death she married Lord Thomas Seymour of Sudeley in 1548. Hardly had she been delivered of their daughter, Mary, that same year, than she died herself – poisoned, some said, by her husband who, according to this version of events, wanted his way clear to press his suit with Princess Elizabeth, soon to be Queen. He survived her by about a year, before being executed for treason (see Tower Hill, City of London). These were strange and exciting times for the institution of marriage.

Greater Manchester

MANCHESTER

JOHN BYROM (1692–1763), poet, mystic, hymnist (author of 'Christians awake!'), diarist and deviser of a system of shorthand, is buried in the cathedral.

At the intersection of Devonshire Street and Hyde Road, its site now covered up by St Gregory's school, a playing field and a bus depot, was the old Ardwick Cemetery. The scientist JOHN DALTON (1766–1844) was buried here. He began his researches (into butterflies and weather forecasting) while he was helping to run his family's boarding house in Kendal, Cumbria. He came to Manchester in 1793 to teach mathematics and science, and it was there that he did the first properly scientific work on 'Daltonism' or colour blindness. He would go on to do important work on the properties and behaviour of gases, while his atomic theory – which revived and refined upon the ancient Greek notion that matter, far from being continuous, was composed of minute particles – is considered to have been the development that made modern chemistry possible.

Famous for his smokey streetscapes populated by ragged-looking stick-figures, the painter L.S. LOWRY (1887–1976) is buried in Southern Cemetery, Barlow Moor Road. Here too is the great Manchester United manager SIR MATT BUSBY (1909–94).

ROCHDALE

In the burial ground of the Friends' Meeting House, George Street, was buried the artist JOHN COLLIER (1708–86), who as Tim Bobbin won fame in his day for his satirical dialect poetry. Here too was buried the politician and Free Trade campaigner JOHN BRIGHT (1811–89), who died, appropriately enough, of Bright's disease (named after its discoverer, the physician Richard Bright, 1789–1858, no relation, who is buried in West London at Kensal Green). With Richard Cobden (see West Lavington, Sussex West), John Bright was the founder of the Anti Corn-Law League. Liberals (in a strictly nineteenth-century sense), they objected strongly to protectionist legislation that forced up the price of food for the poor – and, as a result, industrial wage costs. The victory they won in having such legislation repealed sent a profound shockwave through the nation: it wasn't just the actual impact of the change (though that was real enough) but the symbolic importance of this triumph of the new, industrial establishment over the old, landed one.

Rochdale's most famous daughter, the singer and entertainer GRACIE FIELDS (1898–79), died in Capri and was buried in the Protestant cemetery there.

SALE

At the north end of the Brooklands Cemetery, on the west bank of the Bridgewater Canal, is Salford brewer's son JAMES PRESCOTT JOULE (1818–89), a pupil of John Dalton (see Manchester, above) and in his own right a physicist famous for his work on energy.

SALFORD

SIR CHARLES HALLÉ (1819–95), the distinguished conductor and founder of the famous Manchester symphony orchestra, is buried in the cathedral here.

Hampshire

BINSTED

In Binsted churchyard lies Bernard Law, FIRST VISCOUNT MONTGOMERY OF ALAMEIN (1887–1976), who lived nearby at Isington Mill.

EAST WELLOW

FLORENCE NIGHTINGALE (1820–1910), who spent her youth at nearby Embley Park, ended up in the churchyard here. As a young woman, Nightingale's religious feelings had led to her increasingly turning her back on the fashionable social life her parents had laid on for her. Despite their outraged opposition, she trained as a nurse in hospitals in Germany and France, and was then given the post of Superintendent in London's Hospital for Gentlewomen. Her experience made her the obvious choice to lead a body of nurses into action in the Crimea in 1854, and it was there that she gained her near-mythical status as 'The Lady With the Lamp' and all-round ministering angel. She returned to Britain in 1856, a national heroine, but collapsed the following year, whether from an illness she'd contracted at the front or from the sheer exhaustion consequent upon two years' wartime experience followed by a year's adulation. From that time on she became extremely private in her ways, though she continued to campaign for the professionalization of nursing.

ELLINGHAM

In the church is the tomb of ALICE LISLE (c. 1614–85), mistress of nearby Moyles Court, where she sheltered some fugitives after the Duke of Monmouth's 1685 rebellion. For her pains she became the first victim of Judge Jeffreys' Bloody Assizes and was beheaded at Winchester.

EVERSLEY

In the churchyard, his grave marked with a cross, lies CHARLES KINGSLEY (1819–75), the vicar here for the last thirty years of his life. Famous as the advocate of Muscular Christianity (basically, what Our Saviour would have come up with if he'd had the benefits of an English public-school education – a gospel of manliness, fresh air, cold showers and team sports), Kingsley was also author of the classic children's novel *The Water Babies*. He had a more serious side, too, writing searing social novels such as *Yeast* and *Alton Locke*.

FARNBOROUGH

England isn't the obvious place for a family of Bonapartes to end up, but they had to go somewhere when the Second Empire was brought to its abrupt end in 1870 with France's crushing defeat in the Franco-Prussian war. St Michael's Abbey was built by the empress EUGÉNIE (1826–1920) to provide a worthy resting place for her husband NAPOLEON III (1808–73) and their son, the Prince Imperial, who was killed while fighting for Britain in the Zulu War in 1879. Eugénie joined them herself on her own death.

FORDINGBRIDGE

Asked by a friend what he thought of life, painter AUGUSTUS JOHN (1878–1961) replied: 'There's nothing more terrifying.' He should be able to calm down now, safely dead and buried in an annexe of the cemetery here. John's sister Gwen, Rodin's lover, died and was laid to rest in Dieppe.

HIGHCLERE

A couple of miles to the southwest of the village, at the top of local landmark Beacon Hill, is the grave of Egyptologist George Edward Stanhope Molyneux Herbert, known to his friends as the FIFTH EARL OF CARNARVON (1866–1923). In 1922, his expedition discovered the tomb of Tutankhamun, but he died before the excavation was completed. Many believed he had fallen victim to the curse found inscribed upon the boy-king's tomb, which threatened dire

consequences for anybody who dared disturb it. A warning to all grave-spotters.

HURSLEY

RICHARD CROMWELL (1626–1712), 'Tumbledown Dick', was Lord of the Manor here, and Lord Protector after his father's death in 1685. On the Restoration, in 1659, he had to flee to the Continent for twenty years, never seeing his wife again. But he's said to be buried in the church here beneath the chancel. Outside in the churchyard lies JOHN KEBLE (1792–1866), the leader of the Oxford Movement, which galvanized the conservative wing of the Victorian Church with its call for a return to the (Catholic, High-Church) essentials of Anglicanism. Keble was vicar here from 1836 until his death, and used the royalties from his books, including the enormously popular *The Christian Year* (1827), a collection of devotional verse, to rebuild the church.

LYMINGTON

In the churchyard lies the Victorian poet, COVENTRY PATMORE (1823–96), perhaps unfairly regarded as the epitome of all that is trite and precious in Victorian verse, and notorious in particular for his four-volume panegyric to married love, *The Angel in the House* (1854–62). The first Mrs Patmore died in 1862, but there were plenty more angels where she came from, and Patmore would marry twice more before he died.

LYNDHURST

The ashes of Lewis Carroll's young friend, 'Looking-Glass'

ALICE LIDDELL (1852–1934), as Mrs Hargreaves, are buried in the churchyard here.

MINSTEAD

The creator of Brigadier Gerard, Professor Challenger and, above all, Sherlock Holmes, ARTHUR CONAN DOYLE (1859–1930) was first buried at home at Windlesham, by the summerhouse where he'd liked to work. There was an oak marker with the words 'STEEL TRUE/BLADE STRAIGHT'. Windlesham was sold in 1955, so Arthur and his wife Jean were moved to a new grave beneath an oak tree at the east end of Minstead churchyard, near the new family home at Bignell House. The remains were moved late at night, in a laundry van, to avoid publicity.

NORTH BADDESLEY

The churchyard here has two gravestones to one man, Charles Smith, who was executed in 1822 for shooting at a gamekeeper while he was poaching on Lord Palmerston's estate. The father of gunboat diplomacy rather pacifically sued for his life, but the judge refused. The more sympathetic stone is said to have been put up by William Cobbett.

OTTERBOURNE

CHARLOTTE MARY YONGE (1823–1901), the popular and prolific Victorian novelist, author of over 150 books, lived just across the street from the churchyard in Elderfield house. She had only a short journey to make, therefore, to her final resting place at the foot of the memorial to John Keble (see Hursley for his actual grave), of whose High Church crusade she had been a fervent supporter.

PORTSMOUTH

Outside the west door of the Garrison Church is the grave of SIR CHARLES NAPIER (1782–1853), warrior and wag. Upon conquering the Indian province of Sind, he despatched the simple Latin message, '*peccavi*' – 'I have sinned', ho, ho, ho.

ROMSEY

LORD LOUIS MOUNTBATTEN (1900–79), Mountbatten of Burma, killed by the IRA in County Sligo, is here at the abbey. Despite never having been a good sailor in life, his flamboyant wife LADY EDWINA MOUNTBATTEN (1901–60) had requested burial at sea 'in a sack'. In accordance with at least part of her wishes she had been carried out from Portsmouth on the frigate HMS *Wakeful* and dropped overboard, but in a tasteful wooden coffin. An earlier occupant of Broadlands House, the Victorian statesman Lord Palmerston had intended to be buried here with his ancestors, but his cabinet colleagues insisted on a Westminster Abbey burial.

SELBORNE

GILBERT WHITE (1720–93), naturalist, was born here in the rectory, and lived at The Wakes from the age of ten. He did time at Oxford as student and Fellow, then in 1755 retired to Selborne where, living in The Wakes once more, he served as curate and chronicled the minutiae of the village's natural history until he took his own place in the food chain beneath a simple stone in the churchyard.

The Wakes now serves as a museum not only to White but to two Selborne explorers who might have been buried here had things panned out differently. Frank Oates never made it back from an expedition in Africa in the nineteenth century, but seems none the less to have passed on his luck to his nephew, Captain Lawrence 'I May Be Some Time' Oates, who accompanied Scott to the South Pole in 1911–12.

FUNERAL LABOUR

Disliking the newfangled and, he felt, 'improper custom of burying with the body of the church', naturalist Gilbert White's will specified that he wished to be buried:

> *In the church yard belonging to the parish church of Selborne aforesaid in as plain and private a way as possible without any pall bearers or parade and that six honest day labouring men respect being had to such as have bred up large families may bear me to my grave.*

The fee for carrying the coffin would have been a useful supplement to a poor family's income.

WEST MEON

Beneath the hallowed turf of St John the Evangelist churchyard lies THOMAS LORD (1757–1832), the groundsman-made-good who in 1787 founded Lord's Cricket Ground.

WINCHESTER

THE CATHEDRAL: The site of the grave of ST SWITHUN (d. 862) is marked by a stone outside the cathedral, while another Bishop of Winchester, WILLIAM OF WYKEHAM (1324–1404), is in the Chantry Chapel. William was not only a bishop but twice Chancellor of England, but it is as founder of Winchester School that he is now remembered. His tomb is inscribed with his famous motto, 'Manners Makyth Man'.

The cathedral is rich in royal remains too: on top of the presbytery screen are six chests containing bones rescued from the ruined – indeed now largely disappeared – Old Minster on the same site. Various notables are represented, including CYNEGILS, a seventh-century King of Wessex, and two of his successors from the ninth century, EGBERT and AETHELWULF. The latter was father of King Alfred the Great, whose eldest son EDMUND is also here. Then there's the Danish interloper CNUT (c. 994–1035, reigned 1016–35), famous for trying to stop the waves, and his Saxon queen EMA (d. 1052). She'd already been a royal consort once as queen of the late Aethelred: Cnut married her when he took the throne to avoid problems of succession. Who's who exactly among all this distinguished bone it's impossible to say. Indeed, since they were opened and their contents mixed up in the seventeenth century during the Civil War, it's been impossible even to say who's in which box.

Cnut and Ema's son HARTHACNUT (1019–42, reigned 1040–2) was also supposed to have been buried in the Old Minster, so presumably lies somewhere beneath the present cathedral and its immediate environs. When he died, according to the *Anglo-Saxon Chronicle*, 'his mother, for his soul's salvation, gave to the New Minster the head of St Valentine the Martyr' – so that too must be here somewhere.

The 'New Minster', ironically, predated the Norman cathedral by a couple of centuries, and is now lost pretty much without trace beneath the medieval and modern city of Winchester. That's a pity, given that it was the burial place of, among others, its founder ALFRED THE GREAT (849–99, reigned 871–99). The Norman chronicler William of Malmesbury reports that Alfred was buried in the Old Minster because his new monastery was unfinished, but that 'afterwards, on account of the folly of the canons, asserting that the royal spirit, resuming its carcase, wandered nightly through the buildings, Edward, his son and successor, removed the remains of his father, and gave them a quiet resting place in the New Minster'. Of somewhat later vintage, a large tomb in the choir is said to be that of King William II, or William Rufus (c. 1056–1100), who was killed mysteriously by an arrow while hunting in the New Forest.

There are literary luminaries here too: Compleat Angler IZAAK WALTON (1593–1683), who died nearby at 78 Donne Alley, is buried in the south transept, in the Silkstede Chapel, while JANE AUSTEN (1775–1817) is buried in the north aisle. Not far away is the original Bluestocking, MRS ELIZABETH MONTAGU (1720–1800), whose salons were attended by Dr Johnson among others. The term 'bluestocking' apparently refers to the lax dress code prevailing at these gatherings not for women but for men: the presence of one impoverished young intellectual in his workaday blue woollen stockings, rather than the finer items normally prescribed for evening wear, raised eyebrows among severer social commentators, and gave rise to the name.

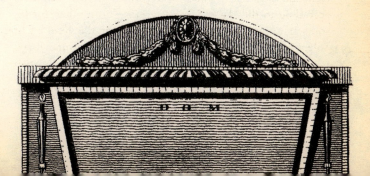

Hereford & Worcester

BREDWARDINE

His grave marked by a white cross, the diarist FRANCIS KILVERT (1841–79) is buried in the graveyard of the church where he was vicar for the last two years of his life. Kilvert's famous diary, discovered in 1937 and published soon afterwards, was kept from 1870–79, here in Bredwardine and in his previous living just over the border at Clyro, Powys, where he was curate. It gives a fresh and vivid picture of life in the Welsh Marches in the Victorian era.

EVESHAM

SIMON DE MONTFORT (c. 1208–65) was buried in what was once the abbey here, and there's a memorial stone to him on the site of the former altar. The Earl of Leicester, de Montfort led a group of barons in revolt against what they regarded as Henry III's high-handed rule. Full of good intentions, they proposed inaugurating a parliamentary system which would represent not only nobles and churchmen but the citizenry of the towns. The rebellion was effectively ended at the Battle of Evesham, at which de Montfort was killed.

GREAT MALVERN

In the churchyard, buried beneath a slab of granite brought from her home country, is the soprano JENNY LIND

(1820–87), the Swedish Nightingale, who lived nearby at Wynds Point.

WAGES FOR SINS

According to John Aubrey, writing in the seventeenth century:

> *In the county of Hereford was an old custom at funerals, to hire poor people, who were to take upon them all the sins of the party deceased. One of them I remember (he was a long, lean, lamentable, poor rascal) lived in a cottage on Ross highway. The manner was that when the corpse was brought out of the house and laid on the bier, a loaf of bread was brought out, and delivered to the sin-eater over the corpse, as also a mazard [cherry] bowl full of beer, which he was to drink up, and sixpence in money, in consideration whereof he took upon him… all the sins of the defunct, and freed him or her from walking after they were dead.*

HEREFORD

The tomb of ST THOMAS DE CANTELUPE (c. 1218–82) is here, in the north transept of the cathedral. Lord Chancellor of England for a few months during 1265, when Simon de Montfort had held power in the realm, and afterwards an adviser to Edward I, Cantelupe disliked the Welsh and the Jews in equal measure. He died in Orvieto while on a trip to Rome in hopes of enlisting the Pope's support in a quarrel with a neighbouring see. According to the custom of the day, his body was boiled to separate the flesh from the bones. The flesh was interred in Italy, the bones brought back here to a shrine in the cathedral, where a series of miracles led to Thomas' canonization in 1320.

LITTLE MALVERN

EDWARD ELGAR (1857–1934), composer, famously, of the Enigma Variations and, more notoriously, of 'Land of Hope and Glory', is buried here beside his wife Alice in St Wulstan's churchyard. He had in fact asked merely to have his name added to his wife's headstone. His body he'd wanted cremated and the ashes scattered at the confluence of the rivers Severn and Teme. This request shocked family members, like Elgar himself staunch Catholics, and it was accordingly overruled.

ROSS-ON-WYE

A cross in the churchyard commemorates over three hundred victims of a plague outbreak of 1637, who were buried in a nearby pit.

WELSH NEWTON

JOHN KEMBLE (c. 1599–1679), who is buried here in the churchyard, was a forebear of the theatrical Kembles of the nineteenth century. His life was not without its own drama, though: a Catholic priest in an age when that wasn't a very comfortable thing to be, he managed to keep a jump or two ahead of the authorities for an astonishing fifty-four years before he was finally caught and martyred.

WEST MALVERN

In the churchyard, graveyard, burial ground or cemetery of St James' Church lies PETER MARK ROGET (1779–1869), who would probably have liked to be remembered as an eminent physician and Secretary of the Royal Society from 1827–49 but is actually famous for a bright idea he had after that: his 1852 *Thesaurus*.

WORCESTER

THE CATHEDRAL: Two saints have their shrines here, ST OSWALD (d. 992) and ST WULFSTAN (d. c. 1095). Little is actually known of their lives, but that didn't stop them from having a huge cult following in medieval times. Hence the presence in the presbytery of the signer of the Magna Carta, KING JOHN 'LACKLAND' (1167–1216, reigned 1199–1216), hoping that some of the saints' grace would rub off on him. King John, according to tradition, had to be buried minus his bowels, taken from his corpse by the abbot of Croxton, Leicestershire, who had tended him after his drenching in the Wash. When John died, the abbot, fearing accusations that he'd poisoned the King, removed the internal organs and kept them in a stone chest in the abbey chapel, where they've been ever since.

More recently, the cathedral would become the home for the ashes of Conservative prime minister STANLEY BALDWIN (1867–1947), which were placed beside those of his wife in the nave. In office for three terms – 1923–4, 1924–9 and 1935–7 – Baldwin was thus prime minister for most of the 1920s and for a crucial couple of years in the 1930s when Hitler's Germany was busy arming itself for war. Baldwin resisted rearmament, and was afterwards blamed by Churchill for leaving Britain unprepared for a world war that had been inevitable. Historians are still arguing. Baldwin wasn't kind to fascists at home: he certainly wouldn't stand for any nonsense from Edward VIII over his marriage with Mrs Simpson, forcing him to abdicate at once. The ashes of American novelist FRANCIS BRETT YOUNG (1884–1954) are also in the cathedral.

Hertfordshire

ALDBURY

Novelist and moralist MRS HUMPHRY WARD (1851–1920) lived near here at Great Stocks, and is buried in the churchyard. Born Mary Augusta Arnold (granddaughter of Thomas Arnold of Rugby, niece of poet and all-round Victorian sage Matthew), she favoured women's education though she was an outspoken campaigner against women's suffrage. Her headstone, topped by the Oxford University motto, *Dominus illuminatio Mea* ('Lord My Light'), has a book to denote her fame as novelist and gives as epitaph some lines from Arthur Hugh Clough which she'd used herself as the epitaph for her most popular fictional hero, Robert Elsmere:

> *Others, I doubt not, if not we,*
> *The issues of our toil shall see,*
> *And, they forgotten and unknown,*
> *Younger children gather as their own*
> *The harvest that the dead had sown.*

Mr Humphry Ward, for many years art critic of *The Times*, joined her in the grave in 1926.

AYOT ST LAWRENCE, NEAR ST ALBANS

The dramatist and socialist GEORGE BERNARD SHAW (1856–1950) lived at Shaw Corner, at the south end of the village; upon his death his ashes were scattered in the garden. He claimed that he had come to live here after seeing a gravestone in the churchyard for a woman who had lived to the age of seventy but whose gravestone none the less lamented, 'Her time was short'. 'I knew that Ayot, where they call a life of seventy years a short one, was the place for me,' said GBS.

HARPENDEN

In the garden of remembrance by the church were scattered the ashes of TV comedian ERIC MORECAMBE (originally Eric Bartholomew, 1926–84).

HATFIELD

Various members of the Cecil family, whose ancestral home is at Hatfield House, were buried in the churchyard. They include LORD ROBERT CECIL, MARQUESS OF SALISBURY (1830–1903), Disraeli's successor as leader of the Conservative Party and prime minister 1885–6, 1886–92 and 1895–1902. Also here is LADY CAROLINE LAMB (1785–1828), for a time Lord Byron's lover. After the affair ended, Lady Caroline slid by degrees into autobiographical fiction and then madness while Byron went off to Greece in search of democracy, glory and shepherd boys. The story goes that, walking out one morning, she chanced upon Byron's funeral procession on its way north (see Hucknall, Nottinghamshire), and that it was this shock which tipped her over the edge into insanity.

KINGS LANGLEY

Buried in the ruined Dominican Friary here – though not before a macabre adventure or two – was the body of Edward II's chief adviser, foster brother, friend (and, it was generally believed, lover) PIERS GAVESTON (d. 1312), Earl of Cornwall. Gaveston was 'executed' by a group of the rebellious Queen Isabella's supporters on Blacklow Hill, near Warwick. Four cobblers, who afterwards found the headless body, public-spiritedly took it to the Earl of Warwick. The noble lord being one of Isabella's men (and indeed one of the murderers), he refused to take delivery, and sent the cobblers packing. Finding themselves with a headless royal favourite on their hands, they neatly sewed the head back on and bore the whole respectfully to Oxford, where they had more luck with the Dominican friars. They were prepared to accept the body, but while they embalmed it, they still wouldn't bury it, since Gaveston had been excommunicated by the then Archbishop of Canterbury, Robert de Winchelsey, another Isabella supporter. Eventually, Edward III having succeeded in standing up to his mother rather more successfully than his father had, the 'French She-Wolf' and her supporters were brought to heel, and Gaveston was given a Christian burial at Kings Langley, where he'd once spent happy times with his royal friend.

SHROUDED IN WOOL

Certificates displayed in the church at Hertingfordbury confirm the corpses had been wrapped in wool shrouds, in accordance with an ordinance of the eighteenth century designed to encourage the wool industry. A French visitor to England, M. Misson, was sufficiently intrigued by this law to give a full account:

> To make these dresses is a particular trade, and there are many that sell nothing else; so that these habits for the dead are always to be had ready made, of what size or price you please, for people of every age and sex. After they have washed the body thoroughly clean, and shaved it, if it be a man, and his beard be grown during his sickness, they put on it a flannel shirt, which has commonly a sleeve purfled about the wrists, and the slit of the shirt down the breast done in the same manner. When these ornaments are not of woollen lace, they are at least edged, and sometimes embroidered with black thread. The shirt should be at least a foot longer than the body, that the feet of the deceased may be wrapped in it, as in a bag. When they have thus folded the end of this shirt close to the feet, they tie the part that is folded down with a piece of woollen thread, as we do our stockings, so that the end of the shirt is done into a kind of tuft. Upon the head they put a cap, which they fasten with a very broad chin cloth, with gloves on the hands, and a cravat round the neck all of woollen ... Instead of a cap, the women have a kind of head-dress, with a forehead-cloth.

NORTHCHURCH

At the church here is the grave of 'Peter', a feral boy found in Hanover, Germany, and brought to England for exhibition in 1726.

PERRY GREEN, NEAR WARE

Sculptor HENRY MOORE (1898–1986), *enfant terrible* of the 1930s avant garde and grand old man of the postwar scene, had a house near here, at Hoglands. He is buried in the village churchyard.

ST ALBANS

THE CATHEDRAL: This houses the shrine of ST ALBAN (d. c. 303) himself, executed by the Romans for harbouring a priest and for refusing to sacrifice to the Roman gods. As the soldier struck the death-blow, according to tradition, his eyes fell out of his head. The shrine was destroyed at the time of the Reformation, but was pieced together again afterwards. Prior to the Reformation what was now the cathedral was actually the abbey church. The abbey being dissolved under Henry VIII, only the church was left, as a mere parish church for the town. With the growth of St Albans in the nineteenth century, the church was awarded its present cathedral status. In the presbytery, near the altar, was buried RICHARD OF WALLINGFORD (c. 1292–1336), an Abbot of St Albans who was also the foremost mathematician of his age and inventor of a famous astronomical clock.

ST MICHAEL's CHURCH: 'It is as natural to die as to be born; and to a little infant, perhaps, the one is as painful as the other...' On thus entering his own third childhood, the

THE DEATH OF BACON

John Aubrey heard the circumstances of Francis Bacon's death from a mutual friend, Thomas Hobbes:

> *Mr. Hobbs told me that the cause of his Lordship's death was trying an Experiment; viz. as he was taking the aire in a Coach with Dr. Witherborne (a Scotchman, Physitian to the King) towards High-gate, snow lay on the ground, and it came into my Lord's thoughts, why flesh might not be preserved in snow, as in Salt. They were resolved they would try the Experiment presently. They alighted out of the Coach and went into a poore woman's house at the bottom of Highgate hill, and bought a Hen, and made the woman exenterate it, and then stuffed the body with Snow, and my Lord did help to doe it himselfe. The Snow so chilled him that he immediately fell so extremely ill, that he could not returne to his Lodging (I suppose then at Graye's Inne) but went to the Earle of Arundel's house at High-gate, where they putt him into a good bed warmed with a Panne, but it was a damp bed that had not been layn-in in about a yeare before, which gave him such a colde that in 2 or 3 dayes as I remember Mr. Hobbes told me, he dyed of Suffocation.*

statesman and scholar FRANCIS BACON, Viscount St Albans (1561–1626), was buried here on the north side of the chancel. Bacon was a man of many parts, though his achievements are not nowadays thought to have included writing Shakespeare. He was an inquiring, adventurous Renaissance man to the end, however, whose remarkable death at the agency of a frozen chicken only highlights how far he was ahead of his time. His Latin epigraph by Sir Henry Wotton, translates:

> *The Light of the Sciences, the Law of eloquence, who after he had unfolded all the Mysteries of Natural and Civil Wisdom, obeyed the Decree of Nature.*

Let the Companions be parted.
Francis Bacon Died on Easter Sunday, 1626.

Bacon is thought to lie here still, though some did later say that his body had been moved, and there are even those who believe he was never here at all, but that he faked his death (in between scribbling scenes of *Hamlet*) in order to escape into exile from a hostile King and Court.

SHENLEY

NICHOLAS HAWKSMOOR (1661–1736) acquired fame in 1985 when he became the subject of a novel by Peter Ackroyd. Wren's assistant in the construction of St Paul's and architect of among other churches St George's, Bloomsbury and St Mary Woolnoth, Mansion House, he lived nearby at Porter's Park and is buried at the parish church.

TEWIN

'Six forest trees – that is a fact – grow out of one of the graves in Tewin churchyard', writes E.M. Forster in his novel *Howard's End*. 'The grave's occupant – that is the legend – is an atheist, who declared that if God existed six forest trees would grow out of her grave.'

Humberside

BEVERLEY

In the Minster here are the remains of ST JOHN OF BEVERLEY (d. 721). St John's relics were reputed to have a calming effect on ferocious animals; bulls wouldn't fight bulldogs set against them in the churchyard here, for example. Englishmen were apparently beyond such influences, however: they marched into battle against the Scots behind the banner of St John, with devastating results.

HULL

Cottingham Cemetery provides the last resting place for PHILIP LARKIN (1922–85), now rather less famous for his poetry than for his views – forcefully expressed in letters published in 1992 – on Blacks, Women, Sex, the Labour Party and other great problems of our time.

RUDSTON

A native of Rudston, the writer and journalist WINIFRED HOLTBY (1898–1935) is buried in All Saints' churchyard. Her most famous novel, *South Riding*, was published posthumously in 1936.

Isle of Wight

BONCHURCH

The eleventh-century old church near the sea may be very picturesque, but it's the graveyard of the new church, above, that boasts ALGERNON CHARLES SWINBURNE (1837–1909). Even the most decadent poet has to have an innocent childhood somewhere, and Swinburne's was here, though his family moved away in the 1860s. Visiting the grave the year after his hero's death, Hardy described the scene in his 'A Singer Asleep':

> In this fair niche above the unslumbering sea,
> That sentrys up and down all night, all day,
> From cove to promontory, from ness to bay,
> The fates have fitly bidden that he should be
>   Pillowed eternally.

By 1910 the fuss surrounding Swinburne's death had had time to die down, and the late singer could indeed sleep quietly. Things hadn't always been so peaceful, though. Inevitably, given the almost diabolical status Swinburne's sensuous, studiously amoral verse had gained him in many quarters, the funeral had proved controversial. The officiating clergyman was severely criticized for having agreed to conduct the ceremony at all (respectable opinion having regarded Swinburne as, quite literally, a corrupter of the nation's youth) while the poet's more doctrinaire followers on the other hand objected to the brief funeral prayer he had offered, overruling – arguably – Swinburne's last request not to have a funeral service but simply to be lowered into the ground while his friends strewed flowers on his coffin. The vicar argued, reasonably enough, that the prayer he'd offered had hardly amounted to a service, that Swinburne's dying instructions had been extremely vague, and that, given that the deceased had specifically requested a churchyard burial, he could hardly object to some minimal religious content in his funeral ceremony.

Kent

ASHFORD

In Bybrook Cemetery is the grave of SIMONE WEIL (1909–43), mystic, philosopher and member of the Free French Government. The effects of the TB from which she suffered were aggravated by her gesture of solidarity in refusing to eat more than the rations allowed her compatriots in occupied France. A stern English coroner, unimpressed by this gallic extravagance, recorded her death as suicide while the balance of the mind was disturbed.

BIRCHINGTON

In All Saints' churchyard, near the south porch of the church, lies the painter and poet DANTE GABRIEL ROSSETTI (1828–82), leader of the Pre-Raphaelite Brotherhood. His grave is topped by a monument in the form of a Celtic cross designed by his one-time teacher, eventual disciple, Ford Madox Brown.

BISHOPSBOURNE

In the church where he served as vicar is the tomb of the REVEREND RICHARD HOOKER (1554–1600). An important

Anglican thinker, his book *Ecclesiastical Polity* argued influentially for a middle way for Anglicanism between Puritanism and Rome.

CANTERBURY

Just outside the town at Fordwich is the partly Norman sculptured tomb which is said once to have housed ST AUGUSTINE OF CANTERBURY (d. 604), Pope Gregory I's missionary to England and founder of the English church. Various Saxon saints were buried in the now-ruined abbey named after him, including ST DUNSTAN (924–88). A man of many parts, Dunstan was skilled in painting and metalworking as well as in the essential pre-Gutenberg accomplishment of transcribing written manuscripts. It had been his (falsely) alleged prowess in blacker arts that led to his losing his place at the court of King Aethelstan (see Malmesbury, Wiltshire) and taking up his religious vocation.

THE CATHEDRAL: This is, of course, the last resting place of THOMAS À BECKET (1118–70), Archbishop of Canterbury 1162–70, the 'turbulent priest' hacked to death within these portals by four barons overzealously devoted to Henry II. A London merchant's son, Thomas was a smart, attractive and ambitious young man with a positive genius for working the aristocratic patronage system. By 1155 he was Royal Chancellor and the King's best friend. He lived lavishly, enjoying the fact and trappings of power and wealth. Technically, at least, he was a clerk in holy orders, hence Henry's bright idea of appointing him to the Canterbury see, which he hoped would annoy the church hierarchy and place his own man in the job. He was successful, initially at least, in the first objective, but quickly found that he'd gravely miscalculated in the second. Thomas went native from the first, giving away his wealth to the poor, transforming his lifestyle and, more important, consistently standing up for the Church against the King. Relations were

THE BECKET FACTOR

The shrine of St Thomas (he was canonized in a lightning-quick three years) would prove a popular place of pilgrimage right up to the Reformation. Six days after his murder in Canterbury Cathedral, a blind woman regained her sight after touching one of Thomas' bloodstained garments, and soon miracles were taking place in the cathedral at a rate of up to ten a day. The cult was soon an industry, the great spiritual rebirth some naïve souls had been hoping would come out of the martyrdom a distant memory as the local clergy cashed in on the Becket Factor, selling not only masses and prayers but vials of the martyr's blood and scraps of his clothing (the apparent limitlessness of both these commodities being something of a miracle in itself). Becket's tomb was smashed during the Reformation, and his bones scattered, but the skull is thought to have been preserved safely under the Corona, or 'Becket's Crown', at the east end of the cathedral.

extremely fraught for some years, Thomas having to flee into exile in France in 1164 after the King ordered his execution for treason. When he returned in 1170, looking set to be as troublesome as ever, Henry finally lost control and in exasperation asked his famous – and, he afterwards insisted, rhetorical – question in the hearing of a group of gung-ho supporters who didn't have to be asked twice: 'Will no one rid me of this turbulent priest?' (Henry II died while campaigning in France, where he is buried at Fontevraud.)

In St Anselm's Chapel, ST ANSELM (1033–1109) himself is buried beside his Italian mentor and predecessor as archbishop of Canterbury, Lanfranc (c. 1005–89), under whom the young Anselm studied philosophy and theology in France. EDWARD, THE BLACK PRINCE (1330–76), son of Edward III and hero of Crécy, is also buried here. He died a year before his father, so never made it beyond the rank of Prince of Wales. Also among those present (along with over fifty bishops) are HENRY IV (1367–1413) and his queen JOAN OF NAVARRE (c. 1370–1437).

ORLANDO GIBBONS (1583–1625), royal keyboardist and composer, is also buried in the cathedral. In addition to his church music, Gibbons wrote beautiful madrigals and music for viols and virginals.

FREDERIC WILLIAM FARRAR (1831–1903), the Dean of Canterbury who put the fear of God into generations of children with his moral shocker *Eric, or Little By Little* (1858) is in the cathedral cloisters cemetery, as is vicar-of-the-airwaves DICK SHEPPARD (1880–1937), actually the Very Reverend Hugh Richard Lawrie Sheppard. In his time at St Martin-in-the-Fields he became a popular broadcaster, delivering sermons over the radio. He had been Dean of Canterbury, 1929–31.

In the grounds of the King's School, near the library he had donated, were scattered the ashes of the writer WILLIAM SOMERSET MAUGHAM (1874–1965), who was an alumnus of the school (though he had, by all accounts, been wretchedly unhappy there).

In the northeast corner of the Catholic Cemetery lies Teodor Józef Konrad Nalecz Korzeniowski, better known as novelist JOSEPH CONRAD (1857–1924). The grey granite headstone bears a couplet from Spenser's *Faerie Queene*, used by Conrad as his epigraph for *The Rover*:

> *Sleep after toyle, port after stormie seas,*
> *Ease after warre, death after life, does greatly please.*

but otherwise makes no reference to his work as writer, not even giving his English *nom de plume*.

According to some accounts, Thomas More's head is in St Dunstan's Church, rescued by his daughter Margaret Roper and placed in the Roper family vault beneath St Nicholas' Chapel. She herself is buried in Chelsea Parish Church, so maybe his head is with her there. The rest of him is in the Tower of London church, St Peter ad Vincula.

On the east side of St Martin's churchyard lies MARY TOURTEL (1874–1948), creator of Rupert Bear, with husband, Herbert Bird Tourtel (1874–1931), the *Daily Express* deputy editor who gave her the original commission in 1920.

DARTFORD

England's first papermaker SIR JOHN SPIELMAN (d. 1626) is buried in the parish church here, while in the public park that was once the churchyard a plaque marks the approximate location (exact position now lost) of the grave of engineer and adventurer RICHARD TREVITHICK (1771–1833). A fairly hapless sort of genius, Trevithick raced a locomotive of his own design against a racehorse at Gower Street, London, in 1808. It might even have won, had it not been derailed before the finish. Trevithick then spent several years in Latin America where he made – and lost – his pile repeatedly before limping back to England where he died in poverty.

EAST FARLEIGH

In St Mary's churchyard is a wooden memorial 'In Memory of Forty-Three Strangers who died of cholera. September 1849. R.I.P.' East-enders come for the hop-picking, they were commemorated by sympathetic local residents. The present memorial is a replacement erected in 1984, by which time the original had pretty much rotted away.

EASTWELL

Among the ruins of St Mary's Church, by tradition, is the grave of RICHARD PLANTAGENET (1469–1550), reputed to be the bastard son of Richard III.

FOLKESTONE

In Cheriton Road Cemetery lies CHARLES STUART CALVERLEY (1831–84), 'Prince of Parodists'. A barrister by profession, a skating accident saw him invalided out in 1865, leaving him ample time to pursue his real love of light verse and wit.

In 1976, Folkestone saw the end of Absolute Beginner COLIN MACINNES (1914–76), its Fish Market providing the curious setting for his funeral, after which his coffin was rowed out to sea and consigned to the deep three miles out. Sixty years earlier, the channel here had provided a watery grave for the Spanish Romantic composer ENRIQUE GRANADOS (1867–1916) and his wife Amparo. They had been visiting London on a concert tour and were among some fifty passengers lost when the English mail-boat the SS *Sussex* was torpedoed by a German U-boat.

GRAVESEND

St George's Church, now the Chapel of Unity, has two windows commemorating the Red Indian Princess POCAHONTAS (1595–1617), who is supposed to have been buried here – there's a statue in the former churchyard. The English adventurer John Smith (see Holborn Viaduct, City of London) claimed that she had saved his life a couple of times when he was at the mercy of her tribe. Cajoled (or coerced, depending which source you believe) back to Jamestown, Virginia in 1612, she was converted to Christianity and baptized Rebecca. The following year she married the Englishman John Rolfe (1585–1622) and in 1616 she came with him on a visit to England, where she was received by royalty. She had already embarked for the return voyage when she died of smallpox off Gravesend. Pocahontas left a son, and several old Virginia families like to claim descent from her. By the present century the colonial tables had begun to turn (not that this had done Pocahontas' people so much good): excavations undertaken by the US government during the 1920s tore up St George's inside and out and unearthed over 150 bodies, outraging local feeling without, however, coming up with any sure-fire Indian Princesses. It has in any case been suggested that there was another burial ground in the neighbourhood for foreigners and those dying offshore, and that Pocahontas may have been there all along.

OLD ROMNEY

Beneath a favourite yew tree in St Clement's churchyard was

buried the artist, film director and gay-rights campaigner DEREK JARMAN (1942–94). He died of AIDS, having recorded his decline in the film *Blue*. His friend the theatre critic Nicholas de Jongh told the congregation at his funeral service: 'All down the exciting road Derek travelled as the first and greatest English gay icon; he blazed a trail. He showed what it was in our cruel, unfeeling times to be an outcast, reviled and persecuted for a sexuality in which he rejoiced and saw no shred of evil.'

RAMSGATE

In St Augustine's Catholic Church, which he had built at his own expense, lies the architect and visionary AUGUSTUS WELBY PUGIN (1812–52). Like Ruskin, Pugin saw in medievalism an opportunity of escaping the soullessness and squalor of the industrial nineteenth century, and found in the gothic style, with its wealth of highly idiosyncratic detail, a means of accommodating the individual genius of each craftsman, otherwise alienated as the mere tools of white-collar architects. Pugin went rather further than Ruskin, however, in adopting the religion of the medieval age.

ROCHESTER

The shrine in the cathedral to ST WILLIAM OF PERTH, murdered in 1201, was long a rival to Becket's as a place of pilgrimage. It seems odd on the face of it that a St William of Perth should have his shrine in Rochester, but it's easily enough explained. The pious young man, who did indeed come from Perth, was passing through the district on a pilgrimage to the Holy Land when his travelling companion turned on him and killed him for his possessions. A mad woman, stumbling upon his body, was miraculously healed, and the rest is ecclesiastical history... There's also a memorial here to Charles Dickens. The novelist was buried in Westminster Abbey by a grateful nation which was not, however, grateful enough to respect his express wish to be interred here in Rochester.

ST MARY IN THE MARSH, ROMNEY MARSH

E. NESBIT (1858–1924) was author of *The Railway Children* (1906) and other children's classics. Her grave on the south side of the churchyard is marked with a simple wooden board carved by her second husband, Captain Tucker.

SALTWOOD

Mr Civilization, the art historian KENNETH CLARK (Lord Clark 1903–83), was buried in the churchyard, by the medieval castle he'd bought in 1953.

SISSINGHURST

In the churchyard here lies SIR HAROLD NICOLSON (1886–1968), who had important careers as diplomat, novelist and literary critic, but is most famous as the long-suffering husband of Vita Sackville-West (see Withyham, East Sussex), with whom he created the beautiful garden at their nearby Sissinghurst Castle home.

SUTTON VALENCE

In the churchyard here lies JOHN WILLES (1777–1852), who is said to have introduced round-arm bowling into cricket. (The same claim is, however, made for Frederick William Lillywhite: see Highgate, North London.)

TROTTISCLIFFE

Painter GRAHAM SUTHERLAND (1903–80) is buried in Trottiscliffe, in the churchyard. Most famous for his landscapes, Sutherland also acquired a certain notoriety for a portrait of Sir Winston Churchill to which its subject strongly objected (claiming that it made him look 'half-witted') and which the outraged Lady Churchill quietly had destroyed a couple of years later. This fact didn't emerge until after her death in 1977 (though Sutherland himself wasn't too surprised). When it did come out it caused a furore, not least because the offending work wasn't even the Churchills' in the first place, but was the property of the nation, so however hideous it may have been it should have been consigned to the flames only by Act of Parliament.

Lancashire

SUNDERLAND

An inscribed gravestone at Sunderland Point recalls a black man, Sambo, who died in 1736.

WALTON-LE-DALE

Around 1580, the Lancashire alchemist and all-round charlatan Sir Edward Kelley, having already had both his ears cut off for 'coining base money', found himself in trouble with the authorities again when he was caught digging up bodies in the churchyard here for his necromantic experiments. He is said to have conducted satanic rites in the churchyard with his friend Sir John Dee (see Mortlake, South London).

Leicestershire

ASHBY-DE-LA-ZOUCH

In a family vault in St Helen's Church lies SELINA HASTINGS, COUNTESS OF HUNTINGDON (1707–91), who first outraged her aristocratic family by embracing Methodism and backing it with her sizeable fortune, which she used to sponsor clergymen and build chapels, then went on to outrage Wesley by siding with George Whitefield in the dispute over Calvinism which divided Methodists in the 1740s. She joined Whitefield to become co-founder of a separate Calvinist branch of the movement. It's odd that her family should have buried her in an Anglican church, but blood will tell, and certain things were expected of a woman of her station.

BELVOIR CASTLE

In the family mausoleum here are the diplomat, statesman and scholar SIR DUFF COOPER (1890–1954) and his socialite wife LADY DIANA COOPER (1892–1986).

DADLINGTON

A large number of unmarked mounds in the churchyard of

St James the Greater are thought to mark the mounds of those killed at the Battle of Bosworth, 1485. There's said to be a mass grave, too, outside the village, while the body of the battle's most distinguished casualty, King Richard III, is believed to have made it as far as Leicester, a few miles to the east.

DISHLEY, NEAR LOUGHBOROUGH

The grave of agricultural pioneer ROBERT BAKEWELL (1725–95) is here, beyond the altar rail in the ruined church. Bakewell experimented with irrigation and innovative feeding techniques and, above all, scientific stock-breeding. He succeeded in more than doubling the average weight for sheep and cattle.

LEICESTER

As Joyce's Stephen Dedalus knew from Doctor Cornwell's spelling book:

> *Wolsey died in Leicester Abbey*
> *Where the abbots buried him.*

The ruined abbey, in what is now Abbey Park, a mile north of the city centre, did indeed provide the last resting place for the ruined CARDINAL WOLSEY (c. 1475–1530), though the exact position of the grave is unknown. As the friend of Henry VIII, Thomas Wolsey became so rich and powerful that his influence rivalled the monarch's, which led to a strongly ambivalent relationship between the two men. Wolsey died while en route to London where he was to answer charges of treason brought by the royal physician. The physician accused the cardinal of bringing 'the King's Majesty into marvellous danger, for knowing himself to have the foul and contagious disease of the great pox, broken out upon him in divers parts of his body, he had come daily to His Grace, blowing upon him with his perilous and infective breath'.

THE BODY OF RICHARD III

A rich but confusing mythology centres upon the body of RICHARD III, CROOKBACK (1452–1485), who having been killed at the Battle of Bosworth, was brought back to Leicester for burial. Laid to rest, very likely in the Greyfriars Church, the bones were, in one account, disinterred at the time of the dissolution of the monasteries and thrown from Bow Bridge into the River Soar. Workmen demolishing the old bridge in 1862 found in the mud of the riverbed the skeleton of a male of more or less (to the nearest ten years or so) the right age. Another view is that he was fished out of the river soon after being thrown in, and reinterred at the east end of the Bridge. A third school of thought believes he was left undisturbed in Greyfriars, which would put him now beneath a private car park on the west side of New Street. Such is mortality.

At Welford Road Cemetery, along with various other local worthies, is THOMAS COOK (1808–92), the first ever travel agent. A cabinet-maker by trade, he worked too as rural missionary for the Baptists and campaigner for the Temperance Movement. It was to a temperance fête at Loughborough that, in 1841, he organized his first excursion, chartering a train to take local citizens for a clean, wholesome day out. The rest is history.

LUTTERWORTH

The proto-Protestant JOHN WYCLIFFE was parish priest here.

Suddenly paralysed while saying mass on Holy Innocents' Day (28 December), 1384, he lost the power of speech and died three days later. Despite his heresies, he was buried in consecrated ground. Those weren't formally denounced till 1415 when a gathering of the western Church at Constance condemned his teachings on a cool three hundred counts. His exhumation was ordered, but the bishop of the day, Repton, ignored the ruling. Repton's successor, Richard Fleming, proved more compliant, and in 1428 the remains were dug up and thrown into the nearby River Swift.

Lincolnshire

BOSTON

Underneath the bell tower of St Botolph's Church is buried the composer JOHN TAVERNER (c. 1490–1545). A native of Boston, Taverner left to go to Christ Church, Oxford, which is where he wrote the music for which he would ultimately be famous. There, however, he came under suspicion for heresy and Wolsey had him cast into a cellar (which reeked, he afterwards reported, of salt fish) along with some other suspects. Taverner was released, being, according to Wolsey, 'but a musitian', and returned to Boston, where he spent the rest of his life, an enthusiastic local representative, it is said, of Thomas Cromwell in his campaign to dissolve the monasteries and bring Catholics to the stake.

CROWLAND

The eleventh–century freedom fighter/terrorist Hereward

the Wake is traditionally held to have been buried at the abbey (now ruined) just outside town. In 1070–71, he led an uprising against the Norman conquerors. From his Isle of Ely fastness – in those days before fenland drainage, surrounded by water and treacherous swamp – he and his men sallied forth to make a nuisance of themselves in the surrounding area.

LINCOLN

THE CATHEDRAL: There are two saint Hughs in Lincoln Cathedral: the first is ST HUGH OF AVALON (c. 1135–1200), who was bishop here and responsible for rebuilding the cathedral, which had been destroyed by an earthquake. He stood out a number of times against the antisemitism of his age, which is ironic given that he was so soon to be joined in the cathedral floor by 'Little Saint Hugh', or HUGH OF LINCOLN (c. 1246–55), who is in the south choir aisle. A young choirboy, he went missing and was afterwards found dead in a Jewish-owned building: he had, it was said, been scourged and crucified in the manner of Christ. Several Jews were promptly put to death as a result, and Hugh became a focal point for medieval antisemitism in Britain, and indeed beyond – all the proof people like Chaucer's Prioress needed that Satan 'hath in Jues herte his waspes nest':

> O yonge Hugh of Lyncoln, slaynd also
> With cursed Jewes, as it is notable
> For it is but a litel while ago...

Also here, in the southeast transept of the choir, is ROBERT GROSSETESTE (c. 1170–1253). Bishop here from 1235 and an energetic campaigner for reform, he was most important as a philosopher of science, doing much to promote the works of Aristotle – up until then the preserve largely of Jewish and Arabic thinkers – in English intellectual life.

By tradition the heart of Edward I's queen Eleanor of Castile (1246–90) is buried beneath the cathedral's splendid east window. She died not far away at Harby, Nottinghamshire. The balance was taken to London, where it lies next to her husband in Westminster Abbey.

SLEAFORD

In the church here is the grave of Frances Brooke (1724–89), author (in *The History of Emily Montagu*, 1766) of the first known Canadian novel.

STAMFORD

The conductor SIR MALCOLM SARGENT (1895–1967) was buried in the town cemetery here, while the churchyard boasts the grave of DANIEL LAMBERT (1770–1809), keeper of Leicester Gaol and reputed to be the fattest ever Englishman. At the time of his death he weighed over fifty-two stone.

Merseyside

FORMBY

Author of well-loved ballads like 'Abdulla Bulbul Ameer', WILLIAM PERCY FRENCH (1854–1920) is buried in St Luke's churchyard. Born into the English landlord class in Ireland, he was a lover of Irish song and folklore. He wrote the lyrics for the traditional air 'The Mountains of Mourne', as well as composing popular pseudo-folksongs like 'Phil the Fluther's Ball' and 'Come Back Paddy Reilly'.

LIVERPOOL

MOUNT PLEASANT: In a little garden near the bottom of Mount Pleasant, all that remains of the Old Unitarian Chapel and its burial ground, lies JOSEPH BLANCO WHITE (1775–1841), who as the young priest José Blanco y Crespo scandalized Spanish clerical opinion both by his unorthodox theological views and his relationship with a woman who bore him a child. Leaving Spain for England in 1810, he went over to Anglicanism and became a leading figure in the literary and religious debates of the 1820s. In the 1830s he ended up in Liverpool, while his spiritual odyssey took him to Unitarianism. He is now commemorated by a plaque erected by the people of his native Seville, who've decided to let bygones be bygones.

ST JAMES' CEMETERY: Though a distinguished states-man, WILLIAM HUSKISSON (1770–1830) is now most famous for having been the first person to die in a railway accident (he was run over by the train at the opening of Stephenson's Liverpool to Manchester Railway). He's buried in the cemetery tucked in behind the Anglican Cathedral, which

towers overhead all the more dizzyingly thanks to the cemetery's site in a deep ravine scooped out by quarrying for the city's construction. It's a very quiet, atmospheric setting, with lots of graves of sea captains, merchants, etc, and with a fine, if now rather dilapidated rotunda, which contains Huskisson himself, along with a good deal of miscellaneous rubbish. (Huskisson was doubly unfortunate in his death and in the embarrassing monument erected to his memory in Pimlico Gardens, London, which shows him bare-shouldered under a Roman toga: 'Boredom rising from the bath,' remarked Sir Osbert Sitwell.)

WALTON: Just off Hornby Road, Walton, opposite the prison entrance on a patch of wasteground which proves, on closer examination, to be a far-flung corner of Walton Park Cemetery, in a paupers' grave together with twelve other men and women, lies Robert Noonan, better known as ROBERT TRESSELL (1870–1911), author of the classic of socialist fiction *The Ragged-Trousered Philanthropists*, who died in Walton Workhouse, which was to become a prison not long afterwards. The grave was marked only recently by a simple memorial, a marble slab inscribed with a verse:

> *Through squalid life they laboured*
> *In sordid grief they died*
> *Those sons of a mighty mother,*
> *Those props of England's pride.*
> *They are gone, there is none*
> *Can undo it, nor save our souls*
> *From the Curse.*
> *But many a million cometh,*
> *And shall they be better or worse?*

PAUPERS' BURIALS

The metamorphosis of Walton Workhouse into Walton Gaol (see Robert Tressell) was appropriate enough. From the time of Oliver Twist well into the present century the struggling poor dreaded the slide into destitution which would see them reduced to the mercy of the parish and incarceration in the workhouse where, in line with the Victorian ethic of 'self-help' (and the perennial British paranoia about 'scroungers'), they would be set jailhouse make-work such as picking oakum, breaking rocks or working treadmills – and on occasion more skilled and fulfilling tasks such as gardening or even coffin-making. Yet if the prospect of life in the workhouse seemed alarming enough, this was as nothing to the fear of dying there. The Poor Law of 1834 had decreed that those who died 'on the parish' should be given the cheapest burial possible: no church bells were to be tolled even, to save expense. Although public outcry led to some softening in the regulations, those who died in the workhouse could still expect to be stored up and carted off to the burial ground in batches. With his head full of visions of a better future, Tressell himself is unlikely to have worried too much about the precise circumstances of his burial. In an age that took the dignity of death very seriously however, this would have been the end his companions most feared, and the prospect of which would have haunted their last days. It was none the less an end to which millions before them had come: it's salutary to recall, in a guide such as this one, that the individual, marked grave of the sort mostly recorded here was a luxury beyond the reach of many people.

It is we must answer and hasten
And open wide the door
For the rich man's hurrying terror,
And the slow foot hope of the poor.

EVERTON CEMETERY: The cemetery (not, misleadingly enough, in Everton, but a couple of miles out in Fazakerley) has become a surprising focus of interest for Native Australians: the head of the Aboriginal leader Yagan, outlawed by the British in 1831, ended up here. After he was shot for the £30 bounty the authorities had set upon him, Yagan's head was brought to England and donated to the Liverpool Royal Institution. They kindly lent it to the city museum, but by 1964 its slow decomposition had gone so far that the museum had it buried in a mass grave here. It's assumed that the Australian authorities will want to have the head exhumed and given a more fitting burial in Yagan's native Western Australia.

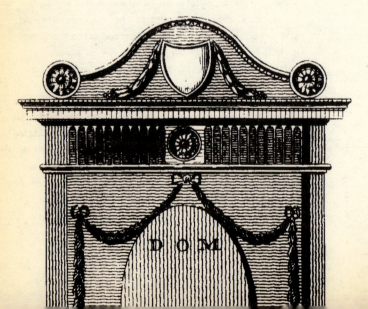

Norfolk

AYLSHAM

In the churchyard here lies the landscape gardener HUMPHRY
REPTON (1752–1818). The leading successor to Capability
Brown (see Fenstanton, Cambridgeshire), Repton moved
further still from the rigidly formal pre-Brownian rules of
landscape gardening to an altogether more unruly, extravagant
ideal of the 'picturesque'. His book, *Observations on the Theory
and Practice of Landscape Gardening* (1803), brought together much
of the experience and insight he had gained down the years.

DITCHINGHAM

A black marble slab in the chancel of the church marks the
grave of SIR HENRY RIDER HAGGARD (1856–1925), author of
hugely popular African romances like *King Solomon's Mines*
(1885) and *She* (1887). The She in Haggard's life was something
of a goldmine herself, being heiress to nearby Ditchingham
Hall, possession of which conferred on her husband the status
of landed squire, which he very much enjoyed.

EAST DEREHAM

St Nicholas' Church occupies the site of St Withburga's, a
seventh-century nunnery. The church boasts not only 'St
Withburga's Bell' but the poet and hymnist WILLIAM
COWPER (1731–1800).

LAMAS

In the Quaker Burial Ground lies ANNA SEWELL (1820–78),
author of *Black Beauty* (1877), with her mother Mary Sewell.

LANGHAM

CAPTAIN FREDERICK MARRYAT (1792–1848), author of many naval novels as well as the classic *Children of the New Forest* (1847), is buried in the churchyard here.

NEW HOUGHTON

The church in the grounds of Houghton Hall contains the family vault of the Walpoles. Whig prime minister Sir ROBERT WALPOLE (1676–1745) is here. Ruthless, corrupt but undeniably great, as prime minister for more than twenty years between 1721 and 1742, Walpole towered over his age, towering too over his son HORACE WALPOLE (1717–97), who was also laid to rest here. Very much in his father's shadow, Walpole branched out in new directions and became creator of England's first Gothic novel, *The Castle of Otranto* (1764) – and, for what it's worth, of its first Gothic mansion at Strawberry Hill, Twickenham. He also left, in over three thousand letters to friends and associates, a rich source of information and insight into the life, the culture and (for he was always, whether he liked it or not, his father's son) the politics of eighteenth-century England.

NORWICH

Like the more famous Hugh of Lincoln a young boy said to have been ritually murdered by Jews, ST WILLIAM OF NORWICH (c. 1132–44) was buried in the cathedral. A different sort of martyr was buried outside the south transept: EDITH CAVELL (1865–1915), the nurse who helped Belgian resistance get British soldiers out of enemy-held areas during the Great War. Captured, she was imprisoned and executed by firing squad, which served merely to hand the British a considerable propaganda coup (boosting recruitment, it was said, by as much as 30 per cent). Her remains were brought back at the end of the war and, after a funeral service in Westminster Abbey, reinterred here.

Outside the gothic church of St Peter Mancroft stands a statue of SIR THOMAS BROWNE (1605–82); the man himself is buried inside. An early grave-spotter, Browne was the author of *Hydrotaphia, Urn Burial* (1658), a study of ancient funerary practices, as well as other idiosyncratic studies of science, language and theology. One way and another Sir Thomas was among the most important and original thinkers of his age. That isn't what he got his knighthood for, though. He won that because in 1671 King Charles II paid a visit to Norwich and was eager to knight one of the city's leading citizens. Since the mayor declined, the knighthood fell to Browne by default.

The tomb of landscape painter JOHN CROME (1769–1821) is in the Church of St George, Colegate.

QUIDENHAM

QUEEN BOUDICCA (d. 62), who led the Iceni in rebellion against the Romans, is said to be buried in Quidenham, beneath a mound near the church. But then she's also said to be buried in London at Parliament Hill, Hampstead, at Tower Hill and even under Charing Cross station (various platforms). Well, she must be somewhere, one supposes, and it might as well be here as anywhere else.

WEST WINCH

Cartoonist, illustrator, writer and designer SIR OSBERT LANCASTER (1908–86) is buried here, in the village churchyard.

WESTON LONGVILLE

'PARSON' JAMES WOODFORDE (1740–1803) was rector here from 1776 until his death. The village was even sleepier then than it is now (it took ten days, for instance, for news to get through of the Storming of the Bastille in 1789), but the place comes joyously alive in Woodforde's five-volume *Diary of a Country Parson*. He was buried in the churchyard, and was much missed, according to parishioner Elizabeth Girling, who wrote to her brother in Manchester:

> We have likewise lost Mr. Woodforde which the parish will have reason to lament, as our new parson Mr. Dell has made the tythe double what it was.

Northamptonshire

FOTHERINGHAY

In the church is the skeleton of that hapless military commander EDWARD, SECOND DUKE OF YORK (1373–1415). An overweight man, he collapsed at Agincourt, where he was commanding the right wing, and apparently suffocated in his armour. His body having been boiled down to remove the flesh, as was the custom then, the skeleton was brought back here for burial. His nephew the Third Duke, Richard, an original contestant in the Wars of the Roses, is also here.

GREAT BRINGTON

In their family chapel in the church of St Mary the Virgin, lie the mortal remains of the Spencers, masters of nearby Althorp Hall and ancestors of DIANA, PRINCESS OF WALES (1961–97). The sometime wife of Prince Charles and thus a former future queen, Diana was to be placed here in her turn when the time came. But such was the outpouring of public emotion after she was killed in a Paris car crash with her companion Dodi Fayed (see Brookwood, page 154) that there were real fears the village might be unable to cope with the flood of visitors expected to journey to what seemed destined to become a secular shrine. She was therefore buried instead on an island in the ornamental lake at Althorp, a beautiful setting landscaped in the eighteenth century by a follower of Capability Brown. Here it was felt that public admission, while permitted at set times of the year, might be more readily controlled.

It is ironic that the world's first postmodern princess should have a send-off which recalled in scale and emotion the great public funerals of the nineteenth century. Crowds lined the London streets to watch her cortege pass, clustering along motorway shoulders and road bridges to cast flowers on to the hearse as it bore the body homeward to Northamptonshire. The death of the 'people's princess' had as yet unmeasurable consequences for the institution of the monarchy.

HARRINGTON

Among those laid to rest in the churchyard here are casualties of the Battle of Naseby, 1645, at which the Parliamentary army led by Thomas Fairfax (see Bilbrough, North Yorkshire) defeated Charles I's Cavaliers in what proved a turning point in the Civil War.

NORTHAMPTON

At the west end of St Peter's Church is the grave of WILLIAM SMITH (1769–1839), the 'father of English geology'. By training an engineer, it was when he was working for the Somerset Coal Canal that he first became interested in geological strata, devising a way of identifying the different layers by the fossils they contained. In 1815 he produced the first ever geological map of England. Smith was staying with friends in Northampton, en route to Birmingham where he was to give a lecture, when what seemed no more than a cold suddenly turned into something far worse.

ROTHWELL

In the crypt of Holy Trinity Church are thousands of bones and skulls found by a sexton when he was digging a grave in 1700. Nobody knows who they belonged to or what they were doing here.

WEEDON LOIS

Across the road from the main graveyard in the churchyard extension, beneath a monument by sculptor Henry Moore, lies the 'genuinely bogus' (Christopher Hassall) poet and critic DAME EDITH SITWELL (1887–1964).

Northumberland

BAMBURGH

The grave of GRACE DARLING (1815–42), heroine, is in

St Aidan's churchyard. In 1838, Grace and her father, keeper of the Longstone Light on the nearby Farne Islands, rowed out in a violent storm and saved five from among the passengers and crew of the shipwrecked steamboat, the *Forfarshire*, even though Grace was sickly with consumption, and would die four years later at the age of twenty-six.

KIRKNEWTON

In the churchyard here lies the Northumberland-born social reformer JOSEPHINE BUTLER (1828–1906), a campaigner against slavery and for women's education, as well, notoriously, as for prostitutes' rights.

KIRKWHELPINGTON

The inventor SIR CHARLES PARSONS (1854–1931) is buried in the graveyard of St Bartholomew's Church. In 1884, Parsons developed a steam turbine which revolutionized electricity generation – at least it would have done had a generator existed that was capable of working with such a powerful motor. In the event, Parsons had to go away and design one himself. He succeeded, however, and taken together his two inventions represented the most important innovation in steam power since Watt. They did indeed revolutionize power generation, making efficient, large-scale power generation possible for the first time. Parsons also built the first ever turbine-driven steamship, the *Turbinia*, in 1897.

MORPETH

In the churchyard, her monument bearing the pre-politically correct inscription 'Greater love hath no man than this, that a man lay down his life for his friends' as well as the motto 'Deeds, not Words', lies EMILY WILDING DAVISON (1872–1913), the suffragette who died after throwing herself in the path of the King's horse during that year's Derby.

OVINGHAM

Side by side in the village churchyard lie the engraver THOMAS BEWICK (1753–1828), famous for his *History of British Birds* (1797–1800) and for having a swan named after him, and his son, ROBERT (1788–1849), a chip off the old block and, from 1812, his father's partner.

THOCKRINGTON

In the churchyard here lies economist and social reformer WILLIAM HENRY BEVERIDGE (1879–1963), the author in 1942 of a famous report sketching the outline of the welfare state as it would be established by the Labour government that would be swept to power after the war in 1945.

Nottinghamshire

BLIDWORTH

One William Scathelock, buried in the churchyard, is traditionally supposed to be Robin Hood's Merrie Man WILL SCARLETT.

HOLBECK

In the churchyard rests LADY OTTOLINE MORRELL

(1873–1938). Virginia Woolf, who became a good friend, was much taken with her beauty: her 'red-gold hair in masses, cheeks as soft as cushions ... and a body really shaped more after my notion of a mermaid's'. Woolf's biographer and Bloomsbury insider Quentin Bell informs his readers that Morrell for her part was in love with Virginia Woolf, but, nothing daunted, goes directly on to claim that Lady Ottoline brought to the Bloomsbury Group 'a very strong heterosexual element'. He sums up her role: 'She brought petticoats, frivolity and champagne to the buns, the buggery and the high thinking of Fitzroy Square.' This may not seem too much of an achievement, but such is fame.

SOUTHWELL DRINKER

The case of Nottinghamshire man John Adams, 'a carrier, who died of drunkenness', so tickled the young Byron that he wrote him a mock epitaph:

> *John Adams lies here, of the parish of Southwell*
> *A Carrier who carried his can to his mouth well:*
> *He carried so much, and he carried so fast,*
> *He could carry no more – so was carried at last;*
> *For, the liquor he drank, being too much for one,*
> *He could not carry off, – so he's now carri-on.*

HOLME PIERREPONT

JOHN OLDHAM (1653–83), the poet, satirist and translator, was buried at the church here.

HUCKNALL

> *Death, so called, is a thing which makes men weep,*
> *And yet a third of Life is passed in sleep.*

GEORGE GORDON, LORD BYRON (1788–1824), at once the ultimate in cynics and the ultimate in Romantics, takes his last, long lie-in in a family vault at the church here (the family seat was at Newstead Abbey, four miles to the north). Byron died, famously, at Missolonghi, where he had gone to do his bit for the Greeks in their fight for liberty from the Turks, though modern scholars strongly suspect that it wasn't so much the swamp fever that killed him as the rigorous course of bleeding his doctors instituted. He had earlier written in a letter:

> I am sure my bones would not rest in an English grave, or my clay mix with the earth of that country. I believe the thought would drive me mad on my deathbed, could I suppose that any of my friends would be base enough to convey my carcass back to your soil.

Be that as it may, he was brought back, and if the aristocracy was frankly ambivalent about the return of such a very prodigal son (see Hatfield, Hertfordshire), the proles were in no doubt that he warranted a hero's welcome. They hadn't forgotten Byron's eloquent attacks on big landowners and big business (and they'd never known about the contempt he had on occasion been known to express in private for the great unwashed: Byron arguably preferred the battle for freedom to be fought abroad). Thousands thronged the route as the cortège made its way slowly through London, and as the hearse progressed northward on its four-day journey through the Midlands, the people turned out in force in every town and village to salute the fallen rebel, the crowds becoming even greater as it neared his Nottinghamshire home.

Byron's daughter AUGUSTA 'ADA' KING, COUNTESS OF

LOVELACE (1815–52) is here as well. A talented mathematician, she helped her friend Charles Babbage in his experiments with computer-like calculating machines and wrote a popular account of his innovations. (The computer language ADA, at one time used as standard by the US military and NATO, was named after her, which would doubtless have made her heart swell with pride.) Ada was also talented at losing money, thanks to her compulsive gambling. She pawned the family diamonds, then when they were redeemed by a relation promptly pawned them again, and still managed to leave a heap of debts when she died, of cancer of the womb. Though she took after Byron in waywardness, she didn't know him well: her request to be buried with her father seems to have owed less to filial devotion to him than to her lifelong desire to annoy her mother, Anne Milbanke, with whom she always had a difficult relationship.

Oxfordshire

BURFORD

Buried in the church is WILLIAM LENTHALL (1591–1662), who as Speaker of the Commons from 1640 to 1653 defied Charles I in Parliament. He lived nearby in the restored Elizabethan house known as The Priory. In 1657 Cromwell, now Lord Protector, made him one of his peers.

CHOLSEY

In the churchyard, having died of natural causes, DAME

AGATHA CHRISTIE (1891–1976) was laid to rest. She wrote a stream of best-selling whodunnits along with, in the never-ending *Mousetrap*, a play. The Queen of Crime was also at least a minor lady-in-waiting in the Court of Love, publishing six romances under the name Mary Westmacott.

ELSFIELD

In St Thomas of Canterbury churchyard, his yarns all spun, lies JOHN BUCHAN, LORD TWEEDSMUIR (1875–1940), the author of imperialist adventure classics like *Prester John* (1910), *The Thirty-Nine Steps* (1915) and *Greenmantle* (1916). His ashes are buried beneath a circular gravestone with four cypresses around.

EWELME

Henry VIII spent his honeymoon with Catherine Howard here, at Manor House, once the home of Alice, Duchess of Suffolk, née Chaucer, whose fifteenth-century tomb is in the church, along with that of her parents: the poet's son Thomas, Speaker of the House of Commons in 1414, and his wife Matilda. Outside in the churchyard is JEROME K. JEROME (1859–1927), who'd lived here for a while during the 1880s, with his wife Ettie.

GODSTOW

The twelfth-century nunnery here is now a ruin. Henry II's mistress ROSAMUND CLIFFORD was buried in its church in 1177. By one tradition she'd retired to Godstow some time before, seized with repentance at her sinful life; by another she'd been murdered by the jealous Queen. Either way, her tomb became a place of pilgrimage. Bishop Hugh of

Lincoln, visiting the nunnery in 1191, was indignant to find a woman with such a colourful past in such a sacred setting, apparently not remembering the story of Mary Magdalen, and had her removed. Later, however, she was discreetly returned.

IDBURY

Designer of the Forth Bridge, Victoria Station, New York's Hudson Tunnel and the original Aswan Dam, the engineer SIR BENJAMIN BAKER (1840–1907) is here, in the churchyard.

KELMSCOTT

In the churchyard near the house where he had lived and which he had made the base for his Arts and Crafts movement, the artist and radical social thinker WILLIAM MORRIS (1834–96) is buried. The Morris family tomb was designed by William's friend and partner Philip Webb. Morris' coffin was brought to Oxfordshire from Paddington in a carriage decorated with green leaves, then borne from the local station in appropriately rustic style, on a haywain. 'The little waggon with its floor of moss and willow branches broke one's heart,' reported Edward Burne-Jones, a friend and disciple: 'The King was being buried, and there was none other left.'

NORTH STOKE

In the churchyard lies the celebrated operatic and recital singer, the contralto DAME CLARA BUTT (1873–1936).

NUFFIELD

WILLIAM RICHARD MORRIS, FIRST VISCOUNT NUFFIELD (1877–1963), the motor magnate and philanthropist, founder of Nuffield College, Oxford, lived here and is buried in Holy Trinity churchyard.

OXFORD

CHRIST CHURCH CATHEDRAL: In the nave, his memorial tablet giving an incorrect date of birth of 1679, is interred the Irish philosopher GEORGE BERKELEY (1685–1753). He argued that there was no such thing as material substance, only collections of ideas or sensations of such substance – hence the notion of the tree in the wood that didn't exist if there was no one there to see it. Having retired from the bishopric of Cloyne, County Cork, the year before, Berkeley had come to live in Oxford, where his son was studying. He lived in Holywell Street; his wife was reading to him from the Bible when he died. Perhaps out of a fear of being buried alive, Berkeley had asked not to be buried until his body was showing tangible signs of corruption, so his funeral didn't take place until a week after his death.

UNIVERSITY CHURCH OF ST MARY THE VIRGIN: Somewhere in the choir is AMY ROBSART (c. 1532–60), the wife of Robert Dudley, Earl of Leicester (see Warwick), Queen Elizabeth I's favourite. When Amy was found dead in mysterious circumstances at the bottom of the stairs in her home it was rumoured that she had been murdered so that her husband could marry the Queen, though if that was really the idea it didn't do Dudley much good. Chivalrous Victorians like Walter Scott got quite exercised about this story, though more recent scholarship suggests that Dudley, while no doubt a bounder, wasn't a murderer, and that Amy's death was probably the result of suicide. The exact whereabouts of her grave are not known.

ST JOHN'S COLLEGE CHAPEL: WILLIAM LAUD (1573–1645), Archbishop of Canterbury, a conservative and a staunch supporter of Charles I's absolutism, shared his master's fate when he was beheaded in the Tower. He was buried in an unmarked coffin at All Hallows' (Tower Hill, City of London), but then after the Restoration the fellows of his old college wanted to have him reinterred with more honour, and he was moved here in 1663. Meanwhile, at Lambeth Palace, the archbishop's pet tortoise grazed on unperturbed by all this to-do. It wouldn't meet its maker until, 108 years after Laud's death, it was stepped upon by a clumsy servant.

ST MARY MAGDALEN CHURCH: Here, at the bottom of Cornmarket, in the space reserved for Trinity men, is the waspish, whimsical mini-biographer JOHN AUBREY (1626–97). His shamelessly scurrilous, cheerfully inaccurate but endlessly illuminating *Brief Lives* gave him a unique place in English Literature and made him a major contributor to the present guide. Given that he lived to the age of seventy his own life was comparatively long.

BROAD STREET: A cross in the roadway in Broad Street by the corner of St Giles – near the Martyrs' Memorial, indeed – marks the place where in 1555–6 three leading churchmen who had helped Henry VIII put together his new creed were burned at the stake by Queen Mary's men for refusing to abandon it. Even before the ascent of Mary, HUGH LATIMER (c. 1485–1555) had run into trouble with Henry VIII for going too far in his rejection of Rome and its ways, while NICHOLAS RIDLEY (c. 1500–55) and THOMAS CRANMER (1489–1556) had both helped write the *Book of Common Prayer* which established a liturgy well to the theological left of the traditional Roman rite. Latimer and Ridley, having proved unbreakable under torture, were put to death in 1555. Cranmer, who recanted, won a reprieve. Consumed with shame, however, he quickly recanted his recantation, and went to the stake the following year, making a point of plunging into the flames the hand with which he had signed his ignoble compromise.

C.S. LEWIS (1898–1963) is buried in Headington Quarry churchyard, with his brother W.H. Lewis. They had lived in the village of Headington. Their epitaph, 'Men must endure their going hence', comes from Shakespeare's *King Lear*. Lewis' fellow-'Inkling', one of a group of spiritually minded, Oxford-based writers, the Christian dramatist CHARLES WILLIAMS (1886–1945), is buried in Holywell (St Cross) churchyard, St Cross Road. Holywell is home for many other distinguished dons, including the essayist and art critic WALTER PATER (1839–94), high priest of late-Victorian aestheticism. Non-academics include KENNETH GRAHAME (1859–1932), whose epitaph, written by his cousin Anthony Hope, reads: 'To the beautiful memory of Kenneth Grahame, husband of Elspeth and father of Alastair, who passed the River on 6th July 1932, leaving childhood and literature through him the more blest for all time.' Grahame's connection with Oxford was a tragic one. His son Alastair while an undergraduate here had committed suicide, lying down on a railway track one night, and it was in his grave that Kenneth was placed. It had been for the young Alastair's bedtime diversion that Kenneth Grahame had first conceived the riverbank tales he published in 1908 as *The Wind in the Willows*. Less wholesome entertainment was later offered by critic and all-round drama phenomenon KENNETH TYNAN (1927–80), who on a momentous evening in 1965 became the first person ever to say 'fuck' on TV. He died in California, in fact, and was cremated in Culver City, but his ashes were brought back to civilization for burial here.

J.R.R. TOLKIEN (1892–1973) was a Catholic, so he couldn't be buried with the other Inklings in Holywell churchyard. Instead he was buried with his wife in the RC section of Wolvercote Cemetery, to the north of the city. The grey granite tombstone is inscribed: 'Edith Mary Tolkien, Lúthien, 1889–1971. John Ronald Reuel Tolkien, Beren, 1892–1973.' These names refer to Tolkien's early poem, the 'Lay of Beren and Lúthien', planned during his courtship of Edith and drafted in Holderness in 1916, just after their marriage, when Tolkien was on leave prior to going to the Western Front. Owing a good deal to Ovid's Orpheus and Eurydice story from the *Metamorphoses*, it describes the fateful first meeting of Beren and Lúthien in a glade of flowering hemlock, all of which seems very far removed from this thoroughly suburban setting.

PIDDINGTON

In the churchyard here is the poet and playwright JOHN DRINKWATER (1882–1937) who, with like-minded fellow poets including James Elroy Flecker and Rupert Brooke (see Cheltenham, Gloucestershire), founded the influential journal *Georgian Poetry*. 'Georgian' verse, as the output of the school came to be known, was a consciously traditionalist reaction to the wild experimentation of Modernists such as T.S. Eliot (see East Coker, Somerset), and generally consisted of gentle, neatly constructed musings on natural and domestic scenes. Unfortunately (though not at all surprisingly) the term 'Georgian' quickly came to be a pejorative one. Drinkwater gained his own love of the countryside from his visits to relatives living near here.

SPELSBURY

Next to his father in the north aisle of the village church lies JOHN WILMOT, EARL OF ROCHESTER (1647–80), poet and libertine. The tomb is unmarked, probably at his own request. His friend Robert Parsons preached the funeral sermon on the text of Luke: 'I say unto you, that likewise joy shall be in heaven over one sinner that repenteth, more than over ninety and nine just persons that need no repentance.' His contemporaries, and early biographers, made much of this deathbed repentance; modern revisionist scholars find it something of a disappointment, and prefer to assume that it was insincere. What we know of Rochester's life is scandalous enough: we were to have known a lot more from the memoirs he left behind at his death. Unfortunately, his family were so horrified when they saw what they contained that they burned them forthwith.

STANTON HARCOURT

Alexander Pope stayed here for a couple of years, a guest of the Harcourt family. That's how he came to know about the Stanton Harcourt Lovers, John Hewet and Sarah Drew, who were killed by lightning while helping with the harvest in 1718. Pope wrote the young couple an impeccably sober and moralistic epitaph, though he couldn't resist another in less reverent vein:

> Here lye two poor Lovers, who had the mishap
> Tho very chaste people, to die of a Clap.

Lady Mary Wortley Montagu saw the funny side too, enjoying the ironies not just of the original story but of Pope's involvement with it:

Here lie John Hughes and Sarah Drew.
Perhaps you'll say, what's that to you?
Believe me, friend, much may be said
On this poor couple that are dead.
On Sunday next they should have married:
But see how oddly things are carried.
On Thursday last it rained and lightened:
These tender lovers, sadly frightened,
Sheltered beneath the cocking hay,
In hopes to pass the storm away.
But the bold thunder found them out
(Commissioned for that end, no doubt)
And, seizing on their trembling breath,
Consigned them to the shades of death.
Who knows if 'twas not kindly done?
For had they seen the next year's sun,
A beaten wife and cuckold swain
Had jointly cursed the marriage chain.
Now they are happy in their doom,
For P[ope] has writ upon their tomb.

The Lovers are commemorated today by a memorial in the churchyard wall, but there's no sign of their grave.

SUTTON COURTENAY

In the churchyard is the grave of the Earl of Oxford and Asquith, in other words HERBERT HENRY ASQUITH (1852–1928). Liberal prime minister from 1908, Asquith found things getting too much when the Great War started, and in 1916 he resigned. He lived nearby with his wife, at their riverside house, The Wharf. Margot Asquith, herself achieving a sort of eminence as socialite and wit, is buried with her husband. She'd married him against her family's wishes. 'When I told my mother of my engagement,' she said, 'she sank upon a settee, put a handkerchief to her eyes, and said: "You might as well marry your groom!"' Curiously enough, she was fascinated by obituaries, and made several stabs at writing her own, though none, in the event, was ever used.

Also here is Eric Blair, better known as the novelist and journalist GEORGE ORWELL (1903–50), who, after witnessing oppression from Burma to Wigan and living the tumult of history in Civil War Spain, settled down in Hebridean seclusion to write his classics *Animal Farm* and *1984*. Unmistakably (if not necessarily unashamedly) English as Orwell's voice always seems, it's none the less odd, perhaps, that a writer with such a burning sense of the imperial and industrialist exploitation on which the English rural idyll was founded should have wanted to be buried in an English country churchyard. He did want it, though, and a friend duly found him a place here.

SWINBROOK

In the churchyard, amid a distinguished collection of seventeenth- and eighteenth-century roll-top tombs, lie the Hons and Rebels NANCY MITFORD (1904–73) and her sister UNITY (1914–48). The former was among other things the inventor of the terms 'U' and 'non-U', while the latter, thanks to her friendship with Adolf Hitler, became a sort of personification of the 'not done'.

UFFINGTON

THOMAS HUGHES (1822–96), author of *Tom Brown's Schooldays* and a Muscular Christian, was born here, and buried in the churchyard.

WOODSTOCK

The chapel at Blenheim Palace contains the tomb of JOHN CHURCHILL, FIRST DUKE OF MARLBOROUGH (1650–1722), a general of great distinction, the victor at Blenheim itself (1704), Ramillies (1706), Oudenarde (1708) and Malplaquet (1709).

His most distinguished descendants are buried a mile and a half to the south, outside the village church in Bladon. Various members of the Churchill family are here, including SIR WINSTON CHURCHILL (1874–1965), the cigar-chewing, V-signing, bulldog-jowled hero of the Second World War, and Lady Clementine Ogilvy Spencer-Churchill (1885–1977). A generation of historians brought up with his praises ringing extravagantly and incessantly in their ears has in recent years been getting its own back with dirt-dishing studies of Churchill's racism and sexism, his arrogance and ruthlessness and his general unpleasantness. Soon, perhaps, counter-revisionists will be advancing the startling new theory that he was a national hero. His parents, LORD RANDOLPH CHURCHILL (1849–95) and LADY CHURCHILL, are buried here too.

WROXTON

The tomb of Frederick, Earl of Guildford, LORD NORTH (1732–92), is here, at All Saints' Church. As prime minister from 1770 to 1782, Lord North has the dishonour (or distinction, depending on how you look at it) of being the man who lost Britain the American colonies.

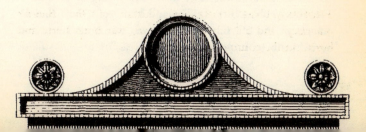

Shropshire

LUDLOW

Outside the Church of St Lawrence by the north wall are the ashes of A.E. HOUSMAN (1859–1936), the Worcestershire Lad who put Shropshire on the map, though it's by no means certain that at the time of the publication of his famous collection in 1896 he'd ever been in the county. Its 'blue remembered hills' did, however, form the western horizon Housman could see from his home in childhood, and thus early came to represent for him something mysterious and romantic.

SHREWSBURY

Strongly associated with the Shrewsbury and Shropshire, where she was brought up, and where most of her best work was set, the novelist MARY WEBB (1881–1927) is buried in the town cemetery.

Beneath the floor of St Margaret's Church, Moreton Say, lie the remains of ROBERT, FIRST BARON CLIVE (1725–74), who as a successful general and then governor of Bengal won the name 'Clive of India'. Returning to England in 1760 to become MP for Shrewsbury, he was promoted to the Lords two years later. Sent back to Calcutta as troubleshooter to take charge of a corrupt colonial government, he restored order in no uncertain terms and returned home in triumph – only to be pursued by claims that, all the time he'd been laying about him at everybody else's little fiddles and kickbacks, he'd had *his* fingers in the till. Clive cut his own throat after attempts were made to impeach him. The reasons for his suicide remain a mystery, however, since he had been innocent of the charges, and by the time he took his own life he must have known that the official enquiry was going to exonerate him. Hence the view that his mind was disturbed as a result of his opium habit, or even that he lashed out with his razor in frustration during an attack of a severe abdominal complaint which was known to cause him agonizing pain.

WHITCHURCH

The tomb of the dashing soldier JOHN TALBOT, EARL OF SHREWSBURY (c. 1388–1453) is here. Talbot kept Ireland in line during a particularly restive stage in its history and hammered the French in a series of brilliant victories. Killed in battle at Bordeaux, he was first buried there, but fifty years later his bones were brought back to England by his grandson, who reinterred them beneath the porch of the church here. The bones were disturbed by restorers working on the church in 1874, and a family of mice was found to have died inside the skull.

Somerset

BECKINGTON

At St George's Church lies the poet SAMUEL DANIEL (1562–1619). In addition to writing some of the Elizabethan age's most beautiful poetry (his sonnets *To Delia* were to be an important influence on Shakespeare's), Daniel was also a humanist in the tradition of Erasmus and Montaigne. He argued eloquently against the colonialist enterprise then gathering momentum, as English conquistadors set off for the Americas in the steps of Ralegh.

BROMPTON REGIS

A brass plaque in the church here bears the epitaph of a girl who died in the seventeenth century at the age of nineteen:

> Reader, Tis worth thy Paines to know
> Who was interred here belowe.
> Here Lyes good nature, Piettie, Witt,
> Though small in volume yet most fairly writ.
> She died young, and so oft times Tis seene
> The fruit God loves He's pleased to pick it greene.

COMBE FLOREY

In St Peter and Paul's churchyard rests the Vile Body of novelist EVELYN WAUGH (1903–66), by now presumably little more than a handful of dust.

DOWLISH WAKE, NEAR ILMINSTER

The explorer JOHN HANNING SPEKE (1827–64) came from Dowlish Wake and is buried in the church. In 1856 he set out with Richard Burton (see Mortlake, South London) in quest of the source of the Nile. Leaving Burton's expedition behind, Speke went on to discover Lake Victoria and to identify it as the great river's source. Burton disputed this claim (though it would be borne out by subsequent exploration), and indeed Speke was due to debate the point with him publicly at the Royal Society on the afternoon of his death. That morning, however, he went out into the Somerset fields to shoot partridge, and ended up accidentally bagging himself.

DOWNSIDE

The abbey here boasts the body of St Oliver Plunkett (see St Giles Street, London West End and Drogheda, Louth, Ireland.)

EAST COKER, NEAR YEOVIL

In the church of St Michael are buried the ashes of T.S. ELIOT (1888–1965). The village was his ancestral home, though Eliot himself had never lived here. A memorial tablet says 'Remember T.S. Eliot, Poet', gives his dates and adds a couple of portentous tags from the 'East Coker' poem of his *Four Quartets*: 'In my beginning is my end' and 'In my end is my beginning'.

Also here lies WILLIAM DAMPIER (1652–1715), the buccaneer and navigator. He circumnavigated the globe three times in all; he is also said to have been the first Englishman in Australia, in 1688.

FROME

In the middle of the lake at Orchardleigh Park, the home of the Duckworth family northwest of Frome, is an island, and on the island is a church. Here, after a good innings, was laid to rest the poet and patriotic drumbeater SIR HENRY NEWBOLT (1862–1938) – author, most notoriously, of 'Vitai Lampada':

There's a breathless hush in the Close tonight—
  Ten to make and the match to win—
A bumping pitch and a blinding light,
  An hour to play and the last man in.
And it's not for the sake of a ribboned coat,
  Or the selfish hope of a season's fame,
But his Captain's hand on his shoulder smote—
  'Play up! play up! and play the game!'

The sand of the desert is sodden red—
  Red with the wreck of a square that broke;
The Gatling's jammed and the Colonel dead,
  And the regiment blind with dust and smoke;
The river of death has brimmed its banks,
  And England's far, and Honour a name;
But the voice of a schoolboy rallies the ranks;
  'Play up! play up! and play the game!'

Generations of schoolboys had to get this off by heart in the days before 'progressive' English teaching when children knew not to split their infinitives, when poetry *was* poetry, not the sort of rhymeless, whining 'self-expression' it is today, and when a good flogging never did anybody any harm.

GLASTONBURY

THE ABBEY: Glastonbury was first put on the mythological map by the arrival of Joseph of Arimathea. He it was who had taken Christ down from the Cross and interred him in his own family tomb. For reasons best known to himself he had, in the process, collected some of the Saviour's blood in the very grail or chalice that had been used at the Last

Supper. He had then brought it with him as he journeyed westward, ending up here, where he died (and, they say, was buried). Afterwards the Holy Grail went missing and, Arthur's Round Table seeming incomplete without it, his knights were forever being sent off in quest of it, killing dragons, rescuing damsels and generally being put to the test along the way. In the ruins of the old abbey, about 50 feet from the south door of the Lady Chapel, King Arthur and Guinevere themselves are traditionally supposed to have been buried. It's arguably a little bit more than a tradition in that we have it on the authority of twelfth-century chronicler Giraldus Cambrensis that the fact was empirically verified. Fire having razed the chapel in 1184, he reports, the monks decided to take advantage of the destruction before rebuilding and dig, testing the old tradition that the legendary king was interred here. Seven feet down, apparently, they found a stone slab and a lead cross marked with a Latin inscription:

HIC IACET SEPULTUS INCLITUS REX ARTURIUS IN INSULA AVALON

(Here lies buried the renowned King Arthur in the Isle of Avalon)

A further nine feet down, the monks came upon a coffin made from a hollowed-out log, containing the bones of a tall man. With it was a smaller skeleton, deemed to be that of Guinevere.

That the monks did actually dig here seems to have been true, at least: archaeologists investigating the site in 1962 found clear traces of their predecessors' excavation, and even identified marks consistent with the removal of a heavy cross from the grave. At the same time, however, it is quite possible that the monks made up the story to raise the abbey's profile and boost its prosperity.

Glastonbury isn't all legends: the abbey still has something to offer for those who prefer a more prosaic, hard-bitten history. Two genuine-article Saxon kings were buried here, though the first, EDGAR (943–75, reigned 959–75), certainly had his mythical aspects. William of Malmesbury described Edgar as the 'honour and delight' of the English, which smacks of mythologizing in itself given that, as he admits, 'There are some persons who endeavour to dim his exceeding glory by saying, that in his earlier years he was cruel to his subjects, and libidinous in respect of virgins.' But such trivial details can do nothing to mar the saintly memory of the man who granted William's monastery its original charter (not, of course, that this could possibly have influenced the chronicler): 'Nor is to be forgotten,' he reminds us:

> that when abbot Eilward opened his tomb in the year of our Lord ten hundred and fifty-two, he found the body unconscious of corruption. This circumstance, instead of inclining him to reverence, served only to increase his audacity; for when the receptacle which he had prepared seemed too small to admit the body, he profaned the royal corpse by cutting it; the blood immediately gushing out in torrents, struck terror into the hearts of the bystanders ... the violator of the sacred body presently became distracted, and not long after, going out of the church, met his death by a broken neck. Nor did the display of royal sanctity stop then; it proceeded still further, a man, lunatic and blind, being there cured.

Buried alongside Edgar is his hapless grandson, EDMUND II, 'IRONSIDE' (c. 993–1016, reigned 1016), who had scarcely ascended the throne when he was rudely dislodged by Cnut (see Winchester, Hampshire).

WHERE KING ARTHUR LIES

There is, of course, a tradition which maintains that King Arthur is not dead at all, only sleeping – awaiting, with a party of his knights, the summons to arise and save England (or Wales, or Scotland, or Britain at large) in its hour of need. A number of sites besides Glastonbury claim the honour of accommodating this distinguished if dormant company: in England there's Cadbury Castle in Somerset, Alderley Edge in Cheshire, Richmond Castle in North Yorkshire and Sewingshields Crags in Northumberland, for instance, while in Wales there are several more, including Caerleon in Gwent and Craig Arthur, near Llangollen, Clwyd. Scotland is something of a laggard in this particular race, but even so it has its own preferred candidate: Eildon Crags, near Melrose, Borders.

LANGPORT

At the parish church is the grave of WALTER BAGEHOT (1826–77), a man of wide interests – and considerable influence on the thinking of his time – who worked in his father's banking and shipping business, edited the *Economist* and wrote about constitutional history, psychology and literature.

MELLS

RONALD KNOX (1888–1957), Bible translator, theologian

and writer of detective fiction, is buried in the churchyard here. Himself a convert to Catholicism, he was mentor to another convert, SIEGFRIED SASSOON (1886–1967). The Jewish foxhunting man, infantry officer and, most famously, poet of the Great War and its miseries, had spent his last few decades living at Heytesbury House, near Warminster, but had requested to be buried here at Mells so that he might be close to his friend.

WEARE

In St Gregory's churchyard is the grave of 'Titter ye not' comedian and actor FRANKIE HOWERD (1917–92).

WELLS

The cathedral here boasts the tomb of THOMAS LINLEY (1733–95), composer of, among other eighteenth-century hits, 'Here's to the Maiden of Bashful Fifteen'.

WEST MONKTON

An inscription in St Augustine's Church commemorates village doctor William Kinglake:

> Contention's doubtfull
> Where two champions bee;
> Thou hast conquered Death,
> Now Death hath conquered thee.

WESTONZOYLAND

In 1685, King James settled the Duke of Monmouth's attempted usurpation a few miles away at Sedgemoor. Many of those killed in the battle are buried in the churchyard here. Monmouth himself, who had fled from the field, leaving his supporters to be slaughtered, was captured in the New Forest and taken to London for trial and execution (see Tower Hill, City of London).

Staffordshire

BURSLEM

In the cemetery of the town he fictionalized as 'Bursley', his ashes placed in his mother's grave, rests ARNOLD BENNETT (1867–1931), author of *Clayhanger*, *Anna of the Five Towns* and various other novels of provincial life set in his native Staffordshire.

DRAYTON BASSETT

SIR ROBERT PEEL (1788–1850), having expanded the manufacturing fortune made by his father up in Lancashire, bought the nearby Drayton Manor and had himself elected as Tory MP for the Tamworth constituency. His tomb is in the parish church. Though prime minister 1841–6, he's now best known for one of his actions as Wellington's Home Secretary: the formation of the Metropolitan Police in 1829. As a longstanding opponent of Catholic emancipation and as PM during the famine years of the 1940s, Peel went down especially badly in Ireland. For Daniel O'Connell, Peel's smile gleamed like 'the silver plate on a coffin'.

NEWCHAPEL

In the churchyard is the grave of JAMES BRINDLEY (1716–72), the distinguished engineer and pioneer in canal construction. Beginning with a waterway to take coal from his patron's mines at Worsley, near Wigan, to Manchester, Brindley went on to build the Bridgewater Canal. The system of canals he inspired would revolutionize bulk transport in the age of industrial revolution, dwindling in importance only very gradually after the rise of the railway.

Suffolk

ALDEBURGH

Women's rights campaigner ELIZABETH GARRETT ANDERSON (1836–1917), Britain's first woman doctor and first woman mayor, is buried in the churchyard as, lying side by side, are composer BENJAMIN BRITTEN (1913–76) and tenor PETER PEARS (1910–86), who lived in the town and founded an annual music festival here. Here too is Britten's friend and amanuensis IMOGEN HOLST (1907–84). The daughter (and biographer) of composer Gustav Holst, she had found a promising pianist's career blighted by illness. She managed none the less to do important work as writer and composer, and as a facilitator for others, organizing and conducting youth choirs.

BOULGE

In St Michael's churchyard lies EDWARD FITZGERALD

(1809–83), the *Rubaiyat* translator, his grave bearing a rose bush grown from a cutting taken from Omar Khayyam's grave at Naishapur, Iran. The church lies in the grounds of Fitzgerald's parents' last house, Boulge Hall. Fitzgerald himself lived in nearby Boulge cottage: an armchair traveller, he never visited the exotic climes whose poetry he translated so memorably.

BURY ST EDMUNDS

ST EDMUND (841–70), King of East Anglia, was given a Bury burial after his murder at the hands of Danish invaders who wanted him to renounce his Christian faith. Defiling the body by cutting off the head, they threw it into thick undergrowth so that the whole body might not be properly entombed. They reckoned without the future saint's miraculous powers, however: the head called out to Edmund's searching followers, and was duly reunited with his body in a shrine in the abbey. Here he would eventually be joined by the medieval poet JOHN LYDGATE (c. 1370–1452) who was born in the nearby village of Lydgate but from the age of thirteen, when he entered the community as a novice, spent most of his life in the monastery. His *The Fall of Princes* warned generations of monarchs of the fickleness of fortune.

DUNWICH

A chunk of churchyard on the clifftop here is all that remains of what was in the Middle Ages a thriving seaport. Ever since the fourteenth century, however, it's been becoming more sea than port, as one storm after another has tugged away at its foundations. Once blest with no fewer than nine churches, Dunwich lost three – along with some four hundred houses – in a tempest of 1326, and since then the town has been eaten inexorably away by the effects of erosion. The last church, All Saints', slid into the sea during the seventeenth century, but a corner of its burial ground endures, and the bones of the dead are still turned up after stormy nights, rather as they were in the churchyard Charlotte Smith found in Middleton-on-Sea, West Sussex.

FRAMLINGHAM

St Michael's Church contains a number of interesting graves, including that of the poet and courtier HENRY HOWARD, EARL OF SURREY (1517–47), who was hanged after his conviction on a treason charge trumped up by Henry VIII. Also here is Henry VIII's bastard son HENRY FITZROY (1519–36) – allegedly poisoned by Anne Boleyn and her brother.

HADLEIGH

It's of some interest that the Danish King GUTHRUM (d. 890), defeated by King Alfred, is said to have been interred here, in a tomb in St Michael's Church. It's not of all that much interest, though, since the said tomb is at least five centuries too late for the story to be true.

ICKWORTH, NEAR BURY ST EDMUNDS

In a family vault, in the church in the park of Ickworth Great House, lies FREDERICK HERVEY, Earl of Bristol and Bishop of Derry (1730–1803). An all-purpose eccentric – politician, rabble-rouser, scholar and sexual intriguer – he was referred to by George III as 'that wicked prelate', though John Wesley praised his good works. He died in Italy and was brought back to England for burial, his coffin having to be placed in a packing case and labelled as an antique statue to overcome prejudice among the ship's crew, who it was believed would feel uncomfortable about the idea of travelling with a corpse for company. This little deception led to the legend that a statue is buried in the body's place, the body having been lost at sea.

KERSEY CHURCHYARD EPITAPH

A defiant epitaph in this Suffolk churchyard says:

> *Reader pass on nor waste thy time*
> *On bad biography or bitter rhyme*
> *For what I am this humble dust enclose,*
> *And what I was is no affair of yours.*

POLSTEAD

Polstead is still notorious as the site of the 'Red Barn Murder'. In 1827 MARIA MARTEN, twenty-six, was shot and stabbed by her lover, William Corder, who buried her in the Red Barn here. She was assumed to have eloped with Corder, but her stepmother dreamed repeatedly that she was in the barn, and eventually her husband went to the barn and found her there. Corder was found living in another part of the country, married to a woman he had met through an advertisement. He was convicted of the murder and hanged. Few physical traces of the story remain: the barn mysteriously burned down one night, and Marten's headstone was chipped away at by souvenir hunters, so comprehensively in the end that the exact whereabouts of the grave were lost. Its approximate position is indicated by a sign.

SOUTH ELMHAM, NEAR FLIXTON

The Canadian writer ELIZABETH SMART (1913–86) spent her later years a few miles north of here at Dell Cottage, Flixton. She is famous for her hot pursuit of English poet George Barker, for whom she conceived a passion after she discovered his work while browsing in a bookshop. They had an affair but he stayed with his wife. She turned their story into *By Grand Central Station I Sat Down and Wept*, not so much a novel as a cry of pain. The other product of their relationship was a daughter, Rose. She died tragically in 1982 when she was still a young woman, a paracetamol overdose bringing to an end a long history of depression and drug abuse, and preceded her mother to the churchyard here.

Surrey

ASH

There is some evidence, though it isn't conclusive, that the bones (or at least most of them) of radical writer and philosopher THOMAS PAINE (1737–1809) were, after much peregrination, finally laid to rest in the churchyard here. He was first buried in New Rochelle, New York, in unconsecrated ground. This outraged his new admirer William Cobbett (formerly, in more conservative days, one of Paine's most derisive critics) so much that he crept into the graveyard late at night and disinterred them, planning to take them back to Britain for a more fitting burial. Landing in Liverpool, he exhibited the bones, hoping to raise the subscription for a proper memorial. Finding less interest than he'd anticipated, he lost interest himself, packed the late radical in a box and took them home to Surrey with him, apparently forgetting all about them. After Cobbett's death (he is buried not far away from here at Farnham, see below), his son tried to auction the bones, but the auctioneer refused, feeling for some reason that the whole thing was in poor taste. After this the story becomes very unclear: the skeleton, or various bits of it, were variously owned by a day labourer, a Unitarian clergyman and a phrenologist. One biographer, Audrey Williams, seems confident enough that the main skeleton, minus any extremities removed by souvenir hunters, lies in the churchyard.

BYFLEET

In the churchyard here is the grave of publisher GEORGE SMITH (1824–1901), the founder in 1882 of the *Dictionary of National Biography*. His own biography was relatively uneventful, though he published some of the biggest
names in Victorian writing,
including Ruskin, Thackeray,
Charlotte Brontë, Browning
and Arnold.

COMPTON

In his parents' grave in
Compton Cemetery are the
ashes of the writer ALDOUS
HUXLEY (1894–1963), brought
back from the Brave New
World to this quiet corner of

the old eight years after his death in California, where he'd been living since 1937. Huxley had a difficult time of it in his early years, losing his mother young and a beloved brother by suicide. Equipped as he was with a heavyweight intellectual ancestry (he was descended not only from the scientific Huxleys but from the Arnolds, Dr Arnold of Rugby being his great-grandfather), he found literary success coming easily. It would not prove entirely enduring, however: all the rage in the 1920s, his reputation declined thereafter, though he maintains a sort of underground reputation. His death from cancer went almost completely unnoticed by the world at large, being overshadowed by that of President Kennedy.

DORKING

In the town cemetery lies GEORGE MEREDITH (1828–1909), the novelist and poet. 'Meredith! Who can define him?' asks a character in Wilde's *The Decay of Lying*:

> *His style is chaos illumined by flashes of lightning. As a writer he has mastered everything, except language: as a novelist he can do everything, except tell a story: as an artist he is everything, except articulate.*

The Egoist (1879) is generally agreed to be a masterpiece by any standards; otherwise, critics have tended to feel that while his novels may be brilliant, they aren't, in the end, very good. Meredith ended up here after he'd been refused a Westminster Abbey burial on account of his freethinking views.

FARNHAM

Next to his grandfather, an agricultural labourer, by St Andrew's Church is WILLIAM COBBETT (1763–1835). After one career as the Tory journalist 'Peter Porcupine', Cobbett then did an about-face and embarked upon a second, far more radical one under his own name, denouncing agrarian poverty and the mismanagement of the country in his famous *Rural Rides*.

FRIMLEY

In the peace of an English churchyard, the American writer BRET HARTE (Francis Brett Harte, 1836–1902) seems a world away from the rowdy western boomtowns he liked to describe in his stories.

GUILDFORD

In the town's Mount Cemetery is the grave of Charles Lutwidge Dodgson, LEWIS CARROLL (1832–98), gone on, one trusts, to some celestial wonderland. The looking-glass of BORIS KARLOFF (1887–1969) showed him one hideous visage after another once he'd captured the imagination of the world as Frankenstein's monster. He doesn't seem to have minded, though. He ended up at the crematorium, his ashes being buried in the garden of remembrance here.

CHARLOTTE SMITH (1749–1806) is buried in the churchyard of Stoke-juxta-Guildford. A novelist and poet, she began writing to support herself after her good-for-nothing husband brought her to the debtor's prison. Of her many novels *Emmeline* (1788) and *The Old Manor House* (1793) proved especially successful in their day, and the former has been recently republished.

LALEHAM

The poet and critic MATTHEW ARNOLD (1822–88) was born here, and is buried in the churchyard with other members of his family. While his poetry – let's not beat about the bush – is dreary and portentous, his criticism and cultural commentary can on occasion be almost sprightly. Like him or not, he was a crucial figure in the intellectual life of the Victorian age.

LEATHERHEAD

In the parish churchyard here lies Sir Anthony Hawkins (1863–1933), aka ANTHONY HOPE, author of the romance classic *The Prisoner of Zenda* and creator of Ruritania.

LIMPSFIELD

Composer FREDERICK DELIUS (1862–1934) is buried in the churchyard here. Born in Yorkshire to German parents, Delius spent most of his adult life abroad, in America and in France, where he died. He was interred temporarily near his home at Grez-sur-Loing while his widow searched for a suitable churchyard in the south of England. He'd wanted to be buried in the south of England because, incredibly, the churchyards there reminded him of the ones in Norway, which for some reason seems to have mattered to him. Mrs Delius' final choice fell upon Limpsfield, where he was later joined by the conductor SIR THOMAS BEECHAM (1879–1961), brought here in 1991 to lie beside his friend after thirty years at Brookwood, near Woking. Concert pianist EILEEN JOYCE (1912–91) and conductor NORMAN DEL MAR (1919–94) complete a formidable musical quartet.

PIRBRIGHT

In St Michael's churchyard is the grave of SIR HENRY MORTON STANLEY (1840–1904), the one who presumed it was Dr Livingstone. A granite standing stone bears his dates and his names both English and African ('Bula Matari'), and the word 'Africa'. Stanley had been expected to have a Westminster Abbey burial, it seems, but the Dean had refused his permission – on the grounds, says Stanley's biographer, of his having been 'a man of blood'. The Dean apparently charged that Stanley had been a womanizer, and violent towards his African servants.

REIGATE

The tomb of Lord High Admiral CHARLES HOWARD OF EFFINGHAM (1536–1624), the brilliant admiral who summoned up the storms that blew away the Spanish Armada of 1588, is here, in the parish church.

SHEPPERTON

In the New Cemetery lies THOMAS LOVE PEACOCK (1785–1866), a poet and novelist in his own right and a friend to most of the other leading writers of his day. Many of them crop up in thinly disguised form in his satirical classics *Headlong Hall* (1816) and *Nightmare Abbey* (1818).

WEST HORSLEY

Beneath the south chapel of the parish church lies the head of SIR WALTER RALEGH (c. 1552–1618). Ralegh is mostly buried in London, at St Margaret's, Westminster (see West End), but his wife, waiting devotedly at the scaffold, snatched up his head as it fell, bundled it into a bag, and took it off as a keepsake. When she died she handed it on to her son. The family eventually thought better of this tradition and gave the wretched heirloom a decent burial here.

WOKING

BROOKWOOD CEMETERY: The Russian Orthodox Chapel at the huge Brookwood Cemetery just outside the town provides the improbable setting for the bones of KING EDWARD THE MARTYR (962–78), brought here from Shaftesbury Abbey, Dorset. The son of King Edgar, St Edward succeeded to the throne after his father's death. His stepmother, Edgar's second wife Elfrida, had other ideas, backing her son Aethelred for the crown. With a group of her servants, she welcomed the young King to her home at Corfe Castle (predecessor of the present, Norman castle there), gave him a cup of wine and, while his attention was thus diverted, stabbed him in the back. They buried him in an unmarked grave but later – after, according to tradition, a series of miracles – it was recovered and brought to Shaftesbury Abbey for a more fitting interment. After this, the King's remains would lie in peace for centuries, but when they were unearthed in the 1930s, the archaeologist – son of the family that owned the land on which the ruined abbey stood – wanted the King to have a proper burial fitting his rank and sanctity, at a site where he could be visited by pilgrims. After protracted negotiations with all the main churches, only the Russian Orthodox Church offered what he considered acceptable terms. So here he is, in a purpose-built chapel.

BROOKWOOD CEMETERY

Brookwood, near Woking, is where in 1854 the imposingly titled Necropolis and National Mausoleum Company opened an enormous state-of-the-art burial ground, joined to the capital by a special rail link

(which would run until 1941 when its Waterloo terminus was destroyed by a German bomb). Some 2,000 acres of land had been bought as the site for what was intended to be the cemetery to end all cemeteries: there was room here, it was believed, for all London's dead to be interred for an indefinite period. Over a quarter of a million bodies have been laid to rest here since, and there are no signs as yet that the cemetery is feeling the strain. The cemetery's rolling parkland seems to go on for ever: the visitor has a feeling of being in open countryside which has become a cemetery only accidentally, and in which it can be almost a surprise to come across a grave. In addition to many thousands of ordinary Londoners, Brookwood has become the last resting place for many hundreds of servicemen. There are military cemeteries here for British, Commonwealth and US war dead, and even a plot for Turkish fliers killed during the Second World War.

You can visit Brookwood, free of charge, all year round, at any time of the day (or, indeed, of the night, for the gates never close).

Anachronistic in a different way is the grave of writer and journalist REBECCA WEST (1892–1983), buried here at her own request – appropriately, perhaps, for a writer who, though she died only in the last decade, was so strongly associated with an earlier time. A militant suffragette, West was famous as a feminist, though women's liberation for her could only ever be of value as part of a wider socialist programme of reform. Her critical trashing of H.G. Wells' 1912 novel *Marriage* led to her meeting the great man (see Poole, Dorset): sparks flew, and the upshot was an affair that lasted ten years and produced a son, Anthony.

From the cemetery's Victorian heyday dates the grave of CHARLES BRADLAUGH (1833–91), social reformer and freethinker. A radical campaigner for birth control, republicanism and anti-imperialism, Bradlaugh still managed to get himself elected to Parliament in 1880; he was ejected from the House by force for refusing to swear on the Bible, stood again and was elected; was re-ejected and re-elected… In 1886 the authorities gave up the unequal struggle and allowed him to take his seat without oath. (His friend and fellow campaigner ANNIE BESANT (1847–1933) died in India where she had gone to pursue her growing interest in Eastern religions, and was cremated on the seashore at Adyar. Annie Besant is most famous now for organizing the Matchgirls' Strike of 1888, when female workers at Bryant & May's East End factory fought a hard but ultimately successful battle for better pay and safer conditions, an early victory for women in the workplace.) The American-born painter JOHN SINGER SARGENT (1856–1925) was also buried here. Still the biggest private cemetery in Europe, Brookwood is particularly popular with Britain's Muslims, making the news in 1997 as the last resting place of DODI FAYED (1955–97). Known as the son of controversial Egyptian businessman Mohammed Al Fayed, and with a reputation as something of a playboy, Dodi acquired a more tragic fame as the friend – some said fiancé – of Diana, Princess of Wales, killed alongside her in a Paris car crash (see Great Brington, page 115).

The crematorium at Brookwood has been a sort of Clapham Junction of the dead, with many notables passing through to other resting places. Among those cremated here are Friedrich Engels (see Eastbourne, East Sussex), theosophists' leader MADAME HELENA PETROVANA BLAVATKSY (1831–91) and Scottish novelist GEORGE MACDONALD (1824–1905), whose ashes were taken to Bordighera, Italy, where his wife had earlier been buried in the British cemetery. Eleanor Marx was cremated here, her ashes subsequently buried in her father's grave at Highgate.

WOTTON

In his family's chapel in St John's Church is JOHN EVELYN (1620–1706), who was born and brought up at nearby Wotton House, though he spent most of his adult life based in Deptford, London. Evelyn's famous *Diary* – which he kept over sixty years from 1641 till his death – offers a vivid and illuminating window on to the characters and events of English history in the second half of the seventeenth century.

Sussex, East

BRIGHTON

ALEISTER CROWLEY (1875–1947), 666, or simply the Beast, to his friends, was cremated at Brighton after a gnostic requiem with readings from his own *Hymn to Pan*, which scandalized the town council. What became of the Beast after that is a mystery. Some sources say that the ashes were stolen away by souvenir hunters; others believe a more mystic hand was at work, snatching the sacred urn from its burial place in the garden of Karl J. Germer, Crowley's successor as head of the Ordo Templi Orientis, or Order of the Golden Dawn. Never modest about his accomplishments or lasting significance, Crowley had in a will of 1931 requested a Westminster Abbey burial, but realism – or something – seems to have set in after that, and in one poem he'd asked his heirs to:

> Bury me in a nameless grave!
> I came from God the world to save.
> I brought them wisdom from above:
> Worship, liberty and love.
> They slew me for I did disparage
> Therefore Religion, Law and Marriage.
> So be my grave without a name
> That earth may swallow up my shame!

EASTBOURNE

A few miles out to sea off Eastbourne lies the urn containing all that remains of FRIEDRICH ENGELS (1820–95), industrialist, political thinker and, of course, collaborator of Karl Marx. His funeral service having been held in the waiting room of Waterloo Station, a special train had taken his coffin, piled high with wreaths and flowers, to Brookwood Crematorium, Woking, Surrey. It was Engels' own request that his urn should be consigned to the waves, and so it was on a stormy day, by Eleanor Marx and some of his closest friends.

FAIRLIGHT

At St Andrew's Church, the impresario who made Gilbert and Sullivan possible, RICHARD D'OYLY CARTE (1844–1901), is buried.

FIRLE, NEAR LEWES

St Peter's churchyard boasts two Bloomsbury Group stalwarts, artist DUNCAN GRANT (1885–1978), and VANESSA BELL (1879–1961), artist and Virginia Woolf's sister, who lived nearby at Charleston.

FLETCHING

In the church, various members of a local Sheffield family share their mausoleum – as in life they did their house – with EDWARD GIBBON (1737–94), a protégé of the family who wrote much of his *Decline and Fall of the Roman Empire* at Sheffield Hall.

GLYNDE

Agriculturalist JOHN ELLMAN (1753–1832) is buried in the churchyard here. His fame will resound down the centuries as the first breeder of the Southdown sheep.

HOVE

Worth a visit if only because it is there is the grave of SIR GEORGE EVEREST (1790–1866) at All Saints' Church. The mountain was named for him in honour of his service as Surveyor General of India.

The ashes of C. AUBREY SMITH (1863–1948), the cricketer and film actor whose credits included *Rebecca* and *The Prisoner of Zenda*, were brought back to England and interred in St Leonard's churchyard.

Another cricketer is buried in the town cemetery: Sir John Berry Hobbs, known to generations of cricket-lovers as JACK HOBBS (1882–1963).

RIPE

The writer and poet MALCOLM LOWRY (1909–57), most famous for *Under the Volcano* (1947), the classic novel of Mexico and alcoholism, spent his last years here at White Cottage, and is buried in the churchyard. Born near Liverpool, he took time out before university to sail as deckhand on a China-bound merchantman. His drink problem being already well established by the time he was a student, his wealthy father recognized that a more productive career was going to be out of the question and allowed him an annuity that enabled him to travel, settling at various times in Mexico and Canada, writing furiously in the (often brief) intervals between drinking bouts.

RODMELL

After she committed suicide by drowning herself in the nearby stream, the ashes of the novelist, critic and feminist VIRGINIA WOOLF (1882–1941) were scattered in the garden of her home at Monk's House. Those of her husband LEONARD WOOLF (1880–1969) would eventually join her there.

ROTTINGDEAN

By the outside wall of the south transept of the church here lies the pre-Raphaelite artist SIR EDWARD BURNE-JONES (1833–98) with his wife Georgiana and their granddaughter, the comic novelist and howling snob ANGELA THIRKELL (1890–1961). A colonel's daughter and lifelong mover in smart society, ENID BAGNOLD (1889–1981) was entitled to be every bit as particular, but managed to deal with the lower middle class without too much trauma in her classic girls' novel *National Velvet* (1935). She, too, is buried in the churchyard.

RYE

In Playden Cemetery lies the novelist and biographer (and, in his youth, Olympic figureskater) E.F. BENSON (1867–1940), who adopted Rye as his home town, even serving as its mayor from 1934 to 1937. In addition to his sporting and civic duties, he managed to find time to write over seventy novels as well as many works of nonfiction. He is best known for his series of *Lucia* books, which were immediately welcomed as comic classics.

WITHYHAM

VITA SACKVILLE-WEST (1892–1962) is here in the Sackville family crypt in the church. She is famous for the garden she created with her husband Harold Nicolson at Sissinghurst, Kent (where he's buried), and for her affairs with other women, most notoriously Virginia Woolf, as well as for her writing – horticultural notes and biographies as well as poetry and (increasingly well-regarded) novels.

Sussex, West

ASHURST

In the churchyard lies MARGARET FAIRLESS DAWSON (née Barber, 1869–1901), who under the name of Michael Fairless, wrote *The Roadmender*, a story of Sussex folk.

BURPHAM

In the churchyard where his parents were buried, the artist

and writer MERVYN PEAKE (1911–68), author of the gothic *Gormenghast* trilogy, was laid to rest. On the tombstone, by way of an upbeat epitaph, is inscribed the opening line of one of his poems:

> *To live at all is miracle enough*

– an impressively philosophical attitude in one whose later life was marred by two nervous breakdowns and by the slow, inexorable progress of a form of Parkinson's Disease which killed him in the end after years of suffering.

BURY

Bury House was the home of the author of *The Forsyte Saga*, JOHN GALSWORTHY (1867–1933), for the last few years of his life. His ashes were scattered on nearby Bury Hill. In youth an idle young gentleman of leisure, he had been encouraged to start writing by the first mate of a ship he was taking on a jaunt to South Africa, 'a Pole called Conrad...a capital chap, though queer to look at.' Back in London, his conscience was stirred by what he saw of slum conditions while collecting rents for his father. Though late in coming, Galsworthy's sense of social justice would be fierce and enduring.

CHICHESTER

In the cathedral, by St Richard's Altar, lies BISHOP GEORGE BELL (1883–1958), leading ecumenist and honorary president of the World Council of Churches. He is commemorated by a plaque fixed on the old stone screen of Bishop Arundel, 1459–77, which was restored and re-erected in his honour. The ashes of composer GUSTAV HOLST (1874–1934) were also buried here, near the memorial to his great musical idol, the Tudor genius Thomas Weelkes, who had been organist in the cathedral more than three centuries earlier.

The son of a local hatter, WILLIAM COLLINS (1721–59) went mad himself in later life, though not before he had produced the work which would make him one of the eighteenth century's finest lyric poets. He was buried in the church of St Andrew Oxmarket, behind East Street, which is now an arts centre.

CRAWLEY

Beside his mother in the cemetery of the Franciscan Friary here is 'Bosie', or LORD ALFRED DOUGLAS (1870–1945), who as a young man got Oscar Wilde into so much trouble. Wilde (1854–1900) had to go into exile after his release from Reading Gaol, dying, as he put it, beyond his means in Paris, where he is buried in the Père Lachaise Cemetery. Bosie ended up converting to both Catholicism and heterosexuality, and switching from decadent verse to respectable journalism. Ironically enough, the new improved Bosie ended up doing time himself, serving six months in Wormwood Scrubs in 1923–4 for criminally libelling Winston Churchill. Another reformed character buried here is CATHERINE WALTERS (1839–1920), also known as 'Skittles', a Liverpool barmaid who went to London to seek her fortune and made it as 'the last Victorian courtesan', friend to artist and aristocrat alike. Wilfred Scawen Blunt (see Worth, below) was among those who fell madly in love with her. It was to her, indeed, that his sonnet sequence *Esther* (1892) was addressed.

HORSTED KEYNES

Interred in the churchyard here is HAROLD MACMILLAN, EARL OF STOCKTON (1894–1986), Tory prime minister from 1957 to 1963. Famous for detecting a 'wind of change' in colonial Africa in the 1950s and for telling the British people they'd 'never had it so good' in the 1960s, Supermac's resignation was attributed to ill-health, though the stuffing had rather been knocked out of his administration by the Profumo affair. Macmillan's brand of High Toryism was marginalized in the 1980s, Margaret Thatcher having whipped up her own wind of change. He denounced her privatization programme memorably (if unavailingly) as 'selling the family silver'.

IFIELD

MARK LEMON (1809–70), a co-founder in 1841 of *Punch* and the magazine's first editor, is buried in the churchyard here. In addition to his journalism, Lemon wrote novels, plays and the libretti for light operas.

LITTLEHAMPTON

In the town cemetery, beneath a simple cross, lies Katharine Parnell, notorious as KITTY O'SHEA (1845–1921), whose adulterous relationship with Charles Stewart Parnell, made public by his British opponents in 1890 after the best part of a decade, put an end to his career – and, for a generation, to any hope of Irish home rule. Though in her way an important figure of its history, she never visited Ireland.

SHIPLEY

In the churchyard, opposite the south door of the church, lies the pianist and composer JOHN IRELAND (1879–1962),

MIDDLETON-UNDER-THE-SEA

Off the coast at Middleton—on-Sea is the old village, a victim to coastal erosion and hence abandoned by its residents in the seventeenth century in favour of a site further inland. The old church was a ruin by the seventeenth century, and along with its churchyard disappearing gradually beneath the waves. Writer Charlotte Smith, visiting Middleton-on-Sea late in the eighteenth century, was moved to write a sonnet as her elegy on a disintegrating country churchyard:

Pressed by the moon, mute arbitress of tides,
*   While the loud equinox its power combines,*
*   The sea no more its swelling surge confines,*
But o'er the shrinking land sublimely rides.
The wild blast, rising from the western cave,
*   Drives the huge billows from their heaving bed,*
*   Tears from their grassy tombs the village dead,*
And breaks the silent sabbath of the grave!
With shells and sea-weed mingled, on the shore
*   Lo! their bones whiten in the frequent wave;*
*   But vain to them the winds and waters rave;*
They hear the warring elements no more:
While I am doomed — by life's long storm
*   oppressed,*
To gaze with envy on their gloomy rest.

She'd have to brave a good deal more of life's long storm before, in 1806, she went to her own gloomy rest in Guildford, Surrey.

his grave marked by a prehistoric sarsen stone. Although Ireland had not lived too far away, this wasn't his local churchyard. A devoted cat-lover, he asked to be buried here on account of Ginger, a tom he'd met in the churchyard when he stopped here one afternoon during a drive, and whom he'd subsequently come back regularly to visit.

WEST GRINSTEAD

In the graveyard of the Catholic Church of Our Lady and St Francis, with his wife and son, lies the writer and cautionary rhymster HILAIRE BELLOC (1870–1953). A spiky conservative satirist, he formed half, with his friend G.K. Chesterton (see Beaconsfield, Buckinghamshire), of the 'Chesterbelloc' animal, a polemical pantomime horse derided – but feared and respected – by liberal and leftist opponents. Of the two, it's Chesterton who has proved more enduring in reputation. Belloc had once written:

> When I am dead, I hope it may be said:
> 'His sins were scarlet, but his books were read'

What's mostly said of Belloc nowadays is that he was a raving fascist. That's a little unfortunate, since it's only half true. (Well, make that three-quarters…) An often brilliant comic writer he did indeed have a much darker side, his jolly, roast-beef-and-beer Englishness (promoted with a foreigner's self-consciousness) being shot through with a rancorous antisemitism, and his old age being spent in mourning for his wife and in increasingly poor health. A stroke in 1942 left him severely handicapped, and he died as grotesquely as the erring child in one of his own Cautionary Verses, falling into the fire as he attempted to poke it.

WEST LAVINGTON

Freetrader RICHARD COBDEN (1804–65) lived at nearby Dunford House and is buried in the churchyard.

WORTH

The poet and orientalist WILFRID SCAWEN BLUNT (1840–1922) was born into a local landowning family and, despite a lifetime's travelling in India, Egypt and Arabia (and an interest in Ireland that got him two months in one of Her Majesty's prisons for speaking out of turn on the nationalism question), he wanted to end his journey here, having his ashes scattered without ritual in Newbuildings Wood.

WORTHING

Novelist and nature-lover RICHARD JEFFERIES (1848–87), perhaps best known for the novel *Bevis, the Story of a Boy* (1882), is here in Broadwater Cemetery. W.H. HUDSON (1841–1922), another naturalist novelist, chose to be buried near him, clearly having found him an inspiration, though to modern tastes Hudson seems the more obviously interesting of the two. Born in Buenos Aires of American parents (his father had come to Argentina to farm sheep after an accident in the Massachusetts brewery where he worked), as a young man Hudson won international fame with his expedition to Patagonia in 1870. Coming to London four years later, he found himself famous but practically destitute, and duly turned to writing. Somewhere between adventure novels and travelogues, Hudson's writings proved hugely popular, offering city-bound readers an instant escape to the wide open pampas. The Argentinians requested that his bones be repatriated for a ceremonial burial there, but the British dug their heels in, though they'd hardly consigned Hudson to the ground than his popularity as writer began to wane. Now, however, with rising green consciousness (Hudson was an early and articulate advocate of the need for active conservation) and a rediscovery of travel literature, he is reaching a new generation of readers.

Given his own early experience as a sheepfarmer's son, Hudson will no doubt feel a certain kinship with Mary Hughes, the subject of the nursery rhyme 'Mary Had a Little Lamb', who was laid to rest here in 1881.

On Highdown Hill, behind the town, Victorian archaeologists unearthed a Saxon cemetery. A more recent occupant is 'Gloomy Miller' John Olliver, who built his tomb here twenty-five years before his death in 1791, and slept each night with a coffin under his bed.

Tyne & Wear

FELLING

South of the town centre at Heworth, a mass grave contains ninety-two victims of an underground explosion at Felling Colliery. The Reverend John Hodgson described the almost apocalyptic scene in his funeral sermon:

> About half past eleven o'clock in the morning of the 25th May, 1812, the neighbouring villages were alarmed by a tremendous explosion in this colliery. The subterraneous fire broke forth with two heavy discharges from the John

Pit, which were, almost instantaneously, followed by one from the William Pit. A slight trembling, as from an earthquake, was felt for about half a mile around the workings; and the noise of the explosion, though dull, was heard to three or four miles distance, and much resembled an unsteady fire of infantry. Immense quantities of dust and small coal accompanied these blasts, and rose high into the air, in the form of an inverted cone. The heaviest part of the ejected matter, such as corves, pieces of wood, and small coal, fell near the pits; but the dust, borne away by a strong west wind, fell in a continued shower from the pit to a distance of a mile and a half. In the village of Heworth, it caused a darkness like that of early twilight, and covered the roads so thickly, that the foot-steps of passengers were strongly imprinted in it . . . As soon as the explosion was heard, the wives and children of the workmen ran to the working-pit. Wildness and terror were pictured in every countenance. The crowd from all sides soon collected to the number of several hundreds, some crying out for a husband, others for a parent or a son, and all deeply affected with an admixture of horror, anxiety, and grief.

The machine being rendered useless by the eruption, the rope of the gin was sent down the pit with all expedition. In the absence of horses, a number of men, whom the wish to be instrumental in rescuing their neighbours from their perilous situation, seemed to supply strength proportionate to the urgency of the occasion, put their shoulders to the starts or shafts of the gin, and wrought it with astonishing expedition. By twelve o'clock, 32 persons, all that survived this dreadful calamity, were brought to day-light. The dead bodies of two boys, numbers one and four, who were miserably scorched and shattered, were also brought up at this time: three boys, viz. numbers two, three, and five, out of the 32 who escaped alive, died within a few hours after the accident. Only twenty-nine persons were, therefore, left to relate what they observed of the appearances and effects of this subterraneous thundering.

One hundred and twenty-one were in the mine when it happened, and eighty-seven remained within the workings. One overman, two wastemen, two deputies, one headsman or putter, (who had a violent toothache) and two masons, in all eight persons, came up at different intervals, a short time before the explosion.

The first of the great mass-disasters of the industrial age, the Felling explosion was the stimulus that eventually led to the development of Sir Humphry Davy's Safety Lamp. Davy (1778–1829), incidentally, died and was buried in Geneva.

HOUGHTON-LE-SPRING

St Michael and All Angels' Church contains the tomb of BERNARD GILPIN (1517–83), who preached here regularly. He lived at Kentmere Hall, Cumbria, but gained his title of 'Apostle of the North' from his missionary work in the farthest byways of Yorkshire and Northumberland – at that time still wildernesses where the conventional clergy seldom ventured.

Warwickshire

CLAVERDON

In a family vault at the church here lies SIR FRANCIS GALTON (1822–1911). A scientist of undoubted ability,

Galton became notorious as pioneer of the 'science' of eugenics. He was firmly convinced that the races differed in their innate qualities (no prizes for guessing who came top in this particular league) and that the human race as a whole could be improved over time by selective breeding. As a traveller in Africa, he had experienced racial differences at first hand, having to maintain discipline among his native bearers. Flogging was effective, he noted in his diary, adding generously that you should avoid hitting the 'nigger' on the head. If this didn't get results, the application of 'Boiling water, hot sand on their naked bodies' surely would.

SHUSTOKE

The antiquary SIR WILLIAM DUGDALE (1605–86) was born at the former rectory and buried in the local church.

STRATFORD-UPON-AVON

CHURCH OF HOLY TRINITY: In the sanctuary of the thirteenth-century Collegiate Church of Holy Trinity is buried whatever remains of English Literature's biggest name, WILLIAM SHAKESPEARE (1564–1616). The Bard's epitaph, traditionally supposed to be his own work, and certainly dating back at least as far as the late seventeenth century, reads:

> *GOOD FREND FOR JESUS' SAKE
> FORBEARE,
> TO DIGG THE DUST ENCLOSED HEARE:
> BLESE BE Ye MAN Yt SPARES THESE STONES.
> AND CURST BE HE Yt MOVES MY BONES.*

This curse has, rather surprisingly, succeeded in seeing off generations of enthusiasts bent on exhuming the great man to find the skeleton of Francis Bacon, the works of Marlowe or whatever other clue to his 'real' (i.e. non-Shakespearean) identity they expect to find. In fact, they'd be most unlikely to find anything at all, so frequently has the low-lying site been flooded over the winters since the sixteenth century. The curse also, it was said at the time, put off Shakespeare's family, who otherwise would have preferred to be buried with him in the same grave. As a result, ANNE HATHAWAY (c. 1556–1623) has a grave to the left of her husband in the chancel, while their children are buried round about. Their daughter Susanna, born in 1583, is nearby with her husband:

> Here lyeth ye body of Susanna, wife to John Hall, gent:
> ye daughter of William Shakespeare, gent: she deceased ye
> 11th of Iuly A.D. 1649, aged 66. Witty above here sexe,
> but that's not all, Wise to salvations was good Mistress
> Hall, Something of Shakespeare was in that, but this
> Wholy of him with whom she's now in blisse.

> Then Passenger, hast nere a teare
> To weepe with her that wept with all? That wept yet set
>   her selfe to chere
> Them up with comforts cordiall. Her love shall live, her
>   mercy spread,
> When thou hast nere a teare to shed.

Of the twins born in 1585, son-and-heir Hamnet died only eleven years later in 1596, while Judith lived on till beyond the Restoration, to die in 1662 at the age of seventy-seven. Their exact whereabouts, whether in the church or outside in the churchyard, are not known.

EVESHAM ROAD CEMETERY: Almost as bright a star in the literary firmament was MARIE CORELLI (1854–1924), the extravagantly eccentric popular novelist who settled locally, having claimed a special affinity with the town's most famous son. Her novels were reactionary in outlook and overblown in style but sold in vast numbers: she was said to be making £10,000 a novel by 1900. Tourists gathered to see her ride with her companion Bertha Vyver in a miniature cart drawn by Shetland ponies, or in a gondola she had had brought from Venice. She was buried in the town cemetery on Evesham Road, her grave marked by a suitably grandiose angel.

WARWICK

Buried in the chapter house at St Mary's Church, in a 'ponderous sarcophagus', is FULKE GREVILLE (1554–1628), First Lord Brooke. He was assassinated by his manservant, who apparently resented some imagined slight. His own epitaph describes him as 'Fulke Grevill, servant to Queene Elizabeth, Conceller to King Iames, and frend to Sir Philip Sidney.' His friendship with Sidney was as important to him as this inscription suggests: he wrote Sidney's biography in 1610 to 1614, though it would not be printed until 1652.

The Beauchamp Chapel contains, as you might expect, various Beauchamps, as well as ROBERT DUDLEY, EARL OF LEICESTER (c. 1532–88), a favourite of Queen Elizabeth – though not of posterity, which has taken exception to his having reputedly murdered his wife Amy Robsart (see Oxford, Oxfordshire) so as to leave the way clear for him to marry the Queen. HRH refused to co-operate in the scheme, angered as she was by his presumption (though not, it seems, by the murder, if such it was). Despite everything, she seems to have retained a soft spot for Dudley to the end.

West Midlands

BIRMINGHAM

Beside her mother in the Key Hill Cemetery lies HARRIET MARTINEAU (1802–76), the novelist and social reformer.

HANDSWORTH OLD CHURCH: Buried here is the engineer-entrepreneur MATTHEW BOULTON (1728–1809). One of the leading figures of Britain's industrial revolution, Boulton was himself an innovator of note, but he was even more important as a talent spotter, finding and sponsoring other inventors, and discovering ways to harness the new steam technology to productive manufacturing processes. Johnson's sidekick James Boswell visited Boulton's Soho, Birmingham plant and seems to have found himself unsure which was the more remarkable, the factory or its owner:

> I wish Johnson had been with us: for it was a scene which I should have been glad to contemplate by his light. The vastness and the contrivance of some of the machinery would have 'matched his mighty mind'. I shall never forget Mr Bolton's expression to me: 'I sell here, Sir, what all the world desires to have, – POWER.' He had about seven hundred people at work. I contemplated him as an iron chieftain, and he seemed to be a father to his tribe.

One positive result of Boulton's power was the support he was able to give to JAMES WATT (1736–1819) in his pathfinding work in steam power. Watt's rotary engine was far more sophisticated than the atmospheric engine designed by Newcomen (see City Road, North Central London), and would eventually transform industry. Watt was also buried here, as was another Boulton protégé, WILLIAM MURDOCK (1754–1839). He too had at one time experimented with steam engines, road-testing his prototype late at night on a lonely lane near his home as he trotted along behind. One night, recalled a friend William Buckle, Murdock had 'heard distant shouting, like to that of despair; it was too dark to discern objects, but he soon found that the cries for assistance proceeded from the worthy pastor, who, going into the town, on business, was met in this lonely road by the fiery monster, whom he subsequently declared he took to be the Evil One *in propria persona*.' Murdock is, however, most famous for his pioneering work in gas lighting. He had his first system up and running in 1792, and by 1803 the Soho works was fully illuminated by gas.

REDNAL: At Rednal, in a little cemetery in the grounds of the retreat house he had established here for the congregation of the Birmingham Oratory, lies JOHN HENRY NEWMAN (1801–90), who in the course of a brilliant career in the Church of England found his Anglicanism getting higher and higher, so much so that in 1845, amid a blaze of publicity and with a number of followers in tow, he took off and went over to Roman Catholicism. His defection inevitably attracted criticism, notably from the proponent of Muscular Christianity Charles Kingsley (see Eversley, Hampshire), who incautiously accused Newman of dishonesty. More brawn than brain, Kingsley was no match for Newman in the ensuing war of words. Newman went on from strength to strength, reaching the rank of Cardinal and helping to found a Catholic university in Dublin, the forerunner of today's University College. He is buried here in the grave of Ambrose St John, an old friend and disciple who had accompanied him on his journey to Rome.

Arguably the wrinkliest poet in English Literature, W.H. AUDEN (1907–73) was brought up in Birmingham, but left the city as a young man. In the end he was buried abroad, in Kirchstettin, the village in Lower Austria where he had liked to spend his summers. Wagner's 'Siegfried Idyll' was played at his funeral.

DUDLEY

In Queen's Cross Cemetery, buried next to his sister Carol Anne, who died in infancy, lies the footballer DUNCAN EDWARDS (1938–58), generally thought to have been the most talented of the 'Busby Babes' killed in the Munich air disaster. Twenty-three people, including eight Manchester United players, died when the team's plane crashed after taking off from Munich on the way back from a European fixture in Belgrade. (Though seriously injured, manager Sir Matt Busby himself would of course live to fight many more seasons at Old Trafford, before his own death and interment at Manchester's Southern Cemetery.)

Wiltshire

ALVEDISTON

In the churchyard here is the grave of SIR ANTHONY EDEN (1897–1977), the Tory prime minister (1955–7) who came unstuck over Suez.

BEMERTON

Beneath the altar in the chancel of the church of which he was vicar for the last three years of his life, 'under no large, nor yet very good, marble grave-stone, without any Inscription', according to Aubrey, lies the religious poet GEORGE HERBERT (1593–1633).

BROAD CHALKE, BETWEEN SALISBURY AND SHAFTESBURY

CECIL BEATON (1904–80), fashion photographer and designer of costumes and sets for films, theatre and ballet, is buried here, in All Saints' churchyard.

BROAD TOWN

The grave of poet and critic GEOFFREY GRIGSON (1905–85) is in the graveyard at Christ Church.

BROMHAM

In the churchyard here rests THOMAS MOORE (1779–1852), the Irish poet, who lived nearby at Sloperton Cottage from 1818 until his death. Moore's *Lalla Rookh* (1817) represented a sort of pinnacle of his age's romancing of the east, but his greatest fame came from his to a large extent forging England's consciousness of his race with his folksy *Irish Melodies*, a collection of lyrics set to traditional airs which took Britain's drawing rooms by storm. Critic William Hazlitt was more sceptical, anticipating the general response of later generations when he accused Moore of converting 'the wild harp of Erin into a musical snuff-box':

> *If these national airs do express the impassioned feeling in his countrymen, the case of Ireland is hopeless. If these*

prettinesses pass for patriotism, if a country can heave from its heart's core only these vapid, varnished sentiments, lip-deep, and let its tears of blood evaporate in an empty conceit, let it be governed as it has been.

HARDENHUISH

Beneath an elaborate monument, all doric columns and naked Greek maidens, are stowed the remains of political economist DAVID RICARDO (1772–1823).

MALMESBURY

WILLIAM OF MALMESBURY (c. 1090–c. 1143) was abbot of the old Benedictine abbey here, but he is more famous as a chronicler, for his *Gesta Regum Anglorum* (Deeds of the Kings of the Angles, c. 1125). He was buried here, as, under the altar of the abbey church, was KING AETHELSTAN (895–940, reigned 924–40). 'His years, though few, were full of glory,' reports William, who could always be relied on to put in a good word for liberal benefactors of his abbey. Historians seem agreed, however, that in his wars on the western and northern peripheries of his kingdom against the Cornish and Welsh, Aethelstan did much to increase the power of Wessex.

MARLBOROUGH

A few miles south of the town, on the slopes of Martinsell, a hill where he'd enjoyed walking with his brothers, the ashes of ANTHONY BLUNT (1907–83), art-historian and Fourth Man, were scattered.

SALISBURY

In the choir of the cathedral lies MARY HERBERT, COUNTESS

OF PEMBROKE (1561–1621), sister of Sir Philip Sidney. 'She was a beautifull Ladie,' wrote Aubrey, 'and had an excellent wit, and had the best breeding that that age could afford. Shee had a pritty sharpe-ovall face. Her haire was of a reddish yellowe.' He goes on, after a somewhat abrupt gear-change, to add:

> She was very salacious, and she had a Contrivance that in the Spring of the yeare, when the Stallions were to leape the Mares, they were to be brought before such a part of the house, where she had a vidette (a hole to peepe out at) to looke on them and please herselfe with their Sport; and then she would act the like sport herselfe with her stallions.

Well, be that as it may, Mary was the instigator and intended audience for her brother's *Arcadia* (it was, he told her, 'done only for you, only to you') and, in the event, its first editor, having to put it into its final shape after her brother's death in 1586. She was also a writer and translator in her own right.

SEVENHAMPTON

IAN FLEMING (1908–65), creator of James Bond, is here with his wife and son, in an unmarked grave in St Andrew's churchyard. They lived nearby at Warneford Place.

TOLLARD ROYAL

In the village church is the tomb of GENERAL AUGUSTUS PITT-RIVERS (1827–1900), who as 'father of English archaeology' was, it might be said, a grave-spotter of sorts. Inheriting an estate in nearby Cranborne Chase in 1880, he devoted the rest of his life to excavating its Bronze Age earthworks.

TROWBRIDGE

In the chancel of St James' is poet GEORGE CRABBE (1754–1832), who was vicar at the church for his last eighteen years, coming here after his wife's death in 1813. Her illness had involved violent mood-changes as well as physical suffering, and Crabbe had had a wretched time of it, but he none the less felt utterly desolate without her. His creativity certainly seems to have ebbed away. Where his long descriptive poems like *The Parish* (1783) and *The Borough* (1810) bring rural life vividly and unsententiously alive, the creator of Peter Grimes never really managed to hit his stride again after his wife's death, and a rather tedious moralizing streak entered his work.

WILSFORD

The physicist SIR OLIVER LODGE (1851–1940), pioneer of radio-telegraphy, is buried in the churchyard here. As early as 1894 he hypothesized that the sun emitted radio waves, though this would not actually be proved until after his death.

Yorkshire, North

BILBROUGH

In a medieval side-chapel of the parish church lies Cromwell's General THOMAS FAIRFAX (1612–71), who lived nearby at Nunappleton House. Commander-in-chief of the New Model Army from 1643, he led the Parliamentary

forces to their great victory at Naseby in 1645. A firm
believer in leading from the front, at Naseby Fairfax
personally wrested a Royalist standard from its bearer in the
thick of the fight. Though he was one of the judges at
Charles I's trial, he disapproved of the king's execution; he
grew increasingly disenchanted with the Commonwealth
and ended up using his influence to ensure the Restoration
of Charles II in 1660.

COXWOLD

In the churchyard here is buried what may be the head of
LAURENCE STERNE (1713–68) – but then again may not.
The Tipperary-born writer's ties to Coxwold seem to have
been comparatively loose. Though he was vicar here in his
last years, the author of *Tristram Shandy* and *A Sentimental
Journey* was never much of a clergyman, and seems to have
used the income the living brought him to support his main
interests, writing and travel. An appropriate air of black
comedy and confusion surrounds his death and burial. His
friend David Garrick had asked in a mock-epitaph:

> *Shall Pride a heap of sculptur'd marble raise,*
> *Some worthless, unmourn'd titled fool to praise;*
> *And shall we not by one poor grave-stone learn*
> *Where Genius, Wit, and Humour, sleep with* Sterne*?*

But in the event the answer was, apparently not. Sterne was
buried quietly in London, in the Bayswater Road burial
ground belonging to St George's, Hanover Square, but his
grave was left unmarked, perhaps to outwit the
resurrectionists who had been plaguing the graveyard in
recent years. A couple of well-wishers erected a stone in

1769 which mourned him in his writerly persona, beginning 'Alas! Poor Yorick'. They don't seem to have known him all that well, though, being unable to pinpoint the exact position of the grave, and getting the date of his death wrong. In 1893 the Sterne estate put up another headstone, a sort of erratum slip in masonry, to correct the first. But from very early on there were rumours that Sterne might not be there at all: he'd been snatched by the resurrectionists, it was said, and sold to a Cambridge professor on whose dissecting table he had come under the knife. One medic with a literary turn having recognized the distinguished (and by now thoroughly mutilated) cadaver, their tutor panicked and had the bones hidden, returning just the head to St George's. Excavations conducted by the Laurence Sterne Trust in 1968, when the site was about to be redeveloped, unearthed a skull that had been sawn neatly in half, apparently in the course of dissection. Its measurements matching those of a bust made in Sterne's lifetime, and thought to be anatomically accurate, it was concluded that it was probably Sterne's, but that if it wasn't he would in any case have enjoyed the joke. It was reinterred at Coxwold, the two headstones from St George's also being set up here.

HUBBERHOLME, NEAR BUCKDEN

The ashes of Good Companion J.B. PRIESTLEY (1894–1984) were buried here, in the parish church. The Bradford-born Priestley left his job as a clerk with a local textiles firm to seek his fortune in the London literary world. He began to make it first as a novelist and then as the author of plays such as *An Inspector Calls* and *I Have Been Here Before*, before reaching a still wider public during the Second World War when his radio broadcasts played an important role in maintaining national morale. In a sense then an establishment figure, Priestley would never lose his youthful radicalism, being a strong early supporter of CND. Though dismissed from the first as 'middlebrow', his work has continued to appeal through revival after revival. It begins to look as if it were destined to last.

NEWBURGH PRIORY

A mile and a half southeast of Coxwold is the house where Cromwell's daughter Mary Fauconberg lived with her husband. By tradition, she got hold of her father's body after the Restoration and placed it here in a bricked-in vault, where it has lain undisturbed ever since (see Cambridge, Cambridgeshire).

SCARBOROUGH

Author ANNE BRONTË (1820–49) came to Scarborough in the hope that it would help ease her tuberculosis, but she died here. She is buried in St Mary's churchyard.

SPOFFORTH

In the churchyard lies JOHN METCALF (1717–1810), known in his day as 'Blind Jack of Knaresborough'. Despite his handicap he was a talented athlete and a sharp judge of horseflesh. He was also an accomplished roadbuilder. A contemporary, John Bew, wrote of his astonishing abilities and his mysterious methods:

> With the assistance only of a long staff, I have several
> times met this man traversing the road, ascending
> precipices, exploring valleys and investigating their several

*extents, forms, and situations, so as to answer his designs
in the best manner. The plans which he makes, and the
estimates he prepares, are done in a manner peculiar to
himself; and of which he cannot well convey the meaning
of to others. His abilities, in this respect, are, nevertheless,
so great, that he finds constant employment. Most of the
roads over the Peak in Derbyshire have been altered by his
directions; particularly those in the vicinity of Buxton: and
he is at this time constructing a new one betwixt
Wilmslow and Congleton to open a communication to the
great London road, without being obliged to pass over the
mountains. I have met this blind projector while engaged in
making his survey. He was alone as usual, and, amongst
other conversations, I made some enquiries respecting this
new road. It was really astonishing to hear with what
accuracy he described its course and the nature of the
different soils through which it was conducted . . .*

TERRINGTON

The eminent historian and historiographer ARNOLD
TOYNBEE (1889–1975) had a home here in later years, and
was laid to rest in the local burial ground.

WHITBY

The clifftop graveyard of St Mary's parish church was used by
Bram Stoker as a setting in *Dracula*. There's a grave, marked
with skull and crossbones, said to belong to a suicide: the evil
count makes a home of just such a grave in Stoker's novel.

There's also a memorial cross here to England's earliest
known poet, CAEDMON (d. 670–80). An unlettered man,
according to Bede, he was for many years a cowherd, before he
found his new vocation when he was divinely inspired one

night to compose a hymn on the Creation. Taken under the protection of the Whitby monks, he went on to produce much more religious verse, very little of which, however, has survived.

YORK

In the western crypt of the Minster is the tomb of ST WILLIAM OF YORK, a twelfth-century saint whose shrine was the scene for a number of miraculous cures before it was destroyed during the Reformation. Nearby is a stone which fell from a great height and landed on the head of a pilgrim to the shrine, but – thanks to the intervention of the saint – without any ill-effects.

DICK TURPIN (1706–39) is in St George's churchyard, George Street. He famously cheated the noose in the south; less well known is that he would only end up swinging in the north instead. The son of an Essex innkeeper, he became an outlaw after he was caught stealing cattle as a young butcher's apprentice. As a highwayman, life grew uncomfortable after he accidentally shot dead his partner. He went to Yorkshire (though actually in a more leisurely, sedate manner than the legend would suggest) and became a horse trader, but was finally convicted of stealing horses and hanged. 'Dick Turpin's Ride' did take place, some sources claim, but it was performed not by Dick Turpin but by an earlier villain, Will Neotson, who was hanged in 1684.

In St Olave's churchyard is the grave of the distinguished artist Sir WILLIAM ETTY (1787–1849), a native of the city. Strongly influenced by Venetian and classical models, he was particularly famous for his nudes.

Beneath the city wall, a little way up from the Royal York Hotel on Station Road, is the burial ground where 185 people who died in the cholera epidemic of 1832 were laid to rest, while to the south of the city, the garden around St Oswald's Hall, Fulford, a converted Norman chapel, was used to bury victims of a much earlier pestilence, the Black Death of 1349.

BEYOND THE GRAVE'S CONFINES

One of a number of ghosts said to haunt Holy Trinity Church, Goodramgate, York, is that of Thomas Percy, Earl of Northumberland (d. 1572), a Catholic who planned an insurrection against Elizabeth I. He was captured and executed, and his head was displayed on a pole before his friends buried it in the church. He is seen here, headless, searching for it.

Yorkshire, South

WENTWORTH

In a grand mausoleum in the grounds of his ancestral home, Wentworth Park, lies CHARLES WATSON-WENTWORTH, SECOND MARQUESS OF ROCKINGHAM (1765–6), the Whig prime minister 1765–6. The mausoleum was built by his nephew and heir Earl Fitzwilliam, and bears a long inscription by Edmund Burke, which concludes sternly:

> *Let his successors, who daily behold this monument, consider that it was not built to entertain the eye, but to instruct the mind. Let them reflect that their conduct will make it their glory or their reproach . . .*
> *Remember; Resemble; Persevere.*

185

Yorkshire, West

HAWORTH

In the family vault in the old church are all the BRONTËS
except Anne, who's in Scarborough. So that leaves, apart
from parents Patrick and Maria Brontë, CHARLOTTE
(1816–55), EMILY (1818–48) and BRANWELL (1817–48).
Matthew Arnold was moved by the sight of Haworth
churchyard to write one of his worst poems, which is going
some; Virginia Woolf, who in 1904 made a pilgrimage to see
the home of the authors of *Wuthering Heights* and *Jane Eyre*,
was struck more felicitously by its atmosphere of death.
Inside the church, the family tomb paid vivid testimony to
the part death had played in the sisters' everyday lives:

> The slab which bears the names of the succession of
> children and of their parents – their births and deaths –
> strikes the eye first. Name follows name; at very short
> intervals they died – Maria the mother, Maria the
> daughter, Elizabeth, Branwell, Emily, Anne, Charlotte,
> and lastly the old father, who outlived them all. Emily was
> only thirty years old, and Charlotte but nine years older.
> 'The sting of death is sin, and the strength of sin is the
> law, but thanks be to God which giveth us the victory
> through our Lord Jesus Christ.' That is the inscription
> which has been placed beneath their names, and with
> reason; for however harsh the struggle, Emily, and
> Charlotte above all, fought to victory.

HEPTONSTALL

In the churchyard is the much fought-over grave of the late

Mrs Ted Hughes, the poet SYLVIA PLATH (1932–63), described on her tombstone – to the outrage of certain sections of the feminist community who want to see her as the women's movement's Thomas à Becket – as Sylvia Plath Hughes. Few writers have polarized opinion so strongly – not just as to the controversial content of her verse but as to its quality, which tends to be seen as either absolutely inspired or utterly fraudulent.

THE DEATH OF ROBIN HOOD

According to legend, Robin, feeling unwell, disregarded the warnings of his anxious henchmen in coming to Kirklees Abbey to have his blood let by the prioress, a cousin of his. She was, it seems, the secret lover of Robin's sworn enemy, Sir Roger of Doncaster, and though she bled him willingly enough, she didn't stop when she should have:

> *Shee laid the blood-irons to Robin Hoods vaine*
> *Alack, the more pitye!*
> *And pearct the vaine, and let out the bloode,*
> *That full red was to see.*
>
> *And first it bled, the thicke, thicke bloode,*
> *And afterwards the thinne,*
> *And well then wist good Robin Hoode*
> *Treason there was within . . .*

By that time, unfortunately, it was too late. Helped to a window by a less than Merry Man, Robin raised his good longbow in his faltering grasp and shot an arrow – where it landed, he was to be buried.

MIRFIELD

It's at least interesting to note that the outlaw–philanthropist ROBIN HOOD is traditionally buried here, at Kirklees Abbey. You can't visit the grave as it's on private property, which would no doubt have amused the outlaw. Robin Hood would, of course, have blithely scaled the wall, KEEP OUT notice or no KEEP OUT notice; less swashbuckling grave-spotters will have to make do with the resting places of his lieutenants, Little John (Hathersage, Derbyshire) and Will Scarlett (Blidworth, Nottinghamshire).

The outlaw's grave slab apparently survived as late as the nineteenth century, but it disappeared then by slow degrees, chunks being taken away as toothache cures by labourers building the Yorkshire and Lancashire railway, an end of which this man of the people would surely have approved. ◆

2

London

Plague Pits

When workers building the foundation for the new Royal Mint in London's East Smithfield started turning up human bones, archaeologists were brought in to excavate systematically. They proceeded to uncover a medieval graveyard – a medieval graveyard that had clearly been stretched beyond its limits. For in addition to a large number of conventional graves, the researchers found two deep trenches, one 73 yards long, the other 136. Each was crammed with skeletons. There could be no doubting what the excavation had revealed: it was on record that Bishop Ralph Stratford had consecrated a cemetery about here in 1349, one of two opened to help ease the strain on the city's churchyards, bursting at the seams thanks to the ravages of the Black Death.

Crossing from Asia into the eastern fringes of Europe at the end of 1347, by the time it abated for no apparent reason in 1350 the bubonic plague had reached Arctic Scandinavia, northwestern Ireland and even Greenland. Thanks to the burgeoning maritime trade of the time the plague travelled far and fast by sea in rat-infested ships. Overland, its spread was surprisingly leisurely: for the people of Europe, who understood nothing of the disease's genesis or propagation, an essential part of the Black Death experience was the agonizing suspense of waiting for the inevitable as the plague seemed to inch its way across the continent, slow but inexorable. There was a time-lag built into the disease's spread, for the plague-bearing fleas would turn to human targets only as a last resort when all the rats in a place were dead, some two weeks after their first arrival in a house or village. Then the human inhabitants would start finding the lymphatic glands of their armpits ballooning out in the painful 'buboes' from which the plague got its name; their skin would erupt in angry blotches; they would feel headachy, feverish and breathless – and within a very few days they would almost certainly be dead.

The people of medieval Europe wouldn't have thanked you for pointing it out, but in theory at least they were lucky, since the bubonic is the least deadly of the plague's three main forms. The highly infectious pneumonic plague, which goes straight to the lungs, filling them up with fluid even before the buboes have a chance to form, tends to carry off its victims within a couple of days, while the thankfully rare septicemic version doesn't wait around to affect either lungs or lymph glands: passing directly into the bloodstream it rushes straight to the brain, bringing about death with 24 hours. The bubonic is the commonest form, however, and there's something about the grotesque swellings it produces that makes it, for all its comparative mildness, the most peculiarly frightening of plagues.

Thanks to the vagaries of chance and the commercial routes of the day, some places got off lightly or were spared completely; others were totally wiped out. The social impact of the plague was profound: the economic routines of centuries were upset as those who could afford to fled. Class hatred flared, the poor resenting the mobility of the rich, believing that those with money were able to escape the plague while they were left behind under sentence of death. This was only partly true, but to have even a hope of escape seemed enviable.

The Black Death is said to have made its British landfall on the Dorset coast, and by the end of 1348 it was threatening London. Dirty and overcrowded, the capital was ill-prepared to fight off an epidemic of this sort. Londoners were soon dying in their hundreds each day and the task of disposing of the bodies was proving impossible – especially as the corporation employees who normally handled this were themselves among the early casualties. The churchyards full to overflowing, Stratford's special relief cemeteries were soon feeling the strain too. The second, at Charterhouse (on the site of what is now St Bartholomew's College of Medicine, in an area that positively bristles with Private signs), was, according to one contemporary observer, receiving two to three hundred bodies a day at the height of the plague. Medieval casualty figures have to be treated with caution; those reports we have suggest astronomical death tolls far in excess of the city's total population. Even so, the Black Death is believed to have claimed up to 30,000 casualties in London alone.

Three centuries later, in 1665, it was back — this time called the Great Plague, but the same old bacillus, the same hideous symptoms and the same horrendous mortality. 'Now the Grave doth open its mouth without measure,' wrote Dr Thomas Vincent, a clergyman who stayed in London throughout:

> *Multitudes, multitudes, in the valley of the shadow of death*
> *thronging daily into Eternity; the Churchyards now are stuft so*
> *full with dead corpses, that they are in many places swell'd two*
> *or three foot higher than they were before, and new ground is*
> *broken up to bury the dead.*

Quacks made a killing – though they might not live to spend it. Nobody really knew what caused the plague, or how it could effectively be treated. Since domestic pets were thought to spread the disease, a bounty of two pence was announced on every cat and dog killed. Pepys reckoned that 40,000 dogs and 200,000 cats were despatched in the space of just a few days. The only ones to benefit were the rats, though of course with the plague raging fiercely they had problems of their own. Their role and that of their fleas would not be understood until the end of the nineteenth century. It was vaguely felt that quarantine might help check the disease's spread – which would have been all very well had the rats not been free to come and go as they pleased. Infected houses were boarded up, their inmates sealed inside, the still-healthy with the already dying in a thousand little private hells. Those who could afford to would naturally bribe officials to record deaths in their households as having been caused by anything except plague. Between the lonely and destitute who died unmissed in the confusion and the well-to-do for whom a different cause of death was falsely recorded, the official death toll of 68,576 was probably under by some thirty thousand.

Either way, that's a lot of bodies to dispose of, and once again mass graves had to be used. In his factional masterpiece *A Journal of the Plague Year*, actually written over half a century after the events it describes but exhaustively researched and utterly convincing, Defoe describes one such pit – one of many across London – at Aldgate:

> *They had supposed this pit would have supplied them for a month or more when they dug it, and some blamed the churchwardens for suffering such a frightful thing, telling them they were making preparations to bury the whole parish, and the like; but time made it appear the churchwardens knew the condition of the parish better than they did: for, the pit being finished the 4th of September, I think, they began to bury in it the 6th, and by the 20th, which was just two weeks, they had thrown into it 1114 bodies . . .*

Defoe's narrator describes a man desperate with grief who follows his dead wife and children to the brink of the pit, and delirious sufferers running to the pit to 'bury themselves'. The plague was a mighty leveller, he realized, watching another wagonload of dead souls arrive:

The cart had in it sixteen or seventeen bodies; some were wrapt up in linen sheets, some in rags, some little other than naked, or so loose that what covering they had fell from them in the shooting out of the cart, and they fell quite naked among the rest; but the matter was not much to them, or the indecency much to any one else, seeing they were all dead, and were to be huddled together into the common grave of mankind, as we may call it, for here was no difference made, but poor and rich went together; there was no other way of burials, neither was it possible there should, for coffins were not to be had for the prodigious numbers that fell in such a calamity as this.

There never has been quite such a calamity as this again in Britain: standards of civic hygiene rose and the black rat was supplanted by the brown. Both species carry the plague bacillus, but their habits are significantly different. Helped along by a series of mild winters, the Thatcherism of the 1980s notoriously produced an explosion in Britain's rat population, thanks to crumbling sewers and collapsing municipal standards, and the cliché now goes that wherever you are you're never more than 25 yards from a rat. But the black rat of Merrie England lived in much closer proximity than that, being far more domesticated and a better climber, scurrying up the walls and scampering through the thatch on terms of considerable intimacy with its human hosts. When it died its fleas fell down into their living space and looked around for something to feed on. The brown rat on the other hand tends to live under the floor when indoors, and more often lives outside in gutters and drains. While it has found its niche living around humans, it prefers where possible to keep them at a distance. Bubonic plague seems in any case to be readily treatable by antibiotics. That isn't the only potential threat, however. Cholera, typhoid and miscellaneous other epidemics recurred through the eighteenth and nineteenth

centuries, while the twentieth century has seen violent outbreaks of flu – nothing on the scale of the earlier plagues, but
quite frightening enough for those who lived through them.

And who's to say it's over yet? As the 1994 outbreak in India
of what was thought to be pneumonic plague made clear, the
plague still has the capacity to wreak havoc. There, large
numbers of people living in squalid and overcrowded conditions
were at the mercy of the sudden upsurge in the domestic rat
population produced by a recent earthquake which disturbed
earlier habitats and created new ones in damaged buildings. For
the time being, plague seems to have become a problem for the
Developing World. The habitants of the developed West
shouldn't allow themselves to become too complacent, however:
reputable epidemiologists in the United States have in the last
few years been expressing concern that the filth, overcrowding
and broken-down facilities of some of America's inner cities
could make them the ideal environment for new outbreaks
among the urban poor.

CENTRAL LONDON

Westminster Abbey

A Mecca for seekers after notable stiffs. Amanda McKittrick Ros, a cult figure of fun among the English literary establishment of the early 1920s, who regarded her as a sort of Irish McGonagall, was perhaps getting her revenge when she wrote:

> *Holy Moses! Take a look!*
> *Flesh decayed in every nook,*
> *Some rare bits of brain lie here,*
> *Mortal loads of beef and beer.*

Given the amount of second-rate statuary strewn about the place, G.K. Chesterton described the Abbey as the nation's lumber-room, and the visitor's impression is indeed one of chaos, with tombs and memorials scattered in bewildering disarray – 'as though,' remarked philosopher's mother Johanna Schopenhauer, visiting London in the early nineteenth century, 'they had somehow been rescued from some disaster and put down anywhere as a temporary measure.' Two centuries on, it's clear that the disorder is here to stay. The guide below attempts to impose some sort of order, dividing the dead into their respective categories and arranging them (roughly) chronologically. To navigate on the ground, you're referred to the Abbey's own leaflet. That's issued free, though to pass into the holy of funereal holies beyond the nave you have to pay (currently £4 – students and o.a.p.s £2, children £1, a rip-off to any normal person, but nothing to discourage the dedicated grave-spotter).

ROYALTY

The paint was scarcely dry when the Abbey's role as a repository for distinguished decay was inaugurated with its founder, EDWARD THE CONFESSOR (c. 1004–66, reigned 1042–66). The *Anglo-Saxon Chronicle* for 1065–6 reports that:

> *King Edward came to Westminster towards Christmas, and there had the abbey church consecrated which he himself had built to the glory of God, St Peter, and all God's saints: the consecration of the church was on Holy Innocents' day [28 December]; and he passed away on the vigil of the Epiphany [6 January, 1066] in this same abbey church.*

The son of Aethelred II, 'The Unready', and Ema, Edward had been sent abroad, out of the way, to be brought up while his mother was otherwise engaged being queen to new king Cnut. The death of his half-brother Harthcnut gave Edward his big chance. 'Ever full of cheer was the blameless king,' reports the *Anglo-Saxon Chronicle*:

> *Though for long in the past, deprived of his land,*
> *He had trodden an exile's path across the wide world,*
> *After Cnut had conquered the race of Aethelred,*

And Danes ruled over this dear land
Of England for twenty-eight years
All told, squandering its riches.
In time he succeeded; noble in armour,
A king of excellent virtues, pure and benign,
Edward the noble protected his fatherland,
His realm and people: until suddenly came
That bitter death, which took so cruelly
The prince from the earth. Angels bore his
Righteous soul within Heaven's light.

Around Edward in what is now known as Edward the Confessor's Chapel lie other royalty, including HENRY III (1207–72, reigned 1216–72), and EDWARD I, LONGSHANKS (1239–1307, reigned 1272–1307) with his queen ELEANOR OF CASTILE (1246–90) (all except her heart, that is: that's traditionally supposed to be in Lincoln Cathedral). The warlike Edward, subjugator of the Welsh, had wanted his bones carried before the English army for inspiration and his heart buried in the Holy Land, but he'd been overruled after his death and his remains come to this rather tamer ending. Chronicler Jean Froissart described the death and burial of their grandson EDWARD III (1312–77, reigned 1327–77), the victor of Crécy, who lies nearby with his queen PHILIPPA OF HAINAULT (c. 1314–69):

On 21 June 1377, the gallant and noble King Edward III departed this life, to the deep distress of the whole realm of England, for he had been a good king for them. His like had not been seen since the days of King Arthur, who once had also been King of England, which in his time was called Great Britain. So King Edward was embalmed and placed with great pomp and reverence on a bier borne by twenty-four knights dressed in black, his three sons and the Duke of Brittany and the Earl of March walking behind him, and carried thus at a slow march through the city of London, the face uncovered. To witness and hear the grief of the people, their sobs and screams and lamentations on that day, would have rended anyone's heart.

So the body of the noble king was taken through London to Westminster and buried beside his wife, Philippa of Hainault, Queen of England, as they had appointed in their lifetime...

RICHARD II (1367–1400, reigned 1377–99) ended up here too, though after he was starved to death in a dungeon in Pontefract Castle by insubordinate nobles he was first buried at Kings Langley, Hertfordshire but afterwards exhumed and brought to the Abbey. A more effective monarch entirely, Agincourt victor HENRY V (1387–1422, reigned 1413–22), is also buried here. HENRY VII (1457–1509, reigned 1485–1509) built his own chapel in the Abbey and was buried here – not, as had always been customary, in a raised tomb, but in a vault beneath the floor, together with his wife Elizabeth of York, who'd died six years earlier in childbirth.

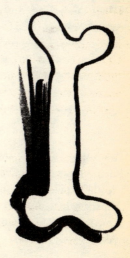

Not far away, at the east end of the chapel aisle, in 'Innocents' Corner', were placed some bones unearthed in the Tower in 1674 and believed to be those of the

'Little Princes', EDWARD V (1470–83, reigned, after a fashion, 1483) and his younger brother, the Duke of York, imprisoned and assumed murdered there by their wicked uncle, Richard Crookback, determined that nothing should stop him ascending the throne himself as Richard III (see Leicester). EDWARD VI (1537–53, reigned 1547–53) is also in the chapel.

On the south side of the Abbey's high altar lies Henry VIII's queen number four, ANNE OF CLEVES (1515–57), a mail-order bride who disappointed from the first, failing to match up to the portrait which Hans Holbein the Younger had been specially sent to Flanders to paint. The marriage annulled within a year, in 1540, Anne seems to have adapted quite well to the wealth and independence her role as discarded queen gave her in her last seventeen years. Back in Henry VII's Chapel are queens MARY I, BLOODY MARY (1516–58, reigned 1553–8) and ELIZABETH I (1533–1603, reigned 1558–1603). Historian John Stow, by that time almost eighty and only two years away from his own death, described the public response to the passing of Queen Bess:

> There was such a generall syghing, groaning and weeping as the like hath not been seene or knowne in the memorie of man, neyther doth any historie mention any people time or state to make such lamentacyon for the death of their soverayne.

It's ironic of course that these scourges of Protestantism and Catholicism respectively should have ended up together in death: a plaque on their tomb asks that we remember 'all those who divided at the reformation by different convictions laid down their lives for Christ and conscience' sake'.

THE DEATH OF MARY, QUEEN OF SCOTS

Robert Wynkfielde was at the execution of Mary, Queen of Scots:

> *lying very still upon the block, one of the executioners holding her slightly with one of his hands, she endured two strokes of the other executioner with an axe, she making very small noise or none at all, and not stirring any part of her from the place where she lay: and so the executioner cut off her head, saving one little gristle, which being cut asunder, he lift up her head to the view of all the assembly and bade God save the Queen. Then, her dress of lawn falling from off her head, it appeared as grey as one of threescore and ten years old, polled very short, her face in a moment being so much altered from the form she had when she was alive, as few could remember her by her dead face. Her lips stirred up and down a quarter of an hour after her head was cut off . . . Then one of the executioners, pulling off her garters, espied her little dog which was crept under her clothes, which could not be gotten forth but by force, yet afterward would not depart from the dead corpse, but came and lay between her head and her shoulders, which being imbrued with her blood was carried away and washed, as all things else were that had any blood was either burned or washed clean, and the executioners sent away with money for their fees, not having any one thing that belonged unto her.*

Distrusted as a potential threat to Elizabeth's power, MARY, QUEEN OF SCOTS (1542–87) had been executed at Fotheringhay Castle and buried ignominiously at Peterborough Cathedral. When the Virgin Queen died, however, the succession passed to Mary's son JAMES VI OF SCOTLAND, I OF ENGLAND (1566–1625, reigned from 1567 in former post, 1603–25 in latter), and he had her brought here for reburial, within spitting distance of her arch-enemy. In due course he would be buried here himself, in the tomb of Henry VII.

Cromwell and his cronies were buried here with the most unrepublican pomp when they died, but they were unceremoniously ejected after the Restoration of the monarchy in 1660 (see Cambridge, Cambridgeshire). The Merry Monarch CHARLES II (1630–85, reigned 1660–85) and joint sovereigns WILLIAM AND MARY – Orange King Billy, William III (1650–1702, reigned 1689–1702) and Mary II (1662–94) – are also in the chapel. Their successor, Mary's sister ANNE (1665–1714, reigned 1702–14) is here too, surrounded by her children, none of whom survived into adulthood. The list of royal tombs in the Abbey ends with GEORGE II (1683–1760, reigned 1727–60), though by this time several (such as Henry VIII, Jane Seymour and Charles I) had already been buried in the Great Chapel at Windsor, as was to become the norm from now on.

POLITICIANS

Most politicians are grouped in the north transept around WILLIAM PITT THE ELDER, Earl of Chatham (1708–78). He stands, noted Johanna Schopenhauer, 'in the stance of an orator; the virtues weep at his feet but it is not clear whether they are touched by his speech or whether he is saying such things as would make virtue cry.' 'In no other cemetery,' wrote a more sympathetic visitor, Macaulay, *do so many great citizens lie within so narrow a space. High over those venerable graves towers the stately monument of Chatham, and from above, his effigy, graven by a cunning hand, seems still, with eagle face and outstretched arm, to bid England be of good cheer, and to hurl defiance at her foes ... And history, while, for the warning of vehement, high, and daring natures, she notes his many errors, will yet deliberately pronounce, that, among the eminent men whose bones lie near his, scarcely one has left a more stainless, and none a more splendid name.*

Among those eminent men whose bones lie near Chatham's is the famous Whig orator CHARLES JAMES FOX (1749–1806), but nearest of all (though his monument is some way off at the west end of the aisle) is WILLIAM PITT THE YOUNGER (1759–1806) who was buried right beside his old man: 'The statue of the father seemed to look with consternation at the vault that was opening to receive his favourite son,' commented Wilberforce in an emotional flight. The Younger Pitt's great friend GEORGE CANNING (1770–1827) is buried opposite him, beside *his* son CHARLES JOHN CANNING (1812–62), First Viceroy of India.

Despite having committed suicide (see Cardington, Bedfordshire), George Canning's sometime duelling partner ROBERT STEWART, VISCOUNT CASTLEREAGH (1769–1822), made it into the Abbey. There was speculation that he had been being blackmailed on account of his homosexuality, and he himself had told friends that he feared he was about to be exposed. But as foreign secretary he had been under a great deal of pressure anyway, and he seems to have been in a general state of paranoia by the time he took his own life. He was of course deeply unpopular in some quarters, and some in the crowd ('thousands', according to the Whig-leaning

Morning Chronicle; fewer than twenty according to Tory friends) jeered and hooted as the cortège went by. His passing left his old enemy Byron in jaunty mood, writing a slew of amiable little epigrams labouring the idea that the departed had cut his country's throat long since, and imagining an appropriate inscription for the tomb:

> *Posterity will ne'er survey*
> *A nobler grave than this:*
> *Here lie the bones of Castlereagh:*
> *Stop, traveller —*

HENRY JOHN PALMERSTON, VISCOUNT PALMERSTON (1784–1865) is another statesman whose passing seems to have evoked a mixed reaction. American author and diplomat Charles Francis Adams, who six months earlier had witnessed the emotional scenes at the funeral of Abraham Lincoln, was shocked at the complete absence of grief on the faces of the crowd, but Palmerston's political ally Lord Shaftesbury saw this apparent impassivity quite differently: 'The crowds were immense, but in wonderful order; silent, deeply reverential… Such a scene has seldom been seen… '

Palmerston himself had wanted a quieter burial among his ancestors at Romsey Abbey, Hampshire, but his cabinet colleagues insisted on an Abbey burial and his widow agreed, on condition that she could be buried with him on her own death. An effective if ruthless promoter of British interests as foreign secretary through much of the 1830s and 1840s, the father of gunboat diplomacy seemed to have reached the end of his career when in 1855, as Aberdeen's administration foundered and all other attempts to form a Whig government failed, the seventy-year-old Palmerston was asked to try. Himself a stripling of fifty-one, Conservative leader

Benjamin Disraeli was not impressed, denouncing Palmerston to a friend in roundly ageist terms as:

> *An impostor, at best only ginger-beer, and not champagne, and now an old painted pantaloon, very deaf, very blind, and with false teeth, which would fall out of his mouth while speaking, if he did not hesitate and halt so in his talk...*

For all that, though ousted in 1858, Palmerston was to return to office in 1859 at the age of seventy-five, while Dizzie and his Tories would have to wait another decade to get hold of the reins of power. An anything but grey eminence in his personal as well as his public life, Palmerston polarized opinions then and afterwards, modern biographers being divided upon whether he was an endearing card for whom 'a pretty face never lost its attraction... ' or just an obnoxious old goat. Those contemporaries without a political interest in taking one side or the other tended to feel strongly ambivalent: Queen Victoria confessed to her diary that she'd never liked or respected Palmerston; but he had, she conceded, been good for the country.

Never prime minister, but all the same a name to conjure with, EDWARD GEORGE EARLE LYTTON BULWER-LYTTON, FIRST BARON LYTTON OF KNEBWORTH (1803–73) was consigned to a resting place in St Edmund's Chapel. A politician and novelist whose authorial manner is, unfortunately, almost as pompous as his title, his historical romances, such as *The Last Days of Pompeii* (1834), were none the less popular in their day. Palmerston's sometime chancellor WILLIAM EWART GLADSTONE (1809–98) was in and out of office as prime minister during the 1870s and 1880s, when he would come to be known as the 'Grand Old

Man'. He joined his predecessors in the north transept when he died, and was in turn joined by his wife when she died in 1900.

Among the politicians in the Abbey are BEATRICE and SIDNEY WEBB, the pioneers of Fabianism and the founders, in 1913, of the *New Statesman* magazine. The ashes of Beatrice (1858–1943) were first placed in an urn on the mantelpiece at home, where Sidney (1859–1947) would point her out to visitors, 'That's Beatrice, you know.' After his death, they were buried together in their garden at Passfield, Suffolk, until their friend Shaw, after long campaigning, managed to get them moved to the Abbey.

Remarkable for being Britain's only Canadian-born prime minister, ANDREW BONAR LAW (1858–1923) is otherwise remembered for his forgettableness. He was for all that a prime minister, so he – or rather, in this case, his ashes – were entitled to his place beneath the Abbey floor. His anti-reputation began immediately after his death, one of his pall-bearers, Herbert Asquith (who didn't exactly set the Thames on fire himself) remarking: 'It is fitting that we should have buried the unknown Prime Minister by the side of the unknown soldier.' There's not much chance of anybody forgetting NEVILLE CHAMBERLAIN (1869–1940), and especially his return from Munich with 'peace in our time'. When war did break out the following year, he served his old enemy Churchill faithfully enough in his War Cabinet, but had to resign soon on account of his failing health. He's buried in the nave, in the south aisle. In the north aisle, meanwhile, lies CLEMENT ATTLEE (1883–1967), who led the Labour Party to its landslide victory of 1945, presiding over its remarkable programme of nationalization, welfarism and decolonization. His foreign secretary, ERNEST BEVIN (1881–1951), darling of the Labour Right, lies nearby. Before he went into Parliament, Bevin was a trade unionist, bringing together over thirty smaller unions to form the mighty Transport and General Workers' Union. As a senior politician he was a staunch supporter of NATO, and notoriously attributed Britain's economic ills to the fact that 'The buggers won't work.'

MISCELLANEOUS GREAT AND, FOR THE MOST PART, GOOD

Somewhere in the Abbey lies RICHARD HAKLUYT (c. 1551–1616), who was Archdeacon of Westminster in his last years. He's most famous, however, for his work as geographer and chronicler. Though he seems never to have ventured further afield than Paris, where he was chaplain to the English ambassador (and, in a small way, a spy), Hakluyt travelled vicariously through the accounts of others. His first book, *Divers Voyages Touching the Discovery of America* (1582), brought together the available records of explorations in the New World to help promote the idea of an English colonizing effort in North America. Between 1598 and 1600 he brought out his enormous *Principal Navigations, Voyages, and Discoveries of the English Nation*, which assembled written and oral testimony not just from the English nation but from explorers of many nationalities to provide the most complete picture possible of the world beyond western Europe.

The soldier GEORGE MONK, DUKE OF ALBEMARLE (1608–70) is here, in the south aisle of Henry VII's Chapel: a smart political operator, one way and another Monk was involved in all the main events of an eventful age. He was a Parliament-leaning general under Charles I, became commander-in-chief and admiral under Cromwell, then, for all his loyalty to the Protectorate, bowed to the inevitable and called for Charles II's restoration. He was knighted and ennobled by the returning monarch. He kept order in London during the Plague year of 1665, then in 1666 commanded the fleet that was defeated by the Dutch, getting back to London just in time to restore order after the Great Fire. In the ambulatory lies hands-on historian EDWARD HYDE, FIRST EARL OF CLARENDON (1609–74), who first played an active part in England's Civil War, as adviser to Charles I and then to Charles II, then settled down to write its most distinguished history.

The Adam Family, who dominated the Scottish – and indeed the British – architectural scene in the eighteenth century, are mostly buried in Edinburgh, in Greyfriars churchyard. The most famous of them all, however, ROBERT ADAM (1728–92) was given an Abbey burial. WILLIAM WILBERFORCE (1759–1833), anti-slavery campaigner and general good influence on Victorian England, is here too, in the north transept, while THOMAS TELFORD (1757–1834), builder of the Menai Bridge, among other great engineering achievements, is in the nave. Here too is DAVID LIVINGSTONE (1813–73), who died upcountry in Africa but was 'Brought by faithful hands over land and sea...', according to his monument in the nave. Actually, other things being equal, the explorer's African servants would simply have buried him where he died: they brought him back the several weeks' journey to the coast not because they were 'faithful hands' but because they feared that otherwise they would be accused of his murder. SIR ROWLAND HILL (1795–1879) is buried in the Chapel of St Paul. The educationalist and administrative reformer is best known as the deviser of the Penny Post, which was introduced in 1840.

WRITERS AND POETS

'Poets' Corner' grew up around *Canterbury Tales*-teller GEOFFREY CHAUCER (c. 1340–1400), who was joined two centuries later by EDMUND SPENSER (c. 1552–99), author of the profoundly influential and stultifyingly boring knightly epic *The Faerie Queen*e (published 1590–99); another Elizabethan poet, MICHAEL DRAYTON (1563–1631) is buried some way off in the north aisle, as is BEN JONSON (c. 1572–1637), whose tomb is inscribed:

> *O RARE BENN JONSON*

which famous epitaph is of course ambiguous, its correct reading poised between the pious humility of Orare Ben Jonson – 'Pray for Ben Jonson' – and the arrogant 'O Rare Ben Jonson', in a manner its subject would have appreciated.

Among the poets in the south transept lies Shropshire farm servant THOMAS PARR, who was reportedly 152 years old at the time of his death in 1635. Neither FRANCIS (dramatist, 1584–1616) nor his brother SIR JOHN (poet, 1583–1627) Beaumont can match that achievement, but they made it here none the less on the strength of their literary attainments, as did ABRAHAM COWLEY (1618–67), a poet with a strong interest in science. Cowley was buried next to Chaucer himself, but posterity hasn't really upheld his age's high regard, and it's a dedicated scholar who gets through his Biblical epic the *Davideis*. All agree that he was a good bloke, though, leaving provision in his will to pay off yearly the creditors of people in prison for small debts.

'All women together ought to let flowers fall upon the tomb of APHRA BEHN [1640–89],' says Virginia Woolf, 'for it was she who earned them the right to speak their minds.' She is to be found in the east walk of the cloisters, near the bottom of the ramp that leads down from the Abbey proper, her gravestone inscribed: 'Here lies a proof that wit can never be/Defence enough against mortality.' Her wit had at least seen her through her life after she was left a widow at the age of twenty-six, enabling her to become Britain's first professional woman writer. MARGARET CAVENDISH, DUCHESS OF NEWCASTLE (c. 1624–74), on the other hand, buried here with her besottedly beloved husband, was the ultimate gentlewoman-amateur, turning her hand to poetry, drama, fiction and biography, as well as to scientific and philosophical exploration. Decidedly eccentric in thought, dress and manner, she was an object of fascinated curiosity when she walked out in London, but there could be no doubting her originality and talent.

MAT'S TOMBSTONE

There are a number of Augustan wits in the Abbey, including MATTHEW PRIOR (1664–1721), who in his other hat as diplomat helped negotiate the 1713 Treaty of Utrecht. A safe, steady chap, Prior took a matter-of-fact view of death – and of the panegyrics that would come after it – as his lines 'For My Own Monument' make clear:

> As Doctors give physic by way of prevention,
> Mat, alive and in health, of his tombstone took care;
> For delays are unsafe, and his pious intention
> May haply be never fulfilled by his heir.
> Then take Mat's word for it, the sculptor is paid;
> That the figure is fine, pray believe your own eye;
> Yet credit but lightly what more may be said,
> For we flatter ourselves, and teach marble to lie...

WILLIAM CONGREVE (1670–1729), dramatist, was buried in the south aisle of the nave after he died of injuries sustained in a carriage accident. JOHN DRYDEN (1631–1700) is here, as is his old rival and his successor (after the Whigs came to power in 1688) as poet laureate THOMAS SHADWELL (c. 1642–92). Both are no doubt turning in their graves, the former at the thought of being so close in death to his sometime usurper, the latter still smarting at Dryden's immortalization of him in *MackFlecknoe*, where the rhymester Flecknoe, personifying all that is crass and tedious in poetry, casts about him in search of a fitting heir:

> Sh— alone my perfect image bears,
> Mature in dullness from his tender years.
> Sh— alone of all my sons is he
> Who stands confirmed in full stupidity.
> The rest to some faint meaning make pretence,
> But Sh— never deviates into sense.

JOHN GAY (1685–1732), the friend of Swift and Pope and the ebullient creator of the *Beggar's Opera* (1728), is here, unfortunately without either his own epitaph upon himself:

> Life is a jest and all things show it,
> I thought so once but now I know it.

or his friend Pope's:

> Well then, poor G— lies underground!
> So there's an end of honest Jack.
> So little Justice here he found,
> 'Tis ten to one he'll ne'er come back.

A severer proposition altogether was DR JOHNSON (1709–84), the surly sage of London. He had earlier written the Latin inscription for his friend Oliver Goldsmith's monument. He had refused requests from friends including Burke, Gibbon, Sheridan and Reynolds to produce a version in English, the vernacular language Goldsmith had done so much to adorn, as he felt it would be a disgrace to the walls of the Abbey. Goldsmith actually had to be buried in the Temple Church, Fleet Street, after it turned out he'd died leaving £2,000 in debts.

JOSEPH ADDISON (1672–1719), the poet, politician and – as contributor to Steele's *Tatler* and then as founder-editor of the *Spectator* – essayist, didn't quite make it into Poets' Corner either, though he has a memorial here (and could in any case hardly have objected to a burial among the kings in the Henry VII Chapel). His last words were, apparently, 'See in what peace a Christian can die!' Let's hope his confidence was justified. Also here is RICHARD BRINSLEY SHERIDAN (1751–1816), the playwright (author of classic comedies such as *The Rivals*, 1775, and *The School For Scandal,* 1777) and manager of the Drury Lane Theatre. In his last years he brought his dramatic skills to bear in the political field, becoming an MP and a great parliamentary orator. At the foot of Addison's statue lies historian THOMAS BABINGTON MACAULAY (1800–59), originator of a particular sort of 'Whig History' that saw the history of humankind as a pre-ordained progression towards a Britain under the rule of the Protestant constitutional monarchy ushered in by the 'Glorious Revolution' of 1688. Not exactly sophisticated to begin with, a vulgarized version of Macaulay's views would help underpin the jingoism of the later British Empire.

Victorian titans CHARLES DICKENS (1812–70), ALFRED, LORD TENNYSON (1809–92) and ROBERT BROWNING

(1812–89) are here. (Browning's wife and fellow-poet Elizabeth Barrett Browning (1806–61) died in Florence and was buried there, in the Protestant cemetery.) In the Abbey rather against his wishes is the lion's share of THOMAS HARDY (1840–1928), whose heart, having first according to a macabre tradition fallen to the share of a pet cat, was buried in Stinsford, Dorset. These giants were later joined by RUDYARD KIPLING (1865–1936), the author of children's classics such as *The Jungle Book* and *Just So Stories*, as well as popular verse such as *The Barrack Room Ballads* and a host of more serious (if equally jingoistic) literature, and JOHN MASEFIELD (1878–1967), the poet, critic and novelist. A place in the Abbey would have been the crowning glory for the career of confirmed anglophile Henry James (1843–1916), who had lived in England for decades and taken citizenship, in a spirit of solidarity, on the outbreak of World War I. His friends hoped he might be granted a place here but the authorities proved unyielding: James was still a parvenu as far as they were concerned. Instead, his ashes had to be ferried ignominiously back to brash, vulgar old America, where they were interred in the family grave in Cambridge, Massachusetts.

ACTORS

A number of the greats of the Restoration stage were given Abbey burials, including some of the first professional actresses ever to work in Britain: prior to this there had been a taboo on women performing, and female parts had been taken by boys in drag. MARY BETTERTON (c. 1637–1712) was interred here, as, in an unmarked grave in the south aisle, was ANNE OLDFIELD (1683–1730). Congreve's favourite lead and a distinguished Shakespearean heroine, ANNE BRACEGIRDLE (c. 1663–1748), lies near Aphra Behn in the cloister.

Eighteenth-century superstar DAVID GARRICK (1717–79) was buried in Poets' Corner after what was practically a state funeral, unprecedented for an actor. The ashes of actor-manager SIR HENRY IRVING (1838–1905) are also here. Born with the surname Brodribb, for some reason he decided to change it. 'Funny, without being vulgar,' said W.S. Gilbert unkindly of his Hamlet; 'How Henry would have loved it!' darlinged Ellen Terry of his funeral. More recently the body of LAURENCE OLIVIER (Lord Olivier, 1907–89) was laid to rest beside that of Garrick.

MUSICIANS

The musicians mostly centre upon HENRY PURCELL (c. 1659–95), who's buried in the north choir aisle, and has an epitaph attributed to Dryden:

> *Here Lyes*
> *HENRY PURCELL Esqr.*
> *Who left this life*
> *And is gone to that Blessed Place*
> *Where only his Harmony*
> *can be exceeded.*

Purcell's teacher, the Newark-born organist and composer JOHN BLOW (1649–1708) is also here. Stating that 'His own Musical Compositions, (Especially his Church Musick) are a far nobler Monument to his Memory, than any other can be rais'd for Him', his memorial obligingly provides a sample, giving a full four-part canon inscribed in stone. Although born in Germany, GEORGE FREDERIC HANDEL (1685–1759) adopted England as his homeland and was the central figure in its musical scene in the mid-eighteenth century. His monument, in Poets' Corner, gives us a quick burst of the *Messiah*, the first of a sheaf of pages the composer clutches in his hand showing, in jumbo type like something out of a children's songbook, the opening lines of the aria 'I Know that My Redeemer Liveth'. Another adoptive Englishman, the pianist and composer MUZIO CLEMENTI (1752–1832), joined the musicians in the Abbey after his death at Evesham, though he was buried in the cloister, along with Haydn's patron the impresario JOHANN PETER SALOMAN (1745–1815) and the composer and musicologist WILLIAM SHIELD (1748–1829). The ashes of RALPH VAUGHAN WILLIAMS (1872–1958) were buried in the north choir aisle of the nave. Composer William Walton (1902–83) is commemorated by a tablet here, but his ashes were buried in the garden of his Italian villa in Ischia. The conductor SIR ADRIAN BOULT (1889–1983) also has a memorial in the north aisle but isn't here himself, having left his body to medical science.

SCHOLARS

The French Protestant refugee ISAAC CASAUBON (1559–1614), now rather unfairly famous for having provided a name for George Eliot's personification of dry, bloodless academicism in *Middlemarch*, is the focal point for the scholars. In 1658 when at the age of sixty-five he was certainly old enough to know better, Izaak Walton scratched his initials in the tomb.

SCIENTISTS

Centring upon SIR ISAAC NEWTON (1642–1727), who is in the central aisle of the nave, are the scientists. SIR JOHN FREDERICK WILLIAM HERSCHEL (1792–1871), who followed his father William (see Slough, Berkshire) into the post of

Royal Astronomer, but also did important pioneering work in optics and photography, is buried in the north aisle of the nave. Belfast-born WILLIAM THOMSON KELVIN (1824–1907), the propounder of the Second Law of Thermodynamics and pioneering researcher into electrical currents, is nearby in the central aisle. Oddly, given his agnostic views, CHARLES DARWIN (1809–82), the great evolutionist, was buried in the Abbey, in the north choir aisle of the nave, while the New Zealand-born atom-smasher Ernest, FIRST BARON RUTHERFORD (1871–1937) is in the central aisle.

West End

BAYSWATER ROAD W2

The burial ground for St George's, Hanover Square was, for reasons of space, sited half a mile away on the Bayswater Road: a block of flats, St George's Fields, covers most of the site now and the nearest thing to an open area remaining is the playground (private, but you can ask permission to look around) of the Hyde Park Nursery School, Hyde Park Place. Laurence Sterne was buried here (but see Coxwold, North Yorkshire), as was another writer, ANN RADCLIFFE (1764–1823), whose gothic masterpiece *The Mysteries of Udolpho* (1794) proved both enormously popular and profoundly influential.

BROADWAY, WESTMINSTER SW1

Nothing now remains of the chapel that stood here

between around 1640 and 1843. During the Civil War, the chapel served not only as a stable for the Roundheads but as an improvised prison for captives taken at the Battle of Worcester. They were kept in such harsh conditions that over a thousand died, to be buried in pits on the Tothill Fields, which lay just southeast of here, between the Abbey and Millbank. Long since built over, Tothill Fields would also take some of the strain during the Plague years of the seventeenth century, mass graves being dug here for victims when the churchyards overflowed. Among those laid to rest more formally in the chapel burial ground, now just a little patch of green by the corner of Victoria Street, was IGNATIUS SANCHO (1729–80), who for many years ran a grocer's shop in Charles Street, Mayfair. Sancho is more famous, however, as one of the first black writers to achieve popular success in Britain, his *Letters* selling out in several editions when they were published two years after his death. A keen musician and a composer of real ability, Sancho was also an enthusiastic theatregoer. (He would have loved to have played Othello but didn't have the voice.) He was a friend of the great actor David Garrick, as well as writers like Sterne and Johnson and many of the other luminaries of the mid-eighteenth century. Born on a slave ship in mid-Atlantic and brought to England at the age of two, Sancho had no recollection of African life, and always regarded himself as an Englishman. But integrated as he was, his eyes were open and he had ears to hear, and if his letters often find him describing his own personal version of the black British experience with wit and good-humoured irony, he was evidently thoroughly alive to the all too serious evils of racism, and could be withering in his denunciation of the slave trade. His West Indian wife, Anne, was buried with him.

AN ADVENTURER'S END

THOMAS 'COLONEL' BLOOD (c. 1618–80), the adventurer who in 1671 had attempted to steal the Crown Jewels and very nearly succeeded, was buried in the chapel that used to stand on Broadway in Westminster. The son of a blacksmith, he'd served the Cromwellian government so well that he was granted estates in Ireland; when these were confiscated by the restored monarchy he was so incensed that he was plotting with fellow malcontents to seize Dublin Castle and assassinate the Lord Protector before the conspiracy was discovered and his confederates executed. Though lucky to be alive, Blood wasn't placated by his merciful treatment – hence the Tower heist. Arrested with the swag, he demanded to speak to the King in person, and was rewarded for his cheek by an interview with Charles II which ended in his being not merely pardoned but given back the Irish estates. A wild man to the last, Blood had got himself into hot water again by the time of his death, having quarrelled violently with his patron, the Duke of Buckingham. Though he was ill, and passed away peacefully in his bed, public awareness of the trouble he was in (along, perhaps, with the implausibility of the idea that such a swashbuckling character could come to such a sedate end) fuelled rumours that the funeral had been a sham to cover up Blood's escape. So feverish did the speculation get that the following week the grave was exhumed, but Blood was found to be lying there all present and correct.

COVENT GARDEN WC2

Designed by Inigo Jones, the original St Paul's Covent Garden burnt down in 1795 and had to be rebuilt. Since Jones' original design was followed, the church looks the same as it did during the Restoration, though the original fittings were all lost. This has been the theatre church since the mid-seventeenth century, and there are scores of memorial plaques to actors and actresses ancient and modern. (Entrances on Henrietta Street, King Street and Bedford Street.)

Playwright WILLIAM WYCHERLEY (c. 1640–1716) was buried here, as was Irish actor CHARLES MACKLIN (actually McLaughlin, c. 1697–1797), one of the great Shylocks of all time. Later the ashes of DAME ELLEN TERRY (1847–1928) would be placed in the south wall. Nearby, to the right of the altar, lies milliner-turned-actress DAME EDITH EVANS (1888–1976). Among the others interred here are GRINLING GIBBONS (1648–1720), a famous woodcarver of the Restoration period.

The scurrilous satirist SAMUEL BUTLER (1612–80), author of the anti-puritanical poem *Hudibras*, won lots of promises of patronage from the Royalist interest for his pains but little in the way of real support. He ended his days in abject poverty, hence his burial here rather than in the Abbey. 'He dyed of a Consumption, September 25,' recalled Aubrey,

> *and buried 27 according to his Appointment, in the Church-yard of Convent Garden; scil. in the north part next the church at the east end. His feet touch the wall. His grave, 2 yards distant from the Pillaster of the Dore, (by his desire) 6 foot deepe. About 25 of his old acquaintance at his Funerall. I myself being one of the eldest, helped to carry the Pall. His coffin covered with black Bayes.*

The Dutch-born painter SIR PETER LELY (originally Pieter Van Der Faes, 1618–80) was buried here too, as was the gallant courtier-turned-highwayman, CLAUDE DUVAL (1643–70), hanged at Tyburn despite the pleas of London's ladies to Charles II. The epitaph on his gravestone in the centre aisle (lost, unfortunately, in the fire of 1795) captured his ambivalent personality:

> Here lies Du Vall: Reader if male thou art,
> Look to thy purse: if female to thy heart.

THOMAS ARNE (1710–78) was baptized in the church, then interred in the churchyard outside. A distinguished composer, he is popularly remembered for the patriotic air 'Rule Britannia' (see Richmond, West London for James Thomson, who wrote the lyrics). The brilliant caricaturist THOMAS ROWLANDSON (1756–1827) was also laid to rest at St Paul's.

DEAN STREET, SOHO W1

Exiled and bankrupt, THEODORE ETIENNE, KING OF CORSICA (d. 1756) wound up here in a humble grave in St Anne's churchyard. And he was lucky at that: he would have been consigned to a mass paupers' grave had not a local tradesman been so tickled by the idea of paying a king's funeral expenses that he decided to help out. The influential Romantic critic and essayist WILLIAM HAZLITT (1778–1830) is in the churchyard too, while in the little chapel under the tower reside the ashes of DOROTHY L. SAYERS (1893–1957), detective novelist and Dante translator, for all her bluestocking eccentricities a straight-down-the-line High Anglican who for many years served as a churchwarden at St Anne's.

LINCOLN'S INN, HOLBORN WC2

JOHN THURLOE (1616–88), Cromwell's secretary of state, lived in the inn, and was buried here; also here is SPENCER PERCEVAL (1762–1812). People always remembered just where they'd been and what they'd been doing when they heard the news of Perceval's death: he was, and fortunately remains, the only British prime minister to be assassinated, and the event sent a profound shockwave through the nation. He was shot in the lobby of the House of Commons by John Bellingham, a bankrupt Liverpool merchant who felt the government (under an earlier and quite different administration) hadn't given him the support it should have done in a disastrous run-in he'd had with the authorities in St Petersburg. Bellingham could not by any stretch of the imagination be described as sane, but the court was in no mood to make allowances: he was found guilty of murder and given the death penalty. He was executed within days and his body was taken to Bart's Hospital for dissection, by order of the court.

MARYLEBONE HIGH STREET W1

What's left of the old St Marylebone Church, about a hundred yards from the top of Marylebone High Street, was laid out as a tiny memorial garden of rest at the time of the Festival of Britain, 1951. A plaque records some of the notables buried here, including JAMES GIBBS (1682–1754), architect of St Martin-in-the-Fields (and indeed the new St Marylebone, just along the street) and JOHN MICHAEL RYSBRACK (c. 1693–1770). A Flemish sculptor who settled in London in 1720, Rysbrack's credits include the Newton memorial in Westminster Abbey. Astronomer JAMES FERGUSON (1710–76) is among those present, as is John's brother CHARLES WESLEY (1708–88), distinguished in his own right as author of 'Hark, the Herald Angels Sing' and other favourite hymns.

St Marylebone is also a good place for artists: the best known is probably GEORGE STUBBS (1724–1806), the creator of racehorse and livestock portraits, but JAMES NORTHCOTE (1746–1831), FRANCIS WHEATLEY (1747–1801) and ALLAN RAMSAY (1713–84) are here too. Ramsay, the son of the famous poet (see Greyfriars, Edinburgh, Lothian), was portrait painter to George III, a friend of Dr Johnson and a correspondent of leading European thinkers such as Rousseau and Voltaire. Here too are the boxer and fencer JAMES FIGG (d. 1736), one of the leading stars of the eighteenth-century sporting scene (he even appears in Hogarth's *The Rake's Progress*), and EDMOND HOYLE (1672–1769), who first codified the rules of whist.

PADDINGTON GREEN W2

In the churchyard at St Mary's is the great tragic actress SARAH SIDDONS (1755–1831), whose statue is nearby on the Green. Nelson's mistress Emma Hamilton had wanted to be buried here, but as things turned out she died in exile in Dieppe, and was laid to rest there.

ST GILES STREET, NEW OXFORD STREET WC1

The poet, dramatist and translator GEORGE CHAPMAN (c. 1560–1634), whose version of Homer would make Keats feel like some watcher in the skies when a new planet swims into his ken, was buried here in the churchyard of St Giles-in-the-Fields in an unmarked grave. His friend William Habington thought it outrageous

> *That Chapmans reverend ashes must*
> *Lye rudely mingled with the vulgar dust.*

A few years later, however, he was granted a memorial, the work of Inigo Jones. It can be seen in a corner of the present church, which dates from 1734.

Chapman was joined fifteen years later by the philosopher EDWARD, LORD HERBERT OF CHERBURY (1583–1648), who left something of a theological time-bomb behind him in his *De Religione Gentilium*, published 1645, which noted certain Common Notions underlying all the main religions of the world and thus, arguably, implied the impossibility of claiming complete authority for any one, such as Christianity. JAMES SHIRLEY (1596–1666) was, it is said, embarking on a career in the Church when Archbishop Laud talked him out of his vocation on account of an unsightly mole he had on his face. (The image-conscious archbishop believed it would hamper his performance as preacher.) Nothing daunted, Shirley set about making himself a successful playwright instead. The poet and satirist ANDREW MARVELL (1621–78) is also here, about the middle of the south aisle. 'Some suspect that he was poysoned by the Jesuites,' reports Aubrey; adding scrupulously, 'but I cannot be positive.' Why on earth the Jesuits should have wanted to do such a thing, he doesn't vouchsafe.

St Giles' has witnessed the deaths of martyrs across the religious spectrum, from the radical Lollard leader Sir John Oldcastle, 'hung and burnt hanging' near the church gate in 1417, to the twelve Catholics denounced by supergrass Titus Oates between 1678 and 1681 as participants in a (completely fictitious, it eventually transpired) 'Popish Plot' to murder Charles II, and buried here in the churchyard, supposedly by the church's north wall. The most famous of these was

Oliver Plunkett, Archbishop of Armagh, who was later exhumed and taken to Germany for safe keeping. Now his head is in Ireland at Drogheda and his body at Downside, Sussex.

As for Titus Oates, nobody knows where he's buried, though many would have loved to jump up and down on his grave. 'Perjurer', announces the *Dictionary of National Biography* after his name, as if that summed him up, which it does to a point, since he does seem to have had a fairly fundamental problem where telling the truth was concerned. After a stay in Spain, for instance, he claimed to have gained a degree from the University of Salamanca, though it's known that he never so much as visited that city. He was more than a perjurer, though – sincere (if verging on the demented) in his anti-Catholic views and not lacking in courage or ingenuity. His time in Spain was in fact spent in Valladolid, where he posed as an ardent Catholic in order to infiltrate the Jesuit College where English priests were trained for return to their homeland as secret missionaries. He managed six months before he was thrown out for misconduct. Unimpressed by his part in the Popish Plot, the Stuart regime had him imprisoned and subjected to annual pillorying, but after 1688 King Billy's Dutchmen gave him not only his liberty but a state pension. Though at last vindicated, he seems none the less to have decided to keep a lower profile after this, living and dying in obscurity. The rakish, raffish Restoration poet SIR CHARLES SEDLEY (c. 1639–1701) could hardly be accused of keeping a low profile: on one occasion he and some aristocratic drinking-buddies narrowly escaped lynching in Covent Garden after mooning the mob in a display apparently intended to demonstrate their superior breeding and intelligence.

PICCADILLY W1

The 'English Hippocrates', physician THOMAS SYDENHAM (1624–89), was buried in St James' churchyard here. His emphasis on observation as against theory had profound implications for medicine then and subsequently. The bluestocking, collage-artist and entertaining memoirist MARY DELANY (1700–88) is also here.

ST MARGARET STREET, WESTMINSTER SW1

Right next door to the Abbey is St Margaret's, Westminster, the House of Commons church. WILLIAM CAXTON (c. 1421–91) lies in the churchyard, the exact site of his grave unknown: valued by St Margaret's for his dedication in auditing the parish accounts, Caxton is better known to posterity for his work with books of another kind. Though he didn't even set up in London until he was in his fifties, after a long apprenticeship in Bruges, Caxton would not only produce England's first printed book, *The Dictes and Sayinges of the Philosophers* (1477), but would go on to print scores more, often translating them himself. A stained-glass window, paid for by subscription of London printers and depicting the great man at work, was damaged in the Blitz, but the lower part, showing Caxton and his press, survived.

The century after Caxton, poet and courtier JOHN SKELTON (c. 1464–1529) was buried before the high altar here. Near him lies all but the head (see West Horsley, Surrey) of SIR WALTER RALEGH (c. 1552–1618). A favourite of Elizabeth's, Ralegh had nothing but trouble under her successor, James I, who started out by having him condemned to death on vague charges of 'treason', then let him off with thirteen years in the tower. Releasing him to undertake an expedition to Guiana, he had him executed when he returned empty-handed from an undertaking that had cost Ralegh the life of his son and his own health. If the mythology is to be believed, Ralegh was a cocky, confident Elizabethan to the last. Feeling the executioner's axe, he commented: 'This is a sharp medicine, but it is a sure cure for all diseases.' He then scornfully rejected the customary blindfold, asking, 'Think you I fear the shadow of the axe, when I fear not the axe itself?'

WENCESLAUS HOLLAR (1607–77), the Czech etcher, is buried here, as, somewhere in the churchyard outside, is ADMIRAL ROBERT BLAKE (1599–1657), England's second greatest naval commander. He was first given a hero's burial in the Abbey, but the Protectorate's heroes were the Restoration's traitors, and in 1661 a mob got into the Abbey and gave it a thorough clearing out, disinterring Blake along with twenty other notables (including Cromwell's mother) and dumping them in a common pit in St Margaret's churchyard.

One writer who, far from resenting his exclusion from the Abbey, will have considered himself lucky to be buried in consecrated ground at all is JOHN CLELAND (1710–89). His novel *Fanny Hill, or The Memoirs of a Woman of Pleasure* made even the shameless eighteenth century blush. As for the nineteenth and most of the twentieth centuries, they didn't know where to put themselves, and the novel disappeared off the literary map more or less completely until it was republished in 1963, between the Lady Chatterley ban and the Beatles' first LP, only to fall foul of the Obscene Publications Act.

ST MARTIN'S PLACE, TRAFALGAR SQUARE WC2

Charles II's favourite mistress NELL GWYNN (1650–87) went to her last bed in the chancel at St-Martin-in-the-Fields. 'Let not poor Nelly starve,' the Merry Monarch is said to have pleaded with his dying breath. There was little danger of that, so nicely had he set her up, and so popular a figure had she become, but she none the less survived him by only a couple of years. ROBERT BOYLE (1627–91) was the first scientist to suggest something like a modern definition of chemical elements, as substances that couldn't be broken down further into different substances, but is most famous as the propounder of Boyle's Law – that given a constant temperature, the volume of gases varies inversely according to pressure. He was buried here, and must still be around somewhere, though the exact location has been lost since the 1720s, when the old church was demolished and the new one built. John Aubrey found him impressive in every respect:

> He is very tall (about six foot high) and streight, very temperate, and vertuouse, and frugall: a Batcheler; keepes a Coach; sojournes with his sister, the Lady Ranulagh. His greatest delight is Chymistrey. He haz at his sister's a noble Laboratory, and severall servants (Prentices to him) to looke to it … At his owne costs and chardges he gott translated and printed the New Testament in Arabique, to send into the Mahometan countreys. He has not only a high renowne in England, but abroad; and when foreigners come to hither, 'tis one of their curiosities to make him a Visit.
> His Works alone may make a Librarie.

ST-MARTIN-IN-THE-FIELDS

At the top of the stairs leading down to the crypt is a plaque erected by the churchwardens, recording vestry decisions of the 1770s:

> ORDERED that in future no Graves be Dug in any of the Vaults under the Church as a Practice thereof will be Prejudicial to and in time Endanger the Foundation of the said Church and ALSO ORDERED at a Vestry Held the 31st Day of March 1774 that in future no corps be Buried in any of the Vaults under the Church but what are in Leaden Coffins.

The Irish-born Restoration playwright GEORGE FARQUHAR (1678–1707) ended up here; an actor then a soldier, he managed to turn both experiences to account in his dramatic work, but none the less died in poverty. The thief and incorrigible escaper JACK SHEPPARD (1702–24) got a Christian burial at St Martin-in-the-Fields, having eluded the waiting dissectionists in death just as he had eluded the authorities so often in life. A major embarrassment to the forces of law and order and a popular hero for ordinary Londoners, Sheppard escaped from Newgate no fewer than five times. Each time he was recaptured – not so difficult, in fact, given the brazen insouciance with which he flaunted himself once outside – the authorities tightened security till they had him fettered to the floor in solitary confinement behind a series of heavy locked doors. Still he managed to free himself. When he was finally brought to book, an estimated 200,000 people turned out to see him safely despatched – and buried, for the crowd prevented the dissectionists' agents from making off with the body. Their skills more socially respectable, the French sculptor LOUIS ROUBILIAC (1695–1762) and the cabinetmaker and designer THOMAS CHIPPENDALE (1718–79) were also interred here.

SAVOY STREET, STRAND WC2

The Chapel of the Savoy (closed Mondays, otherwise open 11.30 a.m. –3.30 p.m.) is all that's left of a hospital built for 'pouer, nedie people' by Henry VII. GAVIN DOUGLAS (c. 1475–1522) is buried here: not only was his 1513 translation of Virgil's *Aeneid* the first rendering of any of the major classical poems into any of the 'English' languages; Douglas was also the first writer consciously to write in 'Scots', thus inaugurating a long and distinguished literary tradition. Such academic points aside, his *Aeneid* is a dazzling technical achievement and a great poem in its own right. Another poet, GEORGE WITHER (1588–1667), was buried here, though his grave is now lost. Wither was executed by the Stuarts for selling his country house to raise money for a troop of horse for Cromwell.

SOUTH AUDLEY STREET, MAYFAIR W1

Two distinguished bluestockings *avant la lettre* were buried here at Grosvenor Chapel. LADY MARY WORTLEY MONTAGU (1689–1762) was an irrepressible character – a poet, a traveller, a gossip and altogether an unavoidable presence on the London literary scene. She was also a tireless campaigner for inoculation, which she had come upon during a visit to Turkey and which she was plugging years before the 'discoveries' of either Jenner (see Berkeley, Gloucestershire) or Jesty (see Worth Matravers, Dorset). The poet, translator and essayist ELIZABETH CARTER (1717–1806) was unfortunately immortalized by Dr Johnson's glowing tribute: 'My old friend, Mrs Carter, could make a pudding as well as translate Epictetus.' A woman of formidable intellect, she had a particular gift for languages. As a child she was taught French, Latin, Greek and Hebrew, then – apparently feeling under-stretched – taught herself Italian, Spanish, German, Portuguese and Arabic. Among the males laid to rest in the Grosvenor Chapel was JOHN WILKES (1727–97), Whig politician and journalist, whose *North Briton* magazine proved a satirical scourge to absolutism and saw him in and out of trouble with the Tory governments of the late eighteenth century.

STRAND WC2

Now the RAF church, St Clement Danes had three centuries' worth of dead when burials were stopped in 1853. In 1956, the contents of the crypt were excavated, gathered together and cremated, for reburial under the South Stair. So while dramatist THOMAS OTWAY (1652–85), author of the recently revived tragedy *Venice Preserv'd*, is here, his remains are mixed in with those of an awful lot of other people, including those of Anne, Mrs John Donne, inspirer (if it can be called an inspiration) of the famous epigram: 'John Donne. Anne Donne. Undone.' She died in 1617, fourteen years before her husband.

North Central

CITY ROAD EC1

Behind the chapel he founded in 1778, sharing a tomb with his sister Mrs Martha Hall (1706–91) and some of his early

ministers, lies JOHN WESLEY (1703–91), first leader of the
Methodists. 'If thou art constrained to bless the instrument,'
his epitaph bids its reader: 'GIVE GOD THE GLORY.' His
mother SUSANNA WESLEY (1669–1742), is just over the road
here, her dazzling white headstone standing out among the
more muted tones in the Bunhill Fields Nonconformist
Burial Ground. Used between 1665 and 1843, but never
consecrated, this site supposedly derived its name from
'Bone Hill', after the bones from the charnel house at
St Paul's were moved here during the sixteenth century.
After that, it provided a home for generations of dissenting
corpses. The graves are mostly fenced off now, but from the
public walkways you can distinguish a number of important
tombs.

Known in the seventeenth century as the 'Calvin of
England', JOHN OWEN (1616–83) was Dean of Christ
Church and Vice-Chancellor of Oxford University, a friend
of Cromwell and an important statesman of the
Commonwealth and Protectorate. He died at home in Ealing
and was given a big funeral here with lots of nobles turning
out to give him a good send off. Pilgrim JOHN BUNYAN
(1628–88) died while on a visit to a friend in Snow Hill,
Holborn – hence his burial here, rather than in his native
Bedfordshire. A Parliamentary general in the Civil War, the
friend and son-in-law of Cromwell, Charles Fleetwood (d.
1692) retired after the Restoration to Stoke Newington, then
a comparatively remote spot. Lost for a long time, his
monument was rediscovered in 1869: by that time, however,
it was seven feet down, so much it seems had the lie of land
changed in Bunhill Fields through two centuries and some
123,000 burials.

Here too is DANIEL DEFOE (1661–1731), writer and
journalist, the author of *Robinson Crusoe* (1719) and *Moll*

Flanders (1722). All his life an outspoken nonconformist, in 1703 Defoe ended up in the pillory for his anti-High Church satire *The Shortest Way With Dissenters*; this treatment rebounded on the authorities, however, when the mob showered him not with the usual rotten fruit, dead cats, etc, but with a hero's acclaim. 'Hark from the tombs a doleful sound,' wrote ISAAC WATTS (1674–1748) in one of his more grotesque flights. Fortunately, the great hymnster, author of such standards as 'O God our help in Ages past', sleeps quietly enough, as, somewhere, does William Blake (1757–1827), artist, poet and prophet. His monument wasn't erected until 1927, and his exact whereabouts are unknown.

Also here, though his tomb is no longer to be seen, is THOMAS NEWCOMEN (1663–1729), who designed the 'atmospheric' steam engine, the first practicable steam engine for industrial use. Though Newcomen's engine was, in theory at least, soon superseded by Watt's more sophisticated rotary engine, in practice Newcomen's – cheaper to run and far easier to maintain – ruled the roost for many decades.

Less famous than all these worthies, but in her own way every bit as remarkable, is Dame Mary Page. 'She departed this life March 11th 1728 in the 56th year of her age,' says the inscription on her tomb. 'In 67 months she was tapp'd 66 times, Had taken away 240 gallons of water, without ever repining at her case or ever fearing the operation.' An example to us all.

Leaving the Fields by the Bunhill Row exit, go up the street to the right for a few yards, then left down Banner Street, and you'll almost immediately see the sign for the Friends Meeting House to your left. The garden behind was once the Quaker Burial Ground: GEORGE FOX (1624–91), founder of the Society of Friends, is there, though the exact position of his grave has been lost.

PANCRAS ROAD NW1

No less a personage than JONATHAN WILD (c. 1682–1725), King of Thieves, put in a fleeting appearance here at Old St Pancras' churchyard – he was 'resurrected' by bodysnatchers within days of his execution and his skeleton now graces a glass case in the Royal College of Surgeons. Wild made a fortune by acting as a broker between the thieves and their victims, organizing the selling-back of swag (from which he would naturally take his own discreet cut), and meanwhile taking an increasingly firm hold of London's gang system, which by the end he was practically running – without of course getting his hands dirty. The judicial process by which the authorities did eventually get Wild to the gallows doesn't bear terribly close scrutiny, though anyone less like driven snow it would be hard to imagine.

Set at what was then the northernmost edge of the city (and is now behind Kings Cross and St Pancras stations), Old St Pancras' churchyard was described by an observer of 1777 as 'a rural place, in some parts entirely covered with docks and nettles, enclosed only by a low hand-rail, and commanding extensive views of open country in every direction'. Composer JOHANN CHRISTIAN BACH (1735–82), the 'London Bach', was among the notables buried here in the late eighteenth century. As the city expanded, however, and the docks and nettles were allowed to run riot unchecked for several decades, the churchyard seems to have taken on an air of dilapidation, to such an extent that by the mid-nineteenth century Mary Shelley was having the remains of her parents Mary Wollstonecraft and William Godwin moved to Bournemouth (see Dorset). She did this despite the strong memories St Pancras' held for her: it had been over her mother's grave that she and her husband Percy Bysshe Shelley had first declared their love. The new St Pancras' was built in 1822 and the old church became a chapel of ease; it was reinstated as a parish church in its own right in 1863. The old churchyard is now a public garden: at its centre stands a gothic monument looking rather like a miniature Albert Memorial for those 'whose graves are now unseen, or the record of whose names may have become obliterated'. Unfortunately, they've mostly been obliterated from this monument too, and those which remain tend to belie the monument's claim that it is commemorating 'names...which have an interest for all time'. Apart from J.C. Bach, the biggest gun here seems to be Sir John Soane (1753–1837), architect of the Bank of England.

PENTONVILLE ROAD N1

Just off the Pentonville Road, in what was the churchyard of St James' Church and is now a public garden named in his honour, lies JOSEPH GRIMALDI (1778–1837) the clown, whose performances at Sadlers Wells were legendary in their day and have influenced all subsequent generations of circus performers.

PRIMROSE HILL NW1

The ashes of the controversial composer ELISABETH LUTYENS (1906–83), 'Twelve-tone Lizzie', were scattered here, where she'd loved to walk. Actually, she'd preferred walking in Regent's Park, and had wanted her ashes scattered over Queen

Mary's Rose Garden, but the park authorities refused and Primrose Hill had to do. Ravaged by arthritis and alcoholism, she was deeply depressed at the time of her death, and there was speculation that she might have committed suicide. There was no real evidence for this, however.

REGENT'S PARK NW1

One man whose ashes were allowed to be scattered here (unlike those of Elisabeth Lutyens, above) was author WILLIAM GERHARDIE (1895–1977). He was born and brought up in St Petersburg, in a household which considered itself British but which spoke French, Russian and German as well as English. During the troubles of 1905, a mob tied his father in a sack: he escaped with his life only because his captors took him for the socialist Keir Hardie. From his teens, Gerhardie grew up in England, but not surprisingly his Russian experiences marked him profoundly, and form the basis for much of his best fiction.

UNIVERSITY COLLEGE LONDON, GOWER STREET WC1

The pioneer political economist and guru of the utilitarian movement JEREMY BENTHAM (1748–1832) helped found UCL. He seems to have believed it conducive to the greatest happiness of the greatest number that his skeleton, kitted out in his clothes and a wax death-mask, should be kept for posterity. It's all been done in accordance with his wishes, his wax face modelled by Jacques Talrich and his head placed in the college safe (which must be nice for the office staff). You can see the great man in his glass case in the south cloister: go through the college's main Gower Street entrance, and the relevant door is across the quadrangle in the right-hand corner.

JEREMY BENTHAM ON HIS OWN CORPSE

My body I give to my dear friend Doctor Southwood Smith to be disposed of... in the manner expressed in the paper annexed to this my will and at the top of which I have written 'Auto Icon' The skeleton he will cause to be put together in such a manner as that the whole figure may be seated in a Chair usually occupied by me when living in the attitude in which I am sitting when engaged in thought in the course of the time employed in writing I direct that the body thus prepared shall be transferred to my executor he will cause the skeleton to be clad in one of the suits of black occasionally worn by me The body so clothed together with the chair and the staff in my latter years bourne by me he will take charge of and for containing the whole apparatus he will cause to be prepared an appropriate box or case and will cause to be engraved in conspicuous characters on a plate to be fixed thereon and also on the labels on the glass cases in which the preparation of the soft parts of my body shall be contained ... my name at length with the letters ob. followed by the day of my decease If it should happen that my personal friends and other disciples should be disposed to meet together on some day or days of the year for the purpose of commemorating the founder of the greatest happiness system of morals and legislations my executor will from time to time cause to be conveyed to the room in which they meet the said box or case with the contents therein to be stationed in such a part of the room as to the assembled company shall so meet.

City

ST PAUL'S CATHEDRAL EC4

Though the present cathedral had of course to be built from scratch after the Great Fire of London, 1666, Old St Paul's dated back to Saxon times. KING AETHELRED II, THE UNREADY (c. 968–1016, reigned 978–1016) was buried here, as, four centuries later, was JOHN OF GAUNT, DUKE OF LANCASTER (1340–99). The truly dominant figure of Richard II's reign, he was regent to the young King and rival to the adult. Other distinguished occupants include, from the Elizabethan period, SIR PHILIP SIDNEY (1554–86), 'whose Fame will never dye, whilest Poetrie lives, was the most accomplished Cavalier of his time,' according to Aubrey: 'He was not only of an excellent witt, but extremely beautiful.' The funeral was a grand affair, as became a noble knight, beloved of the Queen, who had sustained his death wound fighting for Protestantism in the Low Countries. Aubrey, who would see Sidney's leaden coffin when it was exposed by the Great Fire, had already gained a sense of his funeral:

> When I was a boy 9 yeares old, I was with my father at one Mr. Singleton's an Alderman and Wollen-draper in Glocester, who had in his parlour over the Chimney, the whole description of the Funerall, engraved and printed on papers pasted together, which at length was, I beleeve, the length of the room at least; but he had contrived it to be turned upon two Pinnes, that turning one of them made the figures march all in order. It did make such a strong impression on my tender Phantasy that I remember it as if it were but yesterday.

A few years later Sidney would have to move over to make room in his tomb for his father-in-law SIR FRANCIS WALSINGHAM (c. 1530–90), who was laid alongside him. The MP for Banbury, Elizabeth's senior spook and grand Protestant inquisitor, Walsingham was entitled to this last, posthumous favour from Sidney, the appearances his son-in-law had been determined to keep up as courtier, soldier and diplomat having effectively ruined him. In his embarrassment, Walsingham had to ask for a furtive and unceremonious burial at dead of night. Aubrey also had interesting facts to report on the mortal remains of another eminent Elizabethan, JOHN COLET (c. 1467–1519), friend of More and Erasmus, humanist theologian and scholar, dean of the cathedral and founder of St Paul's School. Colet had been buried in Old St Paul's:

> After the Conflagration (his Monument being broken) somebody made a little hole towards the upper edge of his Coffin, which was clowed like the coffin [crust] of a Pye and was full of a Liquour which conserved the body. Mr. Wyld and Ralph Greatorex tasted it and 'twas of a kind of insipid tast, something of an Ironish tast. The Coffin was of Lead, and layd in the Wall about 2 foot H above the surface of the Floore.
>
> This was a strange rare way of conserving a Corps: perhaps it was a Pickle, as for Beefe, whose Saltness in so many years the Lead might sweeten and render insipid. The body felt, to the probe of a stick which they thrust into a chinke, like boyld Brawne.

The Flemish-born painter SIR ANTHONY VAN DYCK (1599–1641) was laid to rest here after dying of Plague in Blackfriars.

The only memorial to survive the fire unscathed (it stands now in the south choir aisle) was that of poet and prelate JOHN DONNE (1572–1631). After a colourful youth, during which he fraternized with smart young aristocrats and wrote passionate and dazzlingly clever love poetry, he moved increasingly towards the Church. Taking orders in 1615, he was appointed Dean of St Paul's six years later. In its own way Donne's manner as priest was as flamboyant as it had ever been in his 'idolatrie': the effigy on his monument shows him naked in his winding sheet. He posed for it when alive, warmed by charcoal fires while sculptor Nicholas Stone worked. Once it was ready, he slept with it standing by his bed. And the performance Donne made of his death didn't end there. According to his biographer Izaak Walton it was his ambition to die in the pulpit, and he very nearly succeeded. On 25 February 1631 he rose from his sickbed to give his last sermon, 'Death's Duell': 'Many that then saw his tears, and heard his faint and hollow voice,' said Walton, felt that 'Dr Donne had preach't his own Funeral Sermon'. In the event, however, he lived to die another day. When death did finally approach for real, Donne 'closed his own eyes; and then disposed his hands and body into such a posture as required not the least alteration by those that came to shroud him'.

THE NEW ST PAUL'S: The new St Paul's was to have many other distinguished occupants, starting, of course, with architect SIR CHRISTOPHER WREN (1632–1723), without whom none of this would have been possible. Entrusted after the Fire with the task of overseeing the rebuilding of the city's churches, of which 84 out of 109 had been destroyed, he designed fifty-one of them personally. St Paul's was to be Wren's masterpiece, but he was matter of fact enough about its construction. Apparently, when the moment came for the foundation stone of the new cathedral to be laid amid the ruins of the old, he simply asked a labourer to bring him the first slab to come to hand. It was, apparently, a gravestone, and inscribed *Resurgam* ('I will rise again'). As the epitaph on Wren's own grave famously runs: *si monumentum requiris, circumspice* ('If you seek his monument, look around').

The first thing you see when you do look around from Wren's grave in the southeast corner of the crypt is the graves of his family, then, stretching away towards the centre of the floor, a collection of Britain's greatest artists, who have always tended to be buried in St Paul's rather than in the Abbey. They include SIR JOSHUA REYNOLDS (1723–92) and his protégé and successor as London's leading portrait-painter SIR THOMAS LAWRENCE (1769–1830). Another fashionable portraitist of the eighteenth century – and a dazzling painter of historical subjects – JOHN OPIE (1761–1807) is here, next to HENRY FUSELI (1741–1825), the strange gothic genius after whom Mary Wollstonecraft had pined painfully. The astonishingly innovative JOSEPH MALLORD WILLIAM TURNER (1775–1851) is here, as is the rather less accomplished but vastly more popular SIR EDWIN LANDSEER (1802–73), who in addition to creating such stirring masterpieces as 'Monarch of the Glen' and such heart-warming ones as 'Dignity and Impudence' also fashioned the lions for the base of Nelson's Column.

Pre-Raphaelite painter WILLIAM HOLMAN HUNT (1827–1910) has his place in the St Paul's pantheon; so too do painter SIR JOHN EVERETT MILLAIS (1829–96) and painter and sculptor FREDERIC LEIGHTON (1830–96). Caricaturist SIR MAX BEERBOHM (1872–1956), half-brother of actor Herbert Beerbohm Tree, is here too. Also a brilliant critic and comic writer, Max Beerbohm was the author of the

Oxford romance *Zuleika Dobson* (1911). The ashes of architect SIR EDWIN LANDSEER LUTYENS (1869–1944) are also here, as are those of the poet Walter de la Mare (1873–1956). A late arrival in this little artists' colony, having lain for some years in Kensal Green before being moved here, the caricaturist GEORGE CRUIKSHANK (1792–1878) lies some way off from the others; at the edge, indeed, of the central area beneath the dome where the rougher sort – military men: admirals and generals – congregate.

Pride of place down here is taken by Britain's two greatest military heroes. First there's the one-armed (and one-eyed) adulterer, HORATIO NELSON (1758–1805), buried amid great pomp and splendour after his death at Trafalgar. After lying in state at Greenwich for three days, he was rowed upriver followed by a water-borne entourage half a mile long, while all the ships flew their flags at half-mast. His coffin spent another night at the Admiralty before being carried in a hearse shaped fore and aft like the *Victory* to St Paul's, where he was placed in a tomb based on the mausoleum Thomas Wolsey had had built for himself over two centuries earlier at Windsor. (Nelson's mistress Emma, Lady Hamilton, died ten years later in depression and abject poverty in Calais: there wasn't enough money for her to be taken back to England for burial as she'd wished, so she was laid to rest on that hostile shore.)

Facing Nelson across the central area of the crypt is that other great military hero of the Napoleonic era, the DUKE OF WELLINGTON (1769–1852). His monument was designed from scratch by the sculptor Alfred Stevens, but wasn't actually completed until 1894, by which time Stevens had been dead almost twenty years. If Wellington the general was a hero, Wellington the prime minister (1828–31) was a villain, passing the deeply unpopular Catholic Emancipation Bill, but the huge national outpouring of grief when he died suggests that all was forgiven and forgotten. You can still see the specially constructed triumphal car in which the Iron Duke was carried through the streets from his lying-in-state at Chelsea Hospital. Other military men buried in St Paul's include ADMIRAL JELLICOE (1859–1935), a hero of a rather British sort whose main achievement seems to have been the sustaining of heavy losses during the 1914 Battle of Jutland, an engagement which saw him the victor but rather a pyrrhic one.

Most of England's great composers are buried or commemorated in the Abbey, but there's a small pocket here: in the northeast corner of the crypt, separated from the artists by the 'Chapel of the Most Excellent Order of the British Empire' (God Bless It), lie WILLIAM BOYCE (c. 1710–79), who had been a choirboy here, his nineteenth-century successor SIR ARTHUR SULLIVAN (1842–1900), the collaborator of W.S. Gilbert (see Stanmore, North London), and the modernist SIR HUBERT PARRY (1848–1918). Just along the aisle from the composers – indeed you have to pass his grave to reach them – is SIR ALEXANDER FLEMING (1881–1955), the discoverer of penicillin.

ALDERMANBURY EC2

The foundation of St Mary's Church remains here; the bomb-damaged fabric was taken down in the mid-1960s and the church reconstructed in Fulton, Missouri. Among those buried here in former times, however, were JOHN HEMINGE (d. 1630) and HENRY CONDELL (d. 1627), Shakespeare's fellow-actors and editors of the First Folio edition of the bard's work, which was published in 1623 and which, despite shortcomings, preserved for posterity classic plays that would otherwise have been lost. Underneath the altar, by tradition, was placed the notorious JUDGE JEFFREYS (George, First Baron Jeffreys, 1648–89), the ruthless instrument of James II's repression at the Bloody Assizes following the Duke of Monmouth's Rebellion of 1685. He was consigned to the Tower by William of Orange's incoming regime in 1688, and ended his days there. Unfortunately, researchers who examined the vault after it was exposed by wartime damage could find no trace of the judge: instead the vault turned out to be occupied by an innocuous London family.

ALDGATE EC3

Painter HANS HOLBEIN THE YOUNGER (c. 1497–1543) is believed to have been buried in the old church on the site of St Katharine Cree. There's no obvious sign of him in the present building which, though much restored after Blitz damage, dates from 1628 to 1630.

BARBICAN EC2

St Giles', Cripplegate, is now a part of the Barbican complex. JOHN FOXE (1516–87), author of a famous book of (Wyclifite and reformist) martyrs, the *Actes and Monuments*, 1563, was buried here, though his exact position is unknown. The explorer and navigator MARTIN FROBISHER (c. 1535–94), who died of wounds sustained in action against the Spanish, is here too – all but his heart and entrails which were buried in St Andrew's, Plymouth (see Devon). Earlier Frobisher had crossed the North Atlantic and sailed up the Canadian coast in hopes of finding a 'Northwest Passage' to the riches of Cathay. Although he didn't get through, he none the less came back from Labrador with 200 tons of gold ore and with the news that there was plenty more where that came from. Unfortunately, it proved on closer examination not to be gold at all, but to be 'worse than good stone' in value. The historian and cartographer JOHN SPEED (1552–1629) is here, as is poet JOHN MILTON (1608–74), author of *Paradise Lost* and other well-loved (or at least well-regarded) classics. He *was* here, next to his father, until 3 August 1790, when souvenir hunters exhumed him – or what they thought was him at least. William Cowper was outraged:

> *Ill fare the hands that heav'd the stones*
> *Where Milton's ashes lay!*
> *That trembled not to grasp his bones*
> *And steal his dust away!*

> *Oh! ill-requited bard! neglect*
> *Thy living worth repaid,*
> *And blind idolatrous respect*
> *As much affronts thee dead.*

BLACKFRIARS EC4

St Anne's, Blackfriars was destroyed in the Great Fire and never rebuilt, but for what it's worth it stood around where Ireland Yard is now, and was the burial place for the composer JOHN DOWLAND (1563–1626), who died during one of London's periodic bouts of the Plague, though his actual cause of death is unknown. A lutenist of genius and a songwriter of rare beauty, Dowland was largely forgotten for several generations, but he has been doing well out of the early-music revival of recent years.

BISHOPSGATE EC2

In addition to SIR JOHN CROSBY (d. 1475), the medieval grocery magnate who became famous as lord mayor and diplomat, St Helen's (currently closed for restoration following the IRA's Bishopsgate bomb) boasts the body of scientist ROBERT HOOKE (1635–1703), whose work on optics, and especially on gravity, anticipated and influenced Newton's. Aubrey gets quite exercised about this aspect of his work, indeed:

> *About 9 or 10 years ago, Mr. Hooke writt to Mr. Isaac Newton, of Trinity College, Cambridge, to make a Demonstration of this theory, not telling him, at first, the proportion of the gravity to the distance, nor what was the curv'd line that was thereby made. Mr. Newton, in his Answer to the letter, did expresse that he had not thought of it; and in his first attempt about it, he calculated the Curve by supposing the attraction to be the same at all distances: upon which, Mr. Hooke sent, in his next letter, the whole of his Hypothesis, scil. that the gravitation was reciprocall to the square of the distance: which is the whole coelastiall theory, concerning which Mr. Newton haz made a demonstration, not at all owning he receiv'd the first Intimation of it from Mr. Hooke. Likewise Mr. Newton haz in the same Booke printed some other Theories and experiments of Mr. Hooke's, without acknowledgeing from whom he had them.*

'This is the greatest Discovery in Nature that ever was since the World's Creation. It never was so much as hinted by any man before,' enthuses Aubrey further, before adding a little wistfully: 'I wish he had writt plainer, and afforded a little more paper.'

CANNON STREET EC4

Somewhere here at St Michael's, Paternoster Royal, though the exact spot is unknown, was buried SIR RICHARD 'DICK'

WHITTINGTON (c. 1358–1423), several times Lord Mayor of London Town. The story about the cat and the bells seems to have arisen centuries after his death and to have no basis in fact. He thrived quite prosaically as a merchant and as moneylender to, among others, Henrys IV and V.

FINSBURY CIRCUS EC2

The church of St Mary, Finsbury Circus, in its former guise as the Catholic Chapel, Moorfields, was for some years the resting place of German composer CARL MARIA VON WEBER (1786–1826). Badly needing the money for his family in Dresden, Weber braved serious consumption to come to London and conduct the world premier of his great opera *Oberon*. He died here and was buried in the chapel. His successor as Kappellmeister Richard Wagner campaigned tirelessly for his return, mobilizing public opinion and raising funds, and Weber was finally disinterred in 1844 and borne ceremoniously back to Dresden. Wagner, who delivered Weber's eulogy, recollected afterwards in his *Life*:

> In my youth, I had learned to love music by way of my admiration of Weber's genius; and the news of his death came as a terrible blow to me. To have come into contact with him again, so to speak, and after so many years by this second funeral, was an event that stirred me to the very depths of my being.

FLEET STREET EC4

ST DUNSTAN'S-IN-THE-WEST: The church was rebuilt in 1831, when its position was moved to enable the street outside to be widened, thus obliterating the burial ground. Still, songwriter THOMAS CAMPION (1567–1620), author of standard numbers like 'Cherry Ripe', was buried here, as was Cavalier poet THOMAS CAREW (1595–1639). Carew was placed beside his father, to whom he'd in fact been something of a disappointment, the old man feeling his son should have been making a go of the diplomatic career he had set up for him rather than being out catching venereal disease and scribbling his sensuous, cynical love poetry.

ST BRIDE'S: This church has been associated with the press since the sixteenth century, when Caxton's assistant WYNKYN DE WORDE (d. c. 1535) was buried here. There have been plenty of people from other walks of life too, though. Tudor maestro THOMAS WEELKES (c. 1575–1623) was one such. His music went largely forgotten until the present century, when it was excitedly rediscovered by the young English composers of the day. Gustav Holst (see Chichester, West Sussex) admired Weelkes' 'fantastic unexpectedness'. Local pawnbroker Mary Frith (c. 1586–1659) was supposedly buried here: she won her fame, or rather notoriety, as 'Roaring Girl' MOLL CUTPURSE, an outrageous drunkard, brawler, cross-dresser and thief.

Drab by comparison, though a colourful enough character enough by any normal standards, was the cavalier poet RICHARD LOVELACE (1618–c. 57). He is also believed to be here, though it's hard to be sure. Once a glittering courtier, an ardent lover and a sophisticated poet, Lovelace paid a particularly heavy price for his commitment to the Civil War's losing side, serving a series of prison terms for his continuing Royalist agitation and, it's thought, ending his days in abject poverty. His biography, therefore, disappears from view in its last days. If he did, as many believe, die in destitution, his grave would have had no great monument in the first place. Besides, any trace wouldn't have survived the torching the church took in the Great Fire of 1666. We're on safer ground with SAMUEL RICHARDSON (1689–1761), whose Salisbury Court workshop was just round the corner. The printer turned novelist was buried in the centre aisle, with his dead children and first wife (he'd be joined afterwards by the second). For reasons best known to themselves, academic critics have been joyously rediscovering Richardson's stultifying, relentlessly moralizing novels in recent years, and a version of *Clarissa* (1747–8) has even been inflicted on the nation's TV viewers in what ought to be the security of their own living rooms.

TEMPLE CHURCH OF ST MARY: GEOFFREY DE MANDEVILLE, EARL OF ESSEX (d. 1144) is here. Appointed Constable of the Tower in 1130, he proved a traitor to King Stephen and the Empress Matilda in turn, eventually having to live as an outlaw in the Fens of Cambridgeshire, where he was finally besieged and killed. Since he had been excommunicated for his crimes he couldn't be buried in consecrated ground, so his body was sealed in lead and hung in a tree, till the Church granted him absolution and he was brought here, to a magnificent marble tomb near the door.

OLIVER GOLDSMITH (1730–74) was laid to rest in the Temple churchyard, the Abbey burial his friends had sought having to be cancelled when it emerged that the Irish poet had left £2,000 in debts. His monument was destroyed in wartime bombing, though a stone to the north of the church marks the approximate site. The playwright JOHN MARSTON (1576–1634), author of *The Malcontent* (1603), was buried in the choir, next to his father, though no sign of these graves has survived.

HART STREET EC3

And so to his last bed here went SAMUEL PEPYS (1633–1703), Secretary of the Navy and diarist, who lived and worked nearby and who worshipped here at St Olave's. He had wanted his friend and fellow diarist John Evelyn to be one of his pall bearers, but Evelyn had to refuse, being indisposed. (He was to survive his friend, as it turned out, by only three years: see Wotton, Surrey.) Pepys is buried by the communion table, alongside his wife Elizabeth. She died before him in 1699, and he it was who had her bust placed in the northeast corner of the church.

'SAINT GHASTLY GRIM'

St Olave's churchyard, Hart Street, has a grotesque gate dating from 1658, elaborately wrought with skulls and spikes. A few years later in 1665, according to the parish register, 326 plague victims were laid to rest here. That thought – and that gate – give the place an especially creepy feel, noticed by Dickens, who in *The Uncommercial Traveller* (1860) described St Olave's under the name of 'Saint Ghastly Grim':

> It is a small small churchyard, with a ferocious strong spiked iron gate, like a jail. This gate is ornamented with skulls and crossbones, larger than the life, wrought in stone; but it likewise came into the mind of Saint Ghastly Grim, that to stick iron spikes a-top of the stone skulls, as though they were impaled, would be a pleasant device. Therefore the skulls grin aloft horribly, thrust through and through with iron spears. Hence, there is attraction of repulsion for me in Saint Ghastly Grim.

HOLBORN CIRCUS EC1

'O, that it were possible, We might hold some two days' conference with the dead!' wrote Jacobean playwright JOHN WEBSTER (c. 1580–c. 1625). He has all the time in the world now. Having despatched characters by the score in bloodthirsty tragedies like *The White Devil* and *The Duchess of Malfi*, Webster is supposed to have gone to his own rest here at St Andrew's, though in truth very little is known about his life, and there's no sign of his grave here today.

More readily locatable in his vault beneath the communion table is HENRY SACHEVERELL (c. 1674–1724) the controversial, nay seditious, high-Tory cleric and Oxford don who on Guy Fawkes' Day 1709 preached a sermon at St Paul's claiming that the Church was in imminent danger from 'false brethren in church and state'. Like others of the Anglican ultra-right he preached the doctrine of 'Non-Resistance' – the view that since monarchs governed by divine right, God's clergy had no business resisting their authority. Where the monarchs concerned were constitutionally minded and Protestant divine right didn't apply, of course: hence in reality the doctrine he preached was one of resistance. In 1713 the Queen took pity on Sacheverell and gave him the living of St Andrew's. Ten years later, falling on the stone doorstep of his Highgate house, he broke two ribs, and never really recovered, declining through a series of complications during the ensuing year. He was buried in a specially prepared vault, but was not to rest in peace. The church's sexton was imprisoned in 1747 for stealing a lead coffin, and in the course of the investigation it emerged that the coffin of SALLY SALISBURY, the most notorious courtesan of her age, had unaccountably been placed alongside Sacheverell's in his private vault. Naturally, the Whig wits swung into action:

> *Lo! to one grave consigned, of rival fame,*
> *A reverend Doctor and a wanton dame.*
> *Well for the world both did to rest retire,*
> *For each, while living, set mankind on fire!*

and:

> *A fit companion for a high-church priest;*
> *He non-resistance taught, and she profest.*

Also buried here, his tomb now in the little chapel at the church's west end, is THOMAS CORAM (1668–1751), a sea-captain who, moved by the plight of babies abandoned on the streets near his Rotherhithe home, dedicated his life to building and running a Foundling Hospital in Lamb's Conduit Fields, north of Red Lion Street. Moralists disapproved, but others were more sympathetic, Hogarth donating pictures for sale and Handel the original manuscript of the *Messiah*, as well as presenting several benefit concerts. Coram was originally buried in the chapel of his hospital, but when that was pulled down his tomb was brought here, along with the chapel's marble font and wooden pulpit, both now installed at St Andrew's. Behind the church, beneath what is now Farringdon Street, lay the Shoe Lane Workhouse burial ground, where the tragic young poet THOMAS CHATTERTON (1752–70) was laid to rest (see Bristol, Avon).

HOLBORN VIADUCT EC1

Among those buried at St Sepulchre without Newgate are ROGER ASCHAM (c. 1515–68), the humanist writer, author of a treatise on education, *The Schoolmaster* (published after his death in 1570), and himself the tutor to the future Queen Elizabeth I; and CAPTAIN JOHN SMITH (1580–1631), the first governor of Virginia, who is in the south aisle. Famous as the adventurer saved from death by Pocahontas (see Gravesend, Kent), Smith had a curious coat of arms. His epitaph explains its origin in exploits further east:

> *Here lyes one conquered that hath conquered kings*
> *Subdu'd large territories, and done things*
> *Which to the World impossible would seem,*
> *But that the truth is held in more esteem.*
> *Shall I report his former Service done*
> *In honour of his God and Christendom?*
> *How that he did divide from Pagans three*
> *Their heads and Lives, Types of his Chivalry,*
> *For which great Service in that Climate done,*
> *Brave Sigismundus, King of Hungarion,*
> *Did give him as a Coat of Arms to wear*
> *These Conquered Heads got by his Sword and Spear...*

It goes on to extol his achievement in North America, noting that Smith drove out heathens to make their lands 'A habitation for our Christian Nation'.

In the Musicians' Chapel, beneath the central window dedicated to St Cecilia, rest the ashes of former St Sepulchre organist SIR HENRY WOOD (1869–1944), the conductor and the visionary who founded the Proms.

KING WILLIAM STREET, BY LONDON BRIDGE

MILES COVERDALE (1488–1568) worked secretly in Cambridge, and then in Antwerp, to produce the first complete English Bible, finally published in 1535. He was rector at St Magnus, Martyr from 1563 to 1566, but was initially buried in St Bartholomew by the Exchange. It was only when that church was demolished in 1840 that he was moved here.

LEADENHALL STREET EC3

JOHN STOW (c. 1525–1605) is buried here at St Andrew Undershaft (currently closed for restoration following an IRA bomb). A tailor and amateur (but distinguished) historian, his *Survey of London*, 1598, is a treasurehouse of information on the City, its history and its traditions. He spent all his money on his research and ended his life in poverty. His widow had a terracotta monument placed on his grave, showing him with quill pen and book: it's survived to this day, and the quill is replaced each year by the Lord Mayor.

NEWGATE STREET EC1

Wren's Christ Church was badly damaged during the Blitz, but the spire survived: it was dismantled for safety, then reassembled in 1960, while the ruined walls and burial ground were landscaped to form a garden. Long before the Wren church, however, there was a church on this site run by the Franciscan friars. ISABELLA OF FRANCE (1292–1358) was buried here. The queen of King Edward II (see Gloucester, Gloucestershire), she'd had a good deal to put up with one way and another, thanks to her husband's preference for male favourites such as Piers Gaveston and Hugh Despenser (see Kings Langley, Hertfordshire), but the implacability with which she pursued her revenge and the ruthlessness and cunning with which she conspired against him would win her the name 'The She-Wolf of France'. This did not, however, stop her having herself buried in the habit of the Franciscan order of the Poor Clares.

Also buried here was SIR THOMAS MALORY (d. 1471), who completed his stirring chronicle of the deeds of King Arthur and his Knights of the Round Table, *Le Morte D'Arthur*, in 1469–70 while he was in prison. It is thought that Malory got into difficulties with Edward IV on account of his allegiance to Warwick, who'd broken with the King and lined up with his Lancastrian opponents in this time of dynastic rivalry. Malory's burial so close to Newgate prison implies, suggests leading scholar Eugene Vinaver, that he was still a prisoner when he died, unpardoned by the King. *Le Morte D'Arthur* was published fifteen years later by William Caxton. 'For herein may be seen noble chyvalre, curtosye, humanyté, frendlynesse, hardynesse, love, frendshyp, cowardyse, murdre, hate, vertue and synne,' says Caxton in his preface: 'Doo after the good and leve the evyl, and it shal brynge you to good fame and renommee.' Actually, if Malory is who scholars think he probably was, he was not exactly a shining example to the young knight errant starting out on his career: Sir Thomas Malory of Newbold Revel, Warwickshire, included rape, armed robbery and cattle rustling among his deeds of chivalry.

Half a century later in 1534, the burial ground would receive another victim of a king's displeasure. ELIZABETH BARTON (c. 1506–34), 'The Holy Maid of Kent', was a sort of English Joan of Arc, a peasant girl who saw visions, made prophecies and worked miracle cures, and thus ended up embroiled in national politics. Adopted by leading partisans of Catherine of Aragon, she was persuaded to take on the thankless task of talking the King out of his intended divorce. She was beheaded at Tyburn for her pains. Many later victims of the scaffold, and others who died in the violence and squalor of Newgate prison, were also laid to rest here.

SHOREDITCH HIGH STREET E1

The churchyard of St Leonard's, Shoreditch (at the corner of Shoreditch High Street and Hackney Road) has been turned into a garden): Henry VIII's jester, WILLIAM SOMMERS (d. 1560), was buried here. Nobody's fool, Sommers had a keen political sense and real influence at the court. Before St Paul's Covent Garden assumed the mantle, St Leonard's was for a time London's theatre church. GABRIEL SPENCER's end was dramatic enough: in 1598 this actor lost a duel with Ben Jonson. Jonson was lucky to escape with his own life: condemned to death for Spencer's murder, he got off only by pleading benefit of clergy. Shakespeare's star tragic actor RICHARD BURBAGE (c. 1569–1619), maker of such roles as Hamlet, Lear and Othello (and, incidentally, by no means a bad painter), was buried at St Leonard's, as was GEORGE LILLO (1693–1739) pioneer of the kitchen-sink drama. Lillo's conscious use of middle-class characters in plays such as *The London Merchant* was a radical departure for the eighteenth century and ensured his swift passage into an oblivion from which the academic drama industry is only just hauling him. Not, however, before he'd influenced big-name continental writers like Lessing and Diderot.

THREADNEEDLE STREET EC2

St Christopher's Church was destroyed in the Fire and never rebuilt; its site is now occupied by the Bank of England, whose entrance hall is thought to be the best guess for the location of the grave of mathematician, astronomer, traveller and all-round Renaissance man THOMAS HARIOT (1560–1621). (You can just make out what appears to be a bronze plaque over the shoulders of the burly, pink-tailcoated bank commissionaires as they eject you from the hallowed portal.) Hariot was given a church burial after his death from cancer, despite his unorthodox views. 'He did not like (or valued not) the olde storie of the Creation of the World. He could not beleeve the old position; he would say *ex nihilo nihil fit* [nothing comes of nothing]. But a *nihilum* killed him at last,' gloats Aubrey, 'for in the top of his Nose came a little red speck (exceeding small) which grew bigger and bigger, and at last killed him.' Another church which stood near here was St Martin Outwich. When it was demolished the remains from the churchyard were moved to Ilford (see East London).

TOWER HILL EC3

Thanks to its proximity to the Tower, various people passed through All Hallows', all more or less the worse for wear. The body of Henry Howard, Earl of Surrey, poet and politician, lay here for a while before its transfer to Framlingham, Suffolk; Archbishop William Laud, executed during the Protectorate, was initially buried here, though after the Restoration he was moved to Oxford.

In the inner yard of the Tower itself, meanwhile, is the Royal Chapel of St Peter ad Vincula. Perhaps London's oldest church, it contains many executees, including ST THOMAS MORE (1478–1535) whose monument, including his own epitaph, is in Chelsea Old Church, where he had been accustomed to worship and where he had had the chapel rebuilt. Another Catholic martyr interred here was BISHOP ST JOHN FISHER (1469–1535). His body, at least, was interred here; the head had another fate.

More and Fisher's old opponent THOMAS CROMWELL, EARL OF ESSEX (c. 1485–1540), Henry VIII's right hand man in the dissolution of monasteries and Protestantization of the

BISHOP FISHER'S HEAD

The head, being parboiled, was pricked upon a pole and set high on London Bridge. And here I cannot omit to declare unto you the miraculous sight of this head which, after it had stood up the space of fourteen days upon the bridge, could not be perceived to waste nor consume; neither for the weather, which was then very hot, neither for the parboiling, but it grew daily fresher and fresher, so that in his lifetime he never looked so well, for his cheeks being beautified with a comely red, the face looked as that it had beholden the people passing by, and would have spoken to them; which many took to be a miracle that Almighty God showed the innocence and holiness of this blessed father.

So wrote a commentator at the time (1535). The crowds thronging to see this marvel so disrupted traffic, it seems, that the authorities ordered the executioner to take the head down and throw it into the river.

realm, himself lost favour with the King after organizing his disastrous fourth marriage to Anne of Cleves, with the result that he ended up here as well. Henry's queen number two, ANNE BOLEYN (c. 1507–36), is another inmate. She was executed on trumped-up charges of adultery and treason, she and her brother being accused, among other things, of having an incestuous relationship and of attempting to shore up their own power by murdering the King's natural son Henry Fitzroy (see Framlingham, Suffolk); CATHERINE HOWARD (c. 1520–42), Henry VIII's fifth wife, was also executed here, though in this case the charge of adultery at least seems to have been true. Afraid that the executioner would botch his task, she had called for a special rehearsal the day before, but it all seems to have passed off smoothly enough on the day. Catherine is said to haunt the gallery at Hampton Court, but any physical remains, at least, are here.

In the reign of Edward VI these victims of the block were followed by others including EDWARD SEYMOUR, THE PROTECTOR SOMERSET (c. 1506–52) (who as Henry VIII's Warden of the Scottish Marches did his bit to foster understanding between the two nations by invading and laying waste to southern Scotland and sacking Edinburgh) and his little brother, the Lord Admiral THOMAS, LORD SEYMOUR OF SUDELEY (c. 1508–49). The former was accused, rather unconvincingly, of sedition; the latter was tactless enough to pursue the hand of Princess Elizabeth before his wife, the widowed queen Catherine Parr, was cold in her Winchcombe, Gloucestershire grave, which seemed to make his ambition seem all too evident.

Then under Mary I came LADY JANE GREY (1537–54), beheaded as a possible rival to HRH, the Earl of Essex, and her father-in-law and sponsor for the succession JOHN DUDLEY, EARL OF WARWICK AND DUKE OF NORTHUMBERLAND (c. 1502–54). JAMES, DUKE OF MONMOUTH (1649–85) was executed here after his ill-advised and ill-fated attempt to supplant James II on the throne. The illegitimate son of Charles II, Monmouth allowed the Earl of Shaftesbury to persuade him to set himself up as a Protestant pretender in competition with the Catholic-leaning Prince James. This led to the Rye House Plot of 1683, the discovery of which forced him to flee to the Netherlands. When Charles II died and James ascended the throne as James II, Monmouth returned to contest his claim. His army was routed at Sedgemoor and, despite grovelling for mercy, he was beheaded, while his followers were hounded by the authorities and had the book thrown at them by Judge Jeffreys at his Bloody Assizes. Monmouth was buried here under the communion table. The above unfortunates were joined in 1746–7 by the Jacobite lords executed after Bonnie Prince Charlie's 1745 rebellion.

UPPER THAMES STREET EC4

The architect INIGO JONES (1573–1652) and writer MARY DELARIVIER MANLEY (c. 1672–1724) were both buried here at St Benet's. Finding that her husband John Manley had neglected to tell her that he was still married to his first wife, she left him (though for all her later indignation it took her three years, once he'd confessed his crime, to get round to it) and was taken in by Charles II's mistress Barbara Villiers, the Duchess of Cleveland (see Chiswick, West London). That friendship came to an abrupt end when the Duchess accused Mary of flirting with her son, and threw her out. From that time on she made a hand-to-mouth living as playwright, Tory journalist, erotic novelist and racy memoirist.

WALBROOK EC4

Somewhere here at St Stephen's were interred the mortal remains of composer JOHN DUNSTABLE (c. 1390–1453), whose pioneering work with counterpoint won him acclaim throughout Christendom. NATHANIEL HODGES (1629–88) won more local – and short-lived – fame, but is worth remembering none the less. A physician, he stayed in London through the Plague Year of 1665, when the rest of the professional classes had fled to the country, and ministered to the populace. His heroism wasn't repaid: his practice fell away afterwards, and he died in Ludgate Prison, where he'd been incarcerated for debt. In a vault beneath the north aisle lies

SIR JOHN VANBRUGH (1664–1726): unfortunately, no trace remains of his gravestone, inscribed with an epitaph said to be the work of fellow-architect Nicholas Hawksmoor:

> Lie heavy on him, Earth! for he
> Laid many heavy loads on thee.

Splendid landmarks like Castle Howard (1701) and Blenheim Palace (1705) don't seem to have proved too onerous, delighting generations of beholders, though Vanbrugh's overambitious design for the Haymarket Theatre would prove a crippling financial burden to him. Vanbrugh's interest in the theatre was more than architectural: he was a successful playwright, beloved of the theatregoers of his day if not by some of the more moralistic critics, who found the frankness of his comic realism objectionable. His *The Relapse* (1696) and *The Provok'd Wife* (1697) have endured as classics.

South of the River

SOUTHWARK CATHEDRAL, ST SAVIOUR'S SE1

Until the Reformation, this church at the south end of London Bridge was known as St Mary Overie. The poet and moralist JOHN GOWER (c. 1330–1408) lies here. A friend of Chaucer, Gower was a generous benefactor of St Mary's priory, and lived here in his last years. His tomb, now in the north aisle, shows his head resting on three of his books.

The Lockyer monument, in the north transept,

commemorates a local pharmacist who filled his last prescription in 1672:

> Here Lockyer lyes interr'd, enough; his name
> Speakes one hath few competitors in fame:
> A Name, soe Greate, we Generallit may scorne
> Inscriptions wch doe vulgar tombes adorne.
> A diminution tis to write in verse
> His eulogies wch most mens mouths rehearse.
> His virtues & his PILLS are too well known
> That envy can't confine them under stone
> But they'll survive his dust and not expire
> Till all things else at th'universall fire.
> This verse is lost, his PILL Embalmes him safe
> To future times without an Epitaph.

Such is fame. In the south choir aisle is LANCELOT ANDREWES (1555–1626), the scholar, sermonizer and general editor of the Authorized Version of the Bible, who rose to the rank of Bishop of Winchester.

Bankside was, of course, theatreland in the seventeenth century. EDMUND SHAKESPEARE, brother of the more famous William, is buried here, as is dramatist PHILIP MASSINGER (1583–1640). 'Death hath a thousand doors to let out life,' he'd once observed. Among the more unusual of these portals must be the one through which passed the man who shares his grave. 'Invited to goe with a Knight into Norfolke or Suffolke in the Plague-time 1625,' reports Aubrey, JOHN FLETCHER (1579–1625) 'stayd but to make himselfe a suite of Cloathes, and while it was makeing, fell sick of the Plague and dyed. ' Aubrey had this, he says, from the unfortunate playwright's tailor, who as it happens was also clerk of St Overie's, so should have known what he was talking about.

Best known for his collaborations with Francis Beaumont, Fletcher is also thought to have worked with Shakespeare on *Henry VIII* and *The Two Noble Kinsmen*. Stone slabs in the floor of the choir record these burials, although they don't indicate the exact positions of the graves, which have long since been forgotten.

BATTERSEA, CHURCH ROAD SW11

In a no-longer marked family vault in St Mary's on Battersea Church Road lies HENRY ST JOHN, FIRST VISCOUNT BOLINGBROKE (1678–1751), who in 1713 negotiated the Treaty of Utrecht, bringing to an end years of war. A more secretive – and ultimately less effective – agent of British policy abroad, BENEDICT ARNOLD (1741–1801) is also about here somewhere. An American general, he passed the plans of West Point, where he was in command, to the British. He fled to England and lived in Battersea till his death. He was removed from his original resting place in the course of renovations to the church a century after his death, and placed with several score other unfortunates in a mass grave. His exact whereabouts cannot, therefore, be pinpointed. The British courier to whom he passed the plans, Major André, was captured by the Americans in 1780 and executed as a spy; he outdid his master in death, though, being buried in Westminster Abbey, in the south aisle of the nave.

KENNINGTON ROAD SE11

Little more than the tower survives of the old church of St Mary's, Newington Butts, and an even older church was demolished in 1720. There it was that Jacobean playwright THOMAS MIDDLETON (1580–1627) was interred. The author of grim tragedies such as *The Changeling* and *Women Beware*

Women and slick, cynical city comedies such as *A Chaste Maid in Cheapside* and *A Mad World, My Masters*, Middleton was also, according to some scholars, responsible for largish chunks of *Macbeth*. London's first public theatres were down here, though by Middleton's day the centre of theatreland had moved north to Bankside.

LAMBETH PALACE ROAD SE1

Here in St Mary's churchyard, now a fragrant museum of gardening, was buried CAPTAIN WILLIAM BLIGH (1754–1817). Having shown himself a model of tact and understanding as captain of the *Bounty*, he was then given the governorship of New South Wales, whereupon he had to be deposed and given a two-year jail sentence on account of the harshness of his rule. A devoted husband, whatever his other shortcomings, he was buried here beside his wife Betsy.

MARYCHURCH STREET, ROTHERHITHE SE16

In the churchyard at St Mary's lies PRINCE LEE BOO (d. 1784), a chief's son from the East Indian Pelau Islands who saved the crew of a London ship from a wreck and was given a trip to London in gratitude. Unfortunately, scarcely had he disembarked than he contracted smallpox, and died soon after.

GREATER LONDON

North

EDMONTON

In the churchyard, side by side in death as in life, are the essayist CHARLES LAMB (1775–1834) and his sister MARY (1764–1847). The two, who collaborated successfully on a collection of *Tales from Shakespeare* (1807), were close and had lived together all their adult lives, Charles having taken responsibility for the care of his mentally disturbed sister after she stabbed their mother to death in a fit of insanity.

FINCHLEY

The scientist and controversialist THOMAS HENRY HUXLEY (1825–95), who famously defended Darwin's evolution theory from its clerical critics, is at St Marylebone Cemetery, East End Road, as is the popularizing newspaper magnate ALFRED CHARLES HARMSWORTH, VISCOUNT NORTHCLIFFE (1865–1922), who exercised a profound, if not necessarily benign, influence on the British press. Also among those present is the man-of-letters SIR EDMUND GOSSE (1845–1928). Admired in his day as essayist and critic, he is now best known for the memoir *Father and Son* (1907), a moving but often funny account of his upbringing in an austerely puritanical, patriarchal home. The great conductor LEOPOLD STOKOWSKI (1882–1977) is here too, while the balletic genius VASLAV NIJINSKY (1890–1950) put in at least a brief appearance, lying here for three years after his death before being exhumed and taken to Montmartre, Paris.

The Pre-Raphaelite painter and associate of William Morris FORD MADOX BROWN (1821–93) is buried at St Pancras and Islington Cemetery, High Road, East Finchley.

GOLDERS GREEN

A star-studded cast has passed through the portals of Golders Green Crematorium. Here it was, for instance, that BRAM STOKER (1847–1912), creator of Count Dracula, was consigned to the flames – perhaps for fear of what he might be capable of if laid to rest in a conventional grave. His ashes reside in an urn in the Eastern Columbarium, where they give disappointingly little sign of returning to life.

Shorthand-inventor ISAAC PITMAN (1813–97) was actually cremated at Brookwood, Surrey, but his family preferred to have his ashes placed at the crematorium here. Not far away in the Ernest George Mausoleum are the ashes of SIGMUND FREUD (1856–1939), the founder of psychoanalysis and – love him or hate him – a central influence on twentieth-century thought. They were placed, along with those of his wife Martha (1861–1951), in a Greek urn from Freud's own collection. The ashes of their daughter ANNA FREUD (1895–1982), herself a psychologist of note, are here too. Not perhaps as important as Freud, but in his way every bit as controversial, was HAVELOCK ELLIS (1859–1939), the psychologist and pioneer of a new field, 'sexology'. Most of his books were banned, at least to the general public, but his views (in addition to maintaining generally that sex was an area worthy of scientific study, he gave specific and vociferous backing to the ideas of birth control, sex education and women's suffrage) proved quietly influential behind the scenes.

PERCY WYNDHAM LEWIS (1884–1957) was for what it's worth the founder of Vorticism, a now largely forgotten modernist mini-movement that united literature and art in the pursuit of a vague aesthetic of concentration into dense vortices of creative energy. More influential by far, albeit on a younger readership, was ENID BLYTON (1897–1968), the creator of Noddy and Big Ears as well as many other well-loved if politically incorrect characters. Too influential by half is CHARLES RENNIE MACKINTOSH (1868–1928), whose distinctively spindly art-nouveau style has in recent years spread like a rash through the less imaginative reaches of Scottish design. Influential in a purely practical way was scientist SIR JAMES DEWAR (1842–1943), who in the 1870s invented the thermos flask and transformed the British picnic.

Golders Green has become the crematorium-of-choice for those in the performing arts. The world of dance has been represented by the Russian ballerina ANNA PAVLOVA (1885–1931) and the influential modernizer DAME MARIE RAMBERT (1888–1982), while many musicians have also ended up here, from the composer SIR ARTHUR BLISS (1891–1975), through ERIC 'Over' COATES (1886–1957), who wrote the 'Dambusters March', to popular bandleaders BILLY COTTON (1899–1969) and VICTOR SILVESTER (1900–78). The pianist DAME MYRA HESS (1890–1966), whose lunchtime recitals at the National Gallery did so much to lift spirits during the London Blitz, was also cremated here.

GOLDERS GREEN CREMATORIUM

There's been a cemetery at Golders Green since the late nineteenth century (the popular actor, composer and playwright IVOR NOVELLO (1893–1951) is among those buried here), but it's the crematorium that has enabled Golders Green to perform for the twentieth century something of the role Highgate played for the nineteenth. It was built in 1902, when it became clear that the crematorium at Brookwood (see Woking, Surrey) wasn't going to be able to meet the growing demand in London for what after initial resistance was slowly coming to be accepted as an appropriate – and for an increasing number of people in the standard-setting worlds of media and the arts the only appropriate – way to go. Well over 284,000 cremations have been carried out to date, far more than at any other British crematorium, and the urns and memorial tablets that seem to cover just about every inch of every wall here can represent only a small fraction of this number. Many had their ashes taken elsewhere, or buried or scattered right here in the crematorium's twelve acres of garden. Long popular with members of the local Jewish community, who had a special shrine built for them in 1959, the crematorium has also been able to cater for those wishing to be cremated according to Hindu rites. The West Indian novelist SHIVA NAIPAUL (1945–85) was one of those to be given a Hindu funeral here.

Golders Green is open 8–7 between April and October and 8–6 from November to March. There's no admission charge for visitors, but for guided tours (inquire at the office, open 9–5) there is a fee.

Singers range from the distinguished contralto KATHLEEN
FERRIER (1912–53) to the crooner MATT MONRO (1930–85).
The 1970s rock-genius MARC BOLAN (1947–76) of T-Rex was
brought here after the Mini driven by his girlfriend crashed
into a tree on Barnes Common. He would be followed two
years later by 'Wild Man of Rock' KEITH MOON, drummer of
The Who, killed by an overdose of the sedatives he was taking
while trying to get over his drink problem. The musically
minded cartoonist GERARD HOFFNUNG (1925–59) was
cremated here, joining *Alice*-illustrator SIR JOHN TENNIEL
(1820–1914) on Golders Green's roll of artistic honour.

St Paul's Covent Garden may still be the 'Theatre Church',
but Golders Green is where the theatrical community come
when they die. The long list of stars of stage and screen
cremated here includes 1930s leading man FRANK LAWTON
(1904–69), comic actress DAME CICELY COURTNEIDGE
(1883–1980) and her husband (and frequently co-star) JACK
HULBERT (1892–1978), DAMES SYBIL THORNDIKE
(1882–1976) and PEGGY ASHCROFT (1907–91), monologuist-
of-genius JOYCE GRENFELL (1910–79), and YOOTHA JOYCE
(1927–80) of TV's *Man about the House* and *George and
Mildred*. PETER SELLERS (1925–80) actually came to scout out
the crematorium a couple of days before he died: his ashes
were placed by his parents' in the garden. The Hungarian-
born film-maker SIR ALEXANDER KORDA (1893–1956)
ended up here, as did the playwright SEAN O'CASEY
(1884–1964). Fate decreed that JOE ORTON (1933–67), the
creator of *Loot* and *What the Butler Saw*, though a playwright
of a completely different generation, should follow O'Casey
only three years later. Orton's ashes were mingled with those
of his lover and murderer Kenneth Halliwell and scattered on
the Garden of Remembrance. The Welsh actor–playwright
EMLYN WILLIAMS (1905–87) was also cremated here.

From the world of light entertainment came music-hall legends VESTA TILLEY (1864–1952) and BUD FLANAGAN (1896–1968), and the Variety star BERNIE WINTERS (1932–91). A newer tradition is represented by the radio comics TOMMY HANDLEY (1892–1949), of ITMA fame, and KENNETH HORNE (1907–69). A rather more serious radio voice was that of GERALD PRIESTLAND (1927–91), famous for his searching talks on religious issues. A.J.P. TAYLOR (1906–90) wasn't technically a broadcaster, but the distinguished historian appeared on TV so often, as one of the first 'media dons', that he might just as well have been.

In the Jewish cemetery on the other side of Hoop Lane lies the cellist JACQUELINE DU PRÉ (1945–87). Her career as performer had been ended in 1973 by the onset of multiple sclerosis, though she'd carried on making an invaluable contribution as a teacher.

HAMPSTEAD

CHURCH ROW: You don't even have to go into St John's churchyard to see the grave of Labour politician HUGH GAITSKELL (1906–63), plainly visible from the pavement outside. Gaitskell was said by some to be selling out his party with the programme of rightward reforms he attempted to introduce after his 1955 election to the leadership; others regard him as a prophetic voice, tragically ignored in his own time yet vindicated forty years later in the triumphant election victory of Tony Blair's 'New Labour'. Attractions inside the graveyard include two important technical innovators: one is the Yorkshire clockmaker JOHN HARRISON (1693–1776), whose chronometer was taken by Cook on his second voyage of discovery to the Pacific in 1772–5. Doggedly accurate whatever the changes in temperature and weather conditions, Harrison's chronometer allowed accurate timekeeping for years on end. This was especially important because, by permitting accurate comparisons between local time and the time at Greenwich, it allowed longitude to be calculated accurately for the first time. Innovator number two is industrial pioneer HENRY CORT (1740–1800). The coal-fired 'reverbatory' furnace he perfected in 1784 allowed 'puddling' – the stirring of the molten metal at high temperatures to burn off impurities – and hence the mass-production of wrought iron of a much higher quality than had ever been achievable in the old, charcoal-fired furnaces.

As befits the modern home of the chattering classes, however, the liberal arts are also well represented in Hampstead. Scottish-born playwright JOANNA BAILLIE (1762–1851) is here, for example. Her work, long forgotten, has been rediscovered lately by feminist critics, though none has yet got as far as endorsing Scott's judgement that Baillie

was 'the best dramatic writer since the days of Shakespeare and Massinger'. Nobody ever compared MAY SINCLAIR (1870–1946) with Shakespeare, but her poetry – as well as novels such as *The Life and Death of Harriett Frean* (1922) – have also been enjoying something of a revival in recent years.

The creator of 'The Hay Wain' and many other well-loved English scenes, the artist JOHN CONSTABLE (1776–1837), long a local resident, is here. Another artist, the nineteenth-century painter GEORGE DU MAURIER (1834–96) is among those buried in the churchyard extension, on the other side of Church Road. Like his granddaughter Daphne (see Fowey, Cornwall), George Du Maurier was also a novelist, and his tombstone bears the closing lines of his most famous work, the bohemian romance *Trilby* (1892):

> *A little trust that when we die*
> *We reap our sowing! and so – good-bye.*

Also here is A.R. ORAGE (1873–1934), the socialist man-of-letters whose journal, *New Age*, from 1907 provided a forum for the liveliest literary and political writers of the age, including Shaw, Chesterton, Belloc, Katherine Mansfield and Ezra Pound. From the 1920s Orage became increasingly concerned with New Ageism in its modern sense, resigning from the journal to concentrate on his interest in the occult and in the teachings of the Russian mystic Gurdjieff. Actors SIR HENRY BEERBOHM TREE (1853–1917) and ANTON WALBROOK (1900–67), and the documentary filmmaker PETER BAYLIS (1910–73), were buried here, as was Michael Llewelyn Davies, the ward of writer and dramatist J.M. Barrie (see Kirriemuir, Tayside).

Beyond, in the adjacent graveyard of the Catholic church, buried beneath sprawling rambler roses, lies the children's writer ELEANOR FARJEON (1881–1965). She came from a Jewish background but had converted to Catholicism in 1951.

HAMPSTEAD CEMETERY, FORTUNE GREEN ROAD: JOSEPH LISTER, First Baron Lister of Lyme Regis (1827–1912), surgeon and pioneer of antiseptics and medical hygiene, was laid to rest here, as was KATE GREENAWAY

(1846–1901), the artist and hugely popular illustrator of children's books. More than 50,000 people turned out to see the cortège of music hall queen MARIE LLOYD (1870–1922) pass on its way to Hampstead. Buried here rather more obscurely, alongside her beloved sister Anne, who had died a year earlier of cancer, was the poet CHARLOTTE MEW (1869–1928). Unable to bear the separation, Charlotte committed suicide by drinking lysol. Both sisters had been haunted by the fear – and perhaps the fact – of insanity, which seemed to have run in their family, and the idea of madness lies at the heart of much of Charlotte Mew's best poetry. A tormented spirit, her last words were, 'Don't keep me, let me go.' The flamboyant French horn player, DENNIS BRAIN (1921–57), the century's leading virtuoso on this peculiarly difficult instrument, was buried here after his tragic death in a car crash. Actress DAME GLADYS COOPER (1888–1971) is here too. She shot to stardom in 1922 when she played Paula in Pinero's *The Second Mrs Tanqueray*: an illustrious career on stage and then in films followed.

HENDON

Buried here at the parish church is the colonial administrator SIR THOMAS STAMFORD RAFFLES (1781–1826), the founder not only of Singapore but of London Zoo.

HIGHGATE

ST MICHAEL'S: Moved here from an earlier resting place in the chapel of the nearby school, the poet and critic SAMUEL TAYLOR COLERIDGE (1772–1834) now shares a vault beneath the centre aisle with the wife he'd ended up loathing – and whom he led, it has to be said, a dog's life. Coleridge was a friend of Wordsworth, and the collaborator with him on the decisive work of the Romantic Revolution, the *Lyrical Ballads* (1798), which broke with the correctnesses and perceived decorum of the eighteenth century with the intention of introducing something more passionate and energetic. Most famous of the poems in this collection was Coleridge's own 'Rime of the Ancient Mariner'. His later opium addiction was the inspiration for his other great anthology-piece, 'Kubla Khan' (1816), but otherwise seems to have been more hindrance than help to his creativity. Not only is much of his later philosophical writing too impossibly abstract and abstruse to be useful; it's at times little more than transcription from the works of German idealist thinkers.

HIGHGATE WESTERN CEMETERY: A guided tour is obligatory for the western part of Highgate Cemetery but it is worth it to see the imposing monuments, feel the incomparable atmosphere and, of course, find some of the most important graves. That of MICHAEL FARADAY (1791–1867), for example. The chemist and electrical pioneer is buried here with his wife Sarah. A century later another eminent scientist, the Polish-born sage JACOB BRONOWSKI (1908–74), famous for his TV series 'The Ascent of Man', would also be buried here. Cricketer FREDERICK WILLIAM LILLYWHITE (1792–1854) is said to have been the man who introduced round-arm bowling – but then so is John Willes (see Sutton Valence, Kent). There's no doubting the distinction of TOM SAYERS (1826–65), last of the great bare-knuckled prizefighters. Some 10,000 people turned out for his funeral. Captured in stone, his mastiff Lion keeps guard on his grave – a fine-looking beast who would, one can't help thinking, have impressed another of the Old Cemetery's occupants, CHARLES CRUFT (1852–1938), the founder in 1886 of the famous dog show.

HIGHGATE CEMETERY

The jewel in London's cemeterial crown, Highgate was opened in 1839. Intended to attract the more prosperous classes then colonizing the districts to the north of the city, the cemetery was from the first conceived along ambitious lines, its grand gates and fine gothic chapels setting a demanding standard for early inmates, who, however, passed the test triumphantly with a wide variety of imposing and original monuments. Artful landscaping, gently winding pathways and a studiously maintained riot of colour from the flowers and shrubs tended year round by a staff of over twenty gardeners all helped maximize the impact of an already majestic hilltop situation, commanding spectacular views over the city to the south. As the management had all along intended, such a setting seemed too beautiful to be left to the dead, and the cemetery was soon a popular spot for weekend strollers from the fashionable class – many of whom would, of course, eventually choose to be buried here themselves.

Split down the middle by Swain's Lane, Highgate is a cemetery of two halves. The 'Old', Western Cemetery can be visited only on official guided tours (£3, concessions £2). You can wander as you please in the Eastern Cemetery, so long as you pay your £1 admission and come between the hours of 10–4 (11–4 weekends) November–March or 10–5 (11–5 weekends) April–October.

On a more literary note, the poet CHRISTINA ROSSETTI (1830–94) was interred near her father and mother in their family plot. Her brother Dante Gabriel isn't here, being in Birchington, Kent, but his wife ELIZABETH SIDDALL is. His mistress until she married him in 1860, Elizabeth died in 1862 of a laudanum overdose. She would afterwards be exhumed so that her widowed husband could retrieve some manuscripts he'd flung into her grave in a dramatic gesture he'd subsequently thought better of. (Highgate's other famous exhumation was that of a shopkeeper whose family believed he'd really been the Duke of Portland, who had staged first his disappearance and then his death. The idea was that the coffin would prove to be full of lead weights, but as it turned out it proved to be full of an elderly shopkeeper.) The novelist RADCLYFFE HALL (1883–1943) is here in the mausoleum built for 'Ladye', Mabel Veronica Batten, with whom she lived till the latter's death in 1916. Ladye's cousin Una Troubridge was her lifelong companion after that. Una died in Rome, but gets a mention on the memorial here. 'John', as Radclyffe Hall preferred to be called, was the author of lesbian classics such as *The Well of Loneliness* (1928), which was prosecuted for obscenity on its first publication and withdrawn from sale.

HIGHGATE EASTERN CEMETERY: Pride of place here is of course taken by KARL MARX (1818–83), who's buried with his daughter ELEANOR (1855–98), but GEORGE ELIOT (1819–80) is here too, with her partner the writer and philosopher GEORGE HENRY LEWES (1817–78). Right behind them is the grave of the radical GEORGE JACOB HOLYOAKE (1817–1906), a leading light in the co-operative movement and, thanks to some ill-advised wisecracks at a public meeting, the last person in Britain to be imprisoned for blasphemy, serving six months in 1842. He was cremated at Golders Green and his ashes were buried here, near the grave of his younger brother and fellow secularist AUSTIN HOLYOAKE (1826–74). A second space in Austin Holyoake's grave (over which had been given a special secularist funeral service which he had written himself) had been intended for his desolate widow, but with her remarriage it seemed the space was going begging. Hence the presence here of his friend the poet and essayist JAMES THOMSON (1834–82), author of that strange masterpiece of post-gothic verse *The City of Dreadful Night* (and not to be confused with the much earlier author of *The Seasons*, who's buried in Richmond, West London).

Another radical thinker, HERBERT SPENCER (1820–1903) also ended his days here. The coiner of the phrase 'survival of the fittest', he contrived to be a social Darwinist before Darwin. Altogether more benign was SIR LESLIE STEPHEN (1832–1904), whose ashes were buried here. An eminent figure in his day, leading light of the intellectual–Christian 'Clapham Sect', he is now more famous as the father of Virginia Woolf. This illustrious company was later joined by the actor SIR RALPH RICHARDSON (1902–83).

ST JOHN'S WOOD

Laid discreetly to rest in the burial ground (now a garden) outside St John's Wood Church, under the pseudonym of Goddard, was JOANNA SOUTHCOTT (c. 1750–1814). Now largely forgotten, Southcott won a huge and fervent following amid the uncertainty of the Enlightenment's *fin de siècle* decade with her claim that she was the woman prophesied in *Revelation*, sent to give birth to the Prince of Peace. The appointed time, early in the next century, came and went, but Southcott's hardcore adherents were undaunted – throughout the nineteenth century, indeed, there would be those who confidently expected her to return from the dead. The landscape painter JOHN SELL COTMAN (1782–1842) never caused such a splash in his lifetime, but his reputation, such as it is, has proved more durable over time.

STANMORE

SIR W.S. GILBERT (1836–1911), the lyrics half of Gilbert and Sullivan (for the latter see St Paul's), lived nearby, and his ashes were buried in St John the Evangelist churchyard. His was a heroic, pathetic end: he died of a heart attack after rescuing a lady from drowning in the swimming lake in the grounds of his house.

STOKE NEWINGTON

Abney Park Cemetery, Stoke Newington High Street, was opened in 1840 to take on the role of Nonconformist Cemetery from Bunhill Fields, by then full to bursting point; within a few years Abney Park was getting crowded itself. Intended as a pleasant park, its shrubs and trees have now been allowed to run wild. Distinguished inmates include the founders of the Salvation Army GENERAL WILLIAM BOOTH (1829–1912) and CATHERINE BOOTH (1829–90), as well as their son BRANWELL BOOTH (1856–1929), his father's successor as General. There's also the quite remarkably unremarkable Mary Hillum (1759–1864) who, according to her gravestone,

> died in the 105th year of her age. She died in the same house in which she was born, scarcely ever slept out of the house in the whole of her life, never travelled either by omnibus or railway and was never more than 15 miles from home.

South

BARNES

Just off Rocks Lane is the tiny Barnes Common Cemetery. Among those buried here is FRANCIS TURNER PALGRAVE (1824–97). His real monument is the anthology of poetry he compiled, *The Golden Treasury* (1875), an enormously, appallingly influential collection which established popular tastes for the best part of a century. Jeanette Pickersgill, whose ashes were laid to rest here in 1885, is of interest only because she was perhaps the first person to be cremated legally in England.

BECKENHAM

In Elmers End Cemetery, his grave marked by a plaque inscribed with bat, ball and stumps as well as name and dates, lies W.G. GRACE (1848–1915), doctor and cricketer. Among other records, the bearded legend was the first cricketer to score 2,000 runs in a single season (2,739 in 1871); the first to reach a hundred centuries (in 1895), and the first to reach 50,000 runs in a career (making a total of 54,896).

BROMLEY

ELIZABETH JOHNSON (d. 1752), the first Mrs Dr Johnson, was buried in the nave of the parish church here, but that was destroyed by bombing in 1941 and the whereabouts of her grave are now unknown. Her tombstone was found during cleaning-up, and was relocated in the rebuilt church of St Peter and St Paul. Boswell never met her – she was before his time, belonging to Johnson's earlier incarnation as Lichfield

Schoolmaster, before he went on to London and fame. Fortunately, old-boy David Garrick was on hand to sketch in this fragment of the master's biography: 'From Mr Garrick's account,' records Boswell, Johnson

> *did not appear to have been profoundly reverenced by his pupils. His oddities of manner, and uncouth gesticulations, could not but be the subject of merriment to them; and, in particular, the young rogues used to listen at the door of his bed-chamber, and peep through the key-hole that they might turn into ridicule his tumultuous and awkward fondness for Mrs Johnson, whom he used to name by the familiar appellation of Tetty or Tetsey, which, like Betty or Betsey, is provincially used as a contraction for Elisabeth, her christian name, but which to us seems ludicrous, when applied to a woman of her age and appearance. Mr Garrick described her to me as very fat, with a bosom of more than ordinary protuberance, with swelled cheeks of a florid red, produced by thick painting, and increased by the liberal use of cordials; flaring and fantastick in her dress, and affected both in her speech and her general behaviour. I have seen Garrick exhibit her, by his exquisite talent for mimickry, so as to excite the heartiest bursts of laughter; but he, probably, as is the case in all such representation, considerably aggravated the picture.*

Absurd she may have been, but Dr Johnson mourned her loss with obvious sincerity.

CHISLEHURST

WILLIAM WILLETT (1856–1915) is buried in St Nicholas' churchyard. He was a builder and, more important, a tireless campaigner for Daylight Saving. He died in sight of the

Promised Land, passing away just before British Summer Time was first introduced in 1916 as a wartime measure. He is commemorated, appropriately enough, by a sundial in nearby Pett's Wood.

CROYDON

In Bandon Hill Cemetery, beneath an elaborate marble headstone featuring an angel with outspread wings, lies black composer SAMUEL COLERIDGE-TAYLOR (1875–1912). The son of a physician from Sierra Leone, Samuel Taylor, and a white lady's companion he met in London, Samuel Jr was deliberately named for the famous poet, which has been known to cause confusion. Though he made it in the conservative environment of the Royal College of Music and the white world of classical music, Coleridge-Taylor never went to special lengths to fit in: he was open in his solidarity with other blacks in both Britain and America and his espousal of the pan-Africanist cause. The inscription on the gravestone concludes with a stave giving four bars of his most famous work, *Hiawatha's Wedding Feast*, setting the words 'Thus departed Hiawatha, Hiawatha, the beloved'.

DULWICH

In the chapel of the school he founded, Dulwich College, is buried the Elizabethan actor-manager EDWARD ALLEYN (1566–1626), whose Rose theatre was a close neighbour and fierce competitor of Shakespeare's Globe.

FARNBOROUGH

THOMAS YOUNG (1773–1829) is buried here, in St Giles' Church. Best known as a physicist and Egyptologist, he had a wide range of interests from languages to maths and optics. His knowledge of Egyptian hieroglyphics was unsurpassed, however, and it was he who first managed to decipher part of the Rosetta Stone, discovered in 1799.

KESTON

Outside the parish church, beneath a monument in the form of a Celtic cross, lies all that remains of novelist Dinah Maria Mulock or MRS CRAIK (1826–87), whose *John Halifax, Gentleman* (1856) is a popular classic.

MORTLAKE

Beneath the chancel floor at St Mary's Parish Church, in the High Street, the mathematician, astrologer – and, many were convinced, necromancer – JOHN DEE (1527–1608) was buried. An inescapable, if shadowy, presence on the Elizabethan scene, Dee's services to legitimate science included pioneering work on the art of navigation, which he saw as part of a grander project aimed at establishing a Protestant English empire to rival the Spanish Catholic one.

In the graveyard of St Mary Magdalen's Catholic Church, North Worple Way, is the curious tent-shaped tomb of the explorer and orientalist SIR RICHARD BURTON (1821–90), a larger-than-life figure who wrote some swashbuckling accounts of his travels. More than a manly hunk, however, Burton was a highly self-conscious writer and a member of Swinburne's circle. His interest in oriental exotica (he produced the first unexpurgated translation of the *Arabian Nights*) shaded into an enthusiasm for erotica: he also translated the *Kama Sutra*.

The Old Mortlake Cemetery in South Worple Way provided the final resting place for SIR EDWIN CHADWICK

(1800–90), the Poor Law Commissioner and campaigner for sewerage and general public hygiene. This would be of minimal interest to grave spotters were it not that his 1843 report on 'The Practice of Interment in Towns' marked a decisive shift in attitudes to burial, a move away from the promiscuous packing of the dead into the narrow confines of city churchyards and towards those spacious, 'scientifically' designed cities of the dead we now recognize as 'cemeteries'.

NORWOOD

The South Metropolitan Cemetery is reached from Norwood High Street. SIR HENRY BESSEMER (1813–98) is buried here. Bessemer found a way of purifying molten iron by blowing hot air through it to burn off the oxide, rather than simply heating it from the outside in the traditional manner. At a stroke, this process made steel-production approximately 150 times as fast as it had been before, with enormous savings in cost. For the first time, steel could be economically manufactured on an industrial scale, opening up a vast range of new technological possibilities. Bessemer may indeed have been, as one historian puts it, not so much a scientist as a 'high-class tinkerer', but his influence on the modern age has been profound.

SIR HIRAM STEVENS MAXIM (1840–1916) had quite an influence too. This American-born engineer was the inventor of the Maxim Gun, an early form of the machine-gun. His baneful influence on the nation's teeth perhaps to some degree offset by his contribution to its high culture, SIR HENRY TATE (1819–99), sugar mogul and founder of the Tate Gallery, is also here. With her *Book of Household Management* (1861), MRS BEETON (née Isabella Mary Mayson, 1836–65) changed the lives of generations of housewives, though her own life was short. A young journalist when she wrote her famous book, she died of puerperal fever at the age of twenty-eight, never actually making it to the sort of distinguished matronhood one tends to imagine for her. ELEANOR RATHBONE (1872–1946) also affected women's lives. As MP she fought doggedly – and at the last, the year before she died, successfully – for the introduction of Family Allowance.

PUTNEY

BRUCE ISMAY (1862–1937) was buried here in the Vale Cemetery, Kingston Road, in a family plot. Chairman of the White Star Line, Ismay thus had the dubious honour of being the owner of the *Titanic*, on whose ill-fated maiden voyage of 1912 he was indeed a passenger. He was said to have saved many lives in the disaster, but there were some who felt he ought to have gone down with his ship, given that over 1600 others, mostly from the cheaper berths, had had to. The American-born sculptor SIR JACOB EPSTEIN (1880–1959) is here, as is novelist DAME IVY COMPTON-BURNETT (1892–1969). A participant – both as victim and villain – of the sort of elaborately oppressive family drama she describes with such chilling humour in her fiction, Compton-Burnett would find a more peaceful mode of existence in later life with her longtime companion Margaret Jourdain.

President of a democratic Russia for a few heady weeks in 1917, the accession to power of socialist ALEXANDER KERENSKY (1881–1970) permitted the return from exile of Bolshevik hard-men Lenin and Trotsky, who overthrew him for his pains, leaving him with no option but to go into exile himself for the rest of his life. Definitely no Bolshevik, radio presenter ROY PLOMLEY (1914–85) none the less sent thousands of distinguished figures into exile on his desert island. He's happily ensconced, let's hope, in some celestial paradise, listening to his eight gramophone records, leafing through his Bible and Shakespeare and rigging up a rude shelter. The Wisconsin-born film director JOSEPH LOSEY (1909–84) was cremated here, as was footballer BOBBY MOORE (1941–93), the West Ham star who led the England team to its 1966 World Cup victory.

STREATHAM

Entered from Oak Row, off Rowan Road, is Streatham Park Cemetery. The pioneer of the 'stream of consciousness' modernist novel, DOROTHY RICHARDSON (1873–1957), is here, her middle name (Miller) given by some Freudian slip as 'Miriam' – the name of the protagonist in her *Pilgrimage* novel sequence.

East

BARKING

ELIZABETH FRY (1780–1845), campaigner for prison reform, was buried in Barking, in the Friends' Burial Ground, opposite the meeting house in North Street (now a Sikh temple). The land was bought by the council a few years ago, and the headstones removed to the Friends' cemetery in Wanstead, but the departed Friends – including Fry – remain.

BARKINGSIDE

In the grounds of the Village Homes for Girls, Tanners Lane, is the grave containing the ashes of Dr Thomas Barnardo (1845–1905), who founded the complex in 1876, only the start of what was to become a considerable organization dedicated to the assistance of vulnerable children. Despite the example he set in his own life, Barnardo never believed that Christian charity towards the disadvantaged could be a substitute for state support. To this end he went in for political lobbying with a cunning and persistence which seemed indecent to purer souls, and he made himself a lot of enemies. Even they, however, would have been surprised to learn that his qualifications as a surgeon and his philanthropic interest in young prostitutes had earned him a place on the suspect list for Jack the Ripper's Whitechapel Murders. As for what he himself would have thought if he'd known, that doesn't bear thinking about.

BLACKHEATH

The ruined old church of St Margaret's, Lee Terrace, is across the street from its nineteenth-century replacement. In its churchyard lie Astronomers Royal Edmond Halley (1656–1742), who correctly predicted the return of the comet which has since borne his name, and John Pond (1767–1836), who played a vital role in modernizing the equipment and methods of the nearby national observatory. In 1833 he published a catalogue of 1,113 stars, their positions determined with unprecedented accuracy.

DEPTFORD

Somewhere in St Nicholas' churchyard lies the poet, playwright, blasphemer, sodomite and secret agent Christopher Marlowe (1564–93) – killed, supposedly, in a tavern brawl. Given the men with whom the 'quarrel over the reckoning' occurred (Ingram Frezer, who stabbed the controversial poet through the eye socket with a '12d. dagger' and was backed by Nicholas Skeres, a servant to the notorious political intriguer the Earl of Essex, and Robert Polway, a known spook), it's hard to believe his fate was quite so haphazard. In all probability, Marlowe, aware that he was in trouble with Her Majesty's Secret Service, was making tracks for the Continent, hoping to take passage on a Deptford boat, when Frezer and friends caught up with him. The fact that he was buried quickly and in considerable secrecy, in an unmarked grave, does nothing to increase one's confidence in the official version.

EAST HAM

In the graveyard of St Mary Magdalen's parish church lies WILLIAM STUKELEY (1687–1765), the antiquarian, scientist, and general enthusiast of 'curiosities'. Stukeley did research of real value at Stonehenge during the 1720s, but as he grew older he got more and more deeply involved in the sort of ethnomystical speculations that would earn him the nickname of 'The Arch-Druid'.

ELTHAM

RICHMAL CROMPTON (1890–1969), creator of *Just William*, was cremated at the crematorium, Rochester Way.

GREENWICH

The old parish church of St Alphege, on Greenwich High Road, should be a port of call for early music enthusiasts. THOMAS TALLIS (c. 1505–85), one of the great composers of the Tudor period, is buried here beneath the chancel. An even earlier composer, WILLIAM NEWARK (c. 1450–1509), was also buried here. A more martial note would be struck by the later addition of the Hero of Quebec, General JAMES WOLFE (1727–1759), who famously scaled the cliffs under fire to capture the Canadian city, then fell in the hour of victory. His body was brought back to England and was laid to rest here in a family vault.

ILFORD

The remains of those interred in St Martin Outwich church-yard, Threadneedle Street, in the City, were brought here, to the cemetery in Clarks Road, when the church was demolished and built over in 1874. Among other faithful departed, these would have included the amiable MRS ABIGAIL VAUGHAN, who died in medieval times having left in her will a sum of four shillings a year towards faggots for burning heretics.

STRATFORD

In an unmarked grave in St Patrick's Catholic Cemetery, Langthorne Road, lies the prostitute MARY KELLY (1864–88), a victim of Jack the Ripper.

WEST HAM

The ashes of LILIAN BAYLIS (1874–1937), the manager who put the Old Vic on the theatrical map and in 1931 effectively re-founded Sadlers Wells, were scattered here in the East London Cemetery, Grange Road.

WHITECHAPEL

Standing out among the graves in the Jewish Burial Ground, Brady Street, is the white-painted, railed-in tomb of NATHAN MEYER ROTHSCHILD (1777–1836), who extended his father's banking empire to London, and in 1815 scored a famous coup when his carefully prepared network of messengers made him first with the news of Napoleon's defeat at Waterloo, leaving him in a position to clean up comprehensively.

West

CHELSEA

In the burial ground of the Royal Hospital, to the east of the hospital itself, lies DR CHARLES BURNEY (1726–1814), the father of the novelist and diarist Fanny Burney (see Bath, Avon) and distinguished in his own right as composer and musicologist (he was the author of a big four-volume *History of Music*, 1776–89). He was organist in the chapel here for many years and had lodgings on the top floor overlooking his final resting place.

Apart from what may be the remains of Thomas More (see Tower Hill, City of London), the Chelsea Old Church of All Saints on Cheyne Walk also boasts the grave of MARY ASTELL (1666–1731), who was laid to rest here in the churchyard. An early polemicist for women's rights she was indeed probably the first feminist writer to reach a wide readership.

MADAME TUSSAUD (1761–1850) is in St Mary's on Cadogan Street. Born in Strasbourg, she got into the waxwork business through her mother, who was housekeeper to Philippe Curtius. She moved to Paris as his assistant, and on his death in 1794 inherited his collection. The following year she married Monsieur Tussaud, but within a few years the couple had separated. Madame Tussaud took her collection to England in 1802 and never looked (or, for that matter, went) back.

CHISWICK

BARBARA VILLIERS, DUCHESS OF CLEVELAND (1641–1709), mistress of Charles II and mother to at least five of his children, is buried here at St Nicholas' Church, Chiswick Mall. The sometime beauty died of dropsy, her looks and energy gone completely, her body swollen to vast bulk. There may be no monument to her, but there's no doubt that she is here, which is more than can be said for Oliver Cromwell, held by one longstanding but almost certainly fanciful tradition to have been buried beneath the floor of the church. Later the painter and cartoonist WILLIAM HOGARTH (1697–1764) was buried in the churchyard here, in his rather grand family vault. Or rather, under it, for when the vault came to be opened in 1789 for his wife Jane to be laid to rest, his coffin was nowhere to be seen. After a shocked pause, it was recalled that the vault had been built only *after* his death and burial, the family having subsequently been aggrandized (though not in fact appreciably enriched) by his work. Further away from the church, the churchyard shades imperceptibly into the local cemetery, and here Hogarth would eventually be joined by another painter, JAMES MCNEILL WHISTLER (1834–1903).

In the grounds of Chiswick House, where he'd enjoyed sitting out on sunny afternoons, were scattered the ashes of MICHAEL FLANDERS (1922–75), the wheelchaired lyrics man of comic singing duo Flanders and Swann. Active – even athletic – until his early twenties, Flanders had then lost the use of his legs through poliomyelitis.

GUNNERSBURY

The novelist, playwright and drama critic CHARLES MORGAN (1894–1958) lies here at the Kensington Cemetery, Gunnersbury Avenue. Highly literary in his style and preoccupations, his reputation has always been greater on the Continent than in his native Britain. TADEUSZ BÒR-KOMOROWSKI (1895–1966) was Commander of the Polish Resistance, 1943–4: he it was who gave the order for the Warsaw Uprising of 1944. Two stones carved with daisies mark the grave of CAROL REED (1906–76), the director of classic films such as *Odd Man Out* (1947) and *The Third Man* (1949), in obscure reference to his mother's house, called 'Daisyfield'.

HANWELL

JONAS HANWAY (1712–86), merchant, traveller, philanthropist and lateral thinker, was buried here, in the parish churchyard. Though famous in his day as author of an *Essay on Tea* (1753), described by an indignant Boswell as a 'violent attack upon that elegant and popular beverage', he lives in history as the originator of the umbrella. A stone's throw away in the Westminster Council Cemetery, in a communal grave among other victims of the Blitz, lies singer and bandleader AL BOWLLY (c. 1890 (he was always vague about his age) to 1941). His big tune was 'Brother Can You Spare a Dime?'

HARROW ON THE HILL

A plaque in the churchyard indicates the grave of John Peachey, of significance now only because the adolescent Lord Byron, a pupil at the nearby school, used to come here to be alone. He revisited the tomb, this 'spot of my youth', in 1807 when he was a grizzled old sage of twenty-one, and recalled the hours he had once passed there, lying musing beneath a spreading elm tree:

> Oft have I thought, 'twould soothe my dying hour,—
> If aught may soothe when life resigns her power,—
> To know some humble grave, some narrow cell,
> Would hide my bosom where it loved to dwell;
> With this fond dream, methinks 'twere sweet to die—
> And here it linger'd, here my heart might lie;
> Here might I sleep where all my hopes arose,
> Scene of my youth, and couch of my repose;
> For ever stretch'd beneath this mantling shade,
> Press'd by the turf where once my childhood play'd...

HESTON

In the parish church, though where exactly isn't clear, since his memorial dates from some decades after his death, is the grave of SIR JOSEPH BANKS (1744–1820), the naturalist who accompanied Captain Cook on his first voyage to the South Seas. The ultimate gentleman–amateur, Banks scorned the European Grand Tour customary for the well-born young man of his day: 'Every blockhead does that; my grand tour shall be one round the whole globe,' he said. Captain and crew had to endure his outrageous demands for special treatment for himself and for his four servants and personal artist, since he was putting up £10,000 towards the costs of the expedition. When, however, Banks insisted that Cook's second ship, the *Resolution*, be fitted with an extra deck just to accommodate himself and his proposed retinue, which was to include a pair of horn players, something in Captain Cook snapped. Banks was not, in fact, the complete buffoon he may seem: his scientific investigations during the expedition and afterwards proved immensely valuable, as did the thousands of paintings and sketches his artist made of the strange flora and fauna the voyagers encountered. He would eventually become President of the Royal Society. (Captain Cook (1728–79) would be buried in the Sandwich Islands, where he was killed in a skirmish with natives.)

KENSAL GREEN

ST MARY'S CATHOLIC CEMETERY: MARY SEACOLE (1805–81) is buried by the avenue near the chapel. She had already built up considerable experience nursing in her native Jamaica and in Panama before in 1854 she went to Crimea with Florence Nightingale – at least, that was the idea before one of Nightingale's assistants took one look at her black face and informed her that there were no further vacancies. So Seacole went out under her own steam, working with heroism and resourcefulness in appalling conditions, and became the first woman into Sebastopol after it fell. In the heat of war, with British forces needing all the medical support they could get, approving dispatches from the front lauded her actions and her saintly presence. Afterwards, however, when the war was over, she was quickly sidelined by the cult of Florence Nightingale, The Lady with the Lamp, a more acceptable icon. Seeing this happening, many objected, *Punch* magazine even publishing an impassioned doggerel appeal on her behalf:

> That berry-brown face, with a kind heart's trace
> Impressed in each wrinkle sly
> Was a sight to behold, though the snow-clouds rolled
> Across that iron sky.

The cold without gave a zest, no doubt,
  To the welcome warmth within:
But her smile, good old soul, lent heat to the coal,
  And power to the pannikin.
No store she set by the epaulette,
  Be it worsted or gold-lace;
For KCB, or plain private SMITH
  She still had one pleasant face...

This appeal, along with those of other influential commentators, led to a short-lived fame for Seacole, but she was soon forgotten, and died in obscurity. GILBERT HARDING (1907–60), TV curmudgeon of *What's My Line?* fame, is buried here, as is the conductor SIR JOHN BARBIROLLI (1899–1970).

KENSAL GREEN CEMETERY: In the spacious cemetery it's easy enough to find, not far from the central avenue, the father and son engineers, SIR MARC ISAMBARD BRUNEL (1769–1849) and ISAMBARD KINGDOM BRUNEL (1806–59). Leaving France after the Revolution, Sir Marc went first to America, working there for some years before coming to England in 1799. A chip off the old block, Isambard Kingdom ended up more famous than his father, his credits including railways, piers, great steamships and (among others) the Clifton Suspension Bridge, Bristol. The essayist and raconteur SYDNEY SMITH (1771–1845) lies buried with his daughter before the Cloisters near the northern edge of the cemetery. The vicar of Combe Florey, Somerset, the Reverend Smith once described country life as 'a kind of healthy grave', but he found the real thing here, being brought to his London town house a few days before his death.

KENSAL GREEN CEMETERY

London's first big commercial cemetery, opened in 1833, Kensal Green has been overshadowed for modern visitors by Highgate, with its spectacular setting and celebrity tombs. This is regrettable, since there's a sense of peace and dignity here that is lacking in Highgate (which on busy weekends can feel more like a funereal theme park) as well as some impressive buildings, an exuberant variety of fine statuary and a distinguished list of inmates. Built on a wide, flat, open site, its graves laid out in neat, disciplined ranks along spacious, sweeping avenues, Kensal Green had none of the rolling contours and winding, shaded ways that would make Highgate such a popular attraction – for the living as well as for the dead. In its aspect of airy openness and order, however, it seemed to offer the healthiest possible contrast to the chaos and claustrophobia of the squalid city churchyards it was designed to supplant.

This orderliness isn't quite so evident now: the cemetery has been allowed to run wild rather, which adds considerably to the atmosphere for the visitor, though it can make the hunt for specific graves frustrating.

Turn right at the Harrow Road entrance for St Mary's Catholic Cemetery, open November–March 8–4 (9.15–4 Sundays), April–October 8–5 (9.15 to 5 Sundays), Bank Holidays 10–1. Turn left at the Harrow Road entrance for Kensal Green Cemetery proper, open April–September 9–6 (9–5 Sundays), October–March 9–5 (10–1 Sundays), Bank Holidays 10–1.30.

Clustered around the E-shaped colonnaded chapel at the heart of the cemetery are various other luminaries. To the west is the fearless tightrope-walker CHARLES BLONDIN (Jean François Gravelet, 1824–97), who in the mid-nineteenth century seems to have commuted back and forth across the Niagara Falls on an almost daily basis, refining his achievement with a variety of gimmicks: doing it blindfolded; carrying a man on his back; walking across on stilts; and even stopping half-way to cook an omelette. ANTHONY TROLLOPE (1815–82) and WILLIAM 'WILKIE' COLLINS (1824–89) had only the critics to fear. Two of the Victorian period's greatest novelists, the former was the Barsetshire chronicler and inventor of the Pallisers (and, during an earlier career as a civil servant, the pillar box), the latter was the author of *The Woman in White* (1860), as well as what's widely held to be the first English detective novel, *The Moonstone* (1868). Collins' mistress, Caroline Graves, was buried beside him here in 1895, the fact being, in a very Victorian way, generally known but officially unrecorded. WILLIAM MAKEPEACE THACKERAY (1811–63) makes up Kensal Green's novelistic triumvirate, though he's buried some way off, in the overgrown wilds of the conservation area beyond the south avenue near the Grand Union Canal, not far from Romantic poet JAMES HENRY LEIGH HUNT (1784–1859).

Further west, beyond Trollope and Collins, lies playwright and screenwriter TERENCE RATTIGAN (1911–77). He was buried in his family's old vault, though his name wasn't added to the monument. To the east of the chapel, working out from the cemetery's central junction, are such notables as the Irish composer MICHAEL WILLIAM BALFE (1808–70), at least those mortal remains that have not ascended to marble halls, and, next to him, the poet and journalist THOMAS HOOD

(1799–1845), whose monumental bust, erected by public subscription, was unfortunately stolen, all but the pedestal, thus robbing the cemetery of what was by all accounts one of its glories. The pedestal of George Cruikshank's memorial also remains, though the popular engraver's body was later transferred to St Paul's.

As Byron's friend and publisher – publisher too of Walter Scott and Jane Austen – JOHN MURRAY (1778–1843) was one of the great literary facilitators of the Romantic age. He was buried at Kensal Green, as were actors WILLIAM CHARLES MACREADY (1793–1873), CHARLES KEMBLE (1775–1854) and his actress daughter FANNY. The physician RICHARD BRIGHT (1789–1858), discoverer of the famous disease, is here too.

Also buried here was CHARLES BABBAGE (1791–1871), whose remarkable 'analytical engines' were ingenious forerunners of the modern computer. The awed reaction recorded in his journal by George Tickner, who saw one of Babbage's machines in 1835, was typical:

> I must say, that during an explanation which lasted between two and three hours, given by himself with great spirit, the wonder at its incomprehensible powers grew upon us every moment. The first thing that struck me was its small size, being only about two feet wide, two feet deep, and two and a half high. The second very striking circumstance was the fact that the inventor himself does not profess to know all the powers of the machine; that he has sometimes been quite surprised at some of its capabilities... The third was that he can set it to do a certain regular operation, as, for instance, counting 1,2,3,4; and then determine that, at any given number, say the 10,000th, it shall change and take a different ratio, like triangular numbers, 1,3,6,9,12. etc. ; and afterwards at any other

given point, say, 10,550, change again to another ratio. The whole, of course, seems incomprehensible, without the exercise of volition and thought.

Babbage's friend Ada King, who did much to publicize his achievements, is buried with her father, Lord Byron, at Hucknall, Nottinghamshire, though her mother, LADY ANNE ISABELLA NOEL BYRON (née Milbanke, 1792–1860), is here, by the centre junction.

Those cremated in the crematorium at Kensal Green include the Queen star FREDDIE MERCURY (1946–91), who died of illnesses associated with AIDS. Born Frederick Bulsara in Zanzibar, Mercury's antecedents weren't quite as exotic as that perhaps sounds. Though his father was of Persian descent, he was in Africa serving as an accountant for the British government.

KENSINGTON

Inside St Mary Abbott's Church on Kensington Church Street, or rather inside its predecessor, for the present building wasn't built until the 1870s, was buried the actress, playwright and novelist ELIZABETH INCHBALD (1753–1821), whose novels *A Simple Story* (1791) and *Nature and Art* (1796) have proved enduring. She spent her last years nearby at Kensington House. Also buried here was the Scottish philosopher JAMES MILL (1773–1836), a friend of the political economist Jeremy Bentham (see University College, North Central London) and a utilitarian true believer. He educated his son John Stuart Mill (1806–73) to within an inch of his life, starting him on Greek at the age of three, and bringing him up to a frightening pitch of intellectual rigour and aesthetic philistinism. In the end, however, he kicked over the traces, falling in love with the poems of Coleridge (despite their evident lack of utility) and with the charms of the feminist polemicist Harriet Taylor (1807–58), whom he subsequently married. While John Stuart Mill never finally abandoned utilitarianism, he certainly made it a lot more human than it had been. He was poleaxed by Harriet's death in France, and from that time on he spent half of each year in Avignon just to be near her grave – a plainly irrational response about which Bentham and his father would have had a thing or two to say. When he himself died, he was of course buried in Avignon beside his beloved wife.

KEW

In St Anne's churchyard, Kew Green, lies THOMAS GAINSBOROUGH (1727–88), portraitist and landscape painter. Nearby is the grave of JOHANN ZOFFANY (1733–1810), a German artist famous in his day for his stage scenes.

RICHMOND

Buried in St Mary Magdalene's Church, Paradise Road, is the poet JAMES THOMSON (1700–48). The exact location of the author of unjustly forgotten works such as *The Seasons* and *The Castle of Indolence* (as well as the unfortunately remembered 'Rule Britannia') is unknown, since he was buried beneath a plain stone, but it's not thought to be anywhere near the monument erected in 1792 in the northwest corner of the church by the Earl of Buchan. Thomson's friend William Collins (see Chichester, West Sussex) commemorated him in an ode:

> In yonder grave a Druid lies,
> Where slowly winds the stealing wave!

The year's best sweets shall duteous rise
To deck its poet's sylvan grave!...

The genial meads, assigned to bless
Thy life, shall mourn thy early doom,
Their hinds and shepherd-girls shall dress
With simple hands thy rural tomb.

Richmond is rather less sylvan now, with relatively few hinds and shepherdesses to the square mile. Also at St Mary's is novelist MARY BRADDON (1837–1915), author in 1862 of *Lady Audley's Secret*, one of the Victorian era's runaway best-sellers.

In the graveyard of St Matthias', Friar's Stile Road, lies EDMUND KEAN (1787–1833), the greatest tragic actor of his age. He was refused an Abbey burial on account of his scandalous lifestyle.

TEDDINGTON

In the Shacklegate Lane Cemetery lies R. D. BLACKMORE (1825–1900), whose grave you'd expect to find in a rather wilder setting beneath a rather more western sky. In fact, the author of *Lorna Doone* did live in Devon for ten years in boyhood, but spent most of his life here in Teddington, his Exmoor being for the most part a purely fictional landscape.

Beneath the reading desk in St Mary's Church, Ferry Road, a stone's throw from the Lock, is the tomb of the seventeenth-century religious writer THOMAS TRAHERNE (1637–74), who was chaplain to the household of local aristocrat Sir Orlando Bridgeman, 1667–72. Traherne's most famous works, including the remarkable *Centuries of*

Meditation, weren't discovered until the end of the nineteenth century, so like Gerard Manley Hopkins (see Dublin), that other great original of religious poetry whose reputation was made posthumously, he seems somehow out of time.

TWICKENHAM

The great Augustan poet ALEXANDER POPE (1688–1744) was buried in the parish church here. His grave is marked by a plain letter P in the middle of the aisle, though Pope had previously written himself a couple of epitaphs. One magnificent piece of sour grapes he entitled 'For one who would not be buried in Westminster-Abbey' (being a Catholic he was of course never going to be asked):

> *Heroes, and Kings! your distance keep:*
> *In peace let one poor Poet sleep,*
> *Who never flatter'd Folks like you:*
> *Let Horace blush, and Virgil too.*

The other, equally defiant, was derided by Dr Johnson for its multiple-choice opening – though to the modern reader it seems refreshing in its matter-of-fact practicality:

> *Under this Marble, or under this Sill,*
> *Or under this Turf, or e'en what they will;*
> *Whatever an heir, or a Friend in his stead,*
> *Or any good Creature shall lay o'er my Head;*
> *Lies He who ne'er car'd, and still cares not a Pin,*
> *What they said, or may say of the Mortal within.*
> *But who living and dying, serene still and free,*
> *Trusts in God, that as well as he was, he shall be.*

WEST BROMPTON

Brompton Cemetery, in the Old Brompton Road, was founded in 1840 as a commercial operation. Its financial fortunes would prove very changeable, but it was always a popular burial place. Early arrivals included the boxer JOHN 'GENTLEMAN' JACKSON (1769–1845), who was English champion 1795–1803 and afterwards became the proprietor of a famous boxing academy in Bond Street which numbered Byron among its elegant students. JOHN SNOW (1813–59) was a pioneer of anaesthetics, using ether and chloroform to help patients through operations. No operation, with or without anaesthetic, could save the poet John Keats. His fiancée FANNY BRAWNE (1800–65) nursed her ailing man as best she could during his illness, but after he died in Italy in 1821 she got on with her life, marrying Louis Lindon, with whom she is buried here. The auctioneer and antiquary SAMUEL LEIGH SOTHEBY (1805–61) wound up here, as did SIR SAMUEL CUNARD (1787–1865), the American-born founder of the Cunard Steam Packet Company, 1840.

Literary luminaries include GEORGE BORROW (1803–81), who wrote about gypsy life in novels such as *Lavengro* and in nonfiction. Borrow's own childhood had been nomadic for the prosaic reason that his father had been an army officer sent to a series of different postings: it was only as a young man that he set off on his wanderings with the Romanies. It's ironic that he should have ended up in such an eminently bourgeois, respectable resting place – more the kind of place, perhaps, that you'd expect to find GEORGE ALFRED HENTY (1832–1902) the author of patriotic yarns for boys and editor of *Union Jack* magazine, 1880–83. 'A place for everything, and everything in its place,' wrote SAMUEL SMILES (1812–1904) the proto-Thatcherite advocate of 'self-help' (i.e. leaving the poor to starve); his own place turned out to be here, as did that of HENRY MEARS (d. 1912), a building contractor and founder, in 1905, of Chelsea Football Club. Music-hall comedian TOM FOY (1866–1917), 'The Yorkshire Lad' ended up here, as did the Suffragette leader EMMELINE PANKHURST (1858–1928). Her daughters Christabel and Sylvia are in Los Angeles and Addis Ababa respectively. The ashes of composer, conductor and critic CONSTANT LAMBERT (1905–51) were also interred here.

WILLESDEN

In St Mary's churchyard, Neasden Road, lies the novelist and playwright CHARLES READE (1814–84), enormously popular in his day, though now remembered only for his epic historical novel of the Reformation, *The Cloister and the Hearth* (1861). ◆

3

Scotland

Death and Resurrection

On 22 February 1794 the following news item appeared in the
Gentleman's Magazine:

> *A hackney coachman, who was apprehended in conveying
> dead bodies, from the burial ground in High-Street, Lambeth,
> was brought before the magistrates, at Union Hall, Borough,
> for examination. The magistrates adjourned the case for a few
> days, and the prisoner was remanded to custody. At the time
> the coach was seized, the body of the late porter to the
> Archbishop of Canterbury, that of a young woman, and two
> children, were found in it. The parish having given permission
> to the friends of such persons as have been buried in this
> ground, to examine whether or not the bodies remained there,
> most of the graves have been opened, and, shocking to say,
> upwards of two hundred of coffins have been taken up empty.
> Large rewards are offered for the apprehending of the parties
> concerned. The opening of the graves, from which circumstance
> a putrid infection might have resulted, is likely to become a
> matter of serious enquiry.*

'Resurrectionists', as they were called, were a peculiar
scourge of the eighteenth and early nineteenth centuries: the
sick had to fear not only death itself but disturbance after it.
Since people looked forward to the resurrection of the body, the
integrity of their physical being was of absolute importance to
them. Certainly they expected to decay in the ground, but that
represented a fair compromise with nature; the idea that their

bodies might be cut up and dispersed, leaving their souls with nothing to wear on the Last Day, was utterly appalling. Yet this was a time when medicine – as a genuinely scientific, modern profession – was in its infancy: great steps were being taken in understanding, great advances were being made in treatment. Serious research – and serious teaching – required human bodies for examination and dissection.

Well understanding the fear people had of being taken apart after death, the Law reserved dissection as an ultimate penalty for those who had most outraged its sense of right. Each year, the bodies of ten of the nastiest murderers or the blackest traitors would officially be handed over to the anatomists for dissection. But this didn't even begin to meet the mushrooming demand of a fast-expanding medical profession. Bodies had to be got somehow, and anatomists would do deals with convicted felons – money up front for themselves or their families in return for the use of their bodies after death. Or they would bribe officials so that after a hanging they might walk off with the body while the executioner turned a blind eye. This system wasn't very much more satisfactory, however. Such was the horror of dissection that the appearance of the anatomists' men at these – public – executions commonly provoked serious rioting, as the crowd attempted to rob the doctors of their prize. The popular thief Jack Sheppard (see St Martin's Place, London West End) was one such victim saved for the grave by the intervention of the mob.

Hence the grim trade of the resurrectionists. Working in teams, with lookouts – for the authorities were soon taking what steps they could to stop them – they would steal into the churchyards at dead of night and work hurriedly to dig up the dead. New graves not only contained fresher corpses but, the soil not yet having settled, were easier to break into. The poor were the most likely victims. The poorest of all were buried in pits in coffinless batches: they could simply be fished out. Those who had managed proper graves had none the less usually had to settle for a cheap, tacky coffin which was easily opened on the spot. The more prosperous you were, the stronger the coffin you could afford, and a heavy casket that had to be sawn painstakingly through would be an obvious deterrent to men working hurriedly at night. People went to extraordinary lengths to protect their mortal remains, resorting to double and triple coffins, often with lead linings, which also helped to preserve the corpse. Resurrectionism was a lucrative business. The going rate for a body in the late eighteenth century was around two guineas; by 1828, a parliamentary committee was told, it had risen to more like eight. Prices varied according to condition, though, and abnormal specimens which could be exhibited afterwards commanded much higher sums – one seven-foot giant went for a staggering £500.

A uniquely terrible crime in the eyes of the ordinary citizen, it was widely believed that the government wasn't doing enough about it. The ruling classes weren't, after all, going to be at risk, since they would have all the protection afforded by heavy multiple coffins placed in fortress-like mausoleums. They were, in addition, going to benefit from the medical advances dissection allowed, since they could pay for treatment. The poor, who were going to provide the bodies without reaping any of the benefits, were convinced that the authorities were tacitly encouraging the commerce in corpses.

The doctors certainly knew what was going on. In Edinburgh, indeed, medical students were said to be paying their tuition fees in bodies rather than cash. A shortage of specimens in Edinburgh was in the 1820s threatening that city's status as a centre for medical training. It was against this background that the story of the most famous bodysnatchers of all, William Burke and William Hare, would be enacted. Strictly speaking, of course, they weren't resurrectionists at all, having invented the new criminal art of 'burking', a practice that had long existed in the public imagination in the form of urban myth but which would now be put into grim practice. The idea first came to the two men when an old man in Mrs Hare's West Port lodging house died owing on his room. Selling the body occurred to them as a possible means of making up the back rent. Taking the corpse up to the medical college, they were steered towards the physician Robert Knox, who gave them seven pounds ten shillings – a small fortune for a couple of labourers, and far more than the original debt. The temptation proved too strong to resist: preying upon vagrants and street people who wouldn't be missed and who would readily be enticed by the offer of food and drink, Burke and Hare murdered fifteen people (twelve women, two handicapped youths and an elderly man), receiving ten to fifteen pounds a go from a grateful Knox, before their macabre scheme was discovered by neighbours.

The public outcry was furious, especially against Knox, who was considered to have encouraged the killers, who certainly must have known something untoward was going on, and who seemed even to have destroyed evidence of what had been going on – yet who was being left untouched by the Law, not even being called upon to testify at the trial. Popular anger was inflamed still further by the press and, it's generally believed, by the dynasty of time-servers that ran the city's medical establishment, for whom Knox – a brilliant medic, however personally unlikeable – had represented a major threat. Rising up in its indignation the populace rioted, marching upon Knox's Newington Place home, smashing windows and hanging the doctor in effigy. There were calls for hanging in fact, for Knox and for Hare, who had escaped the noose by turning King's Evidence against his partner. In the event it was only Burke who swung. His skeleton ended up in the Edinburgh University Museum.

Forced into action by events in Edinburgh, the government set about passing legislation that would put an end to burking and bodysnatching once and for all. Their handling of the problem was awesome in its aplomb: by the terms of the Anatomy Act of 1832, only those with 'lawful custody' of the body could give it over for dissection, and this permission had to be clearly and explicitly given. Which sounded good until you realized that those with 'lawful custody' would include not only grieving relatives but workhouse authorities and, where sufficient funds weren't available for a proper funeral, parish officials. There was no danger now of the bodies of the poor being dug up by resurrectionists; there was no need for it, since they would be passed directly on to the dissectionists by the relevant authorities. Bodysnatching was no longer a crime but a nationalized industry. The fear that haunted people of dying 'on the parish' did wonders for their work ethic; Friendly and Burial Societies sprang up in their hundreds across the country so that people could save against the day they died. The Victorians' obsessive concern with death and mourning and their exaggerated taste for funereal pomp were to some extent rooted in this fear: the hour of your death was now more than ever the defining moment in life; the moment at which your worth and status were established, when it was decided whether or not your time on earth had been justified.

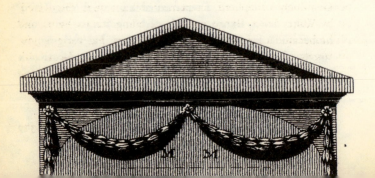

Borders

CHIRNSIDE

In the churchyard here is the grave of racing driver JIM CLARK (1936–68), winner of the Formula One World Championship in 1963 and again in 1965, when he also won the Indianapolis 500, becoming the first non-American to do so since 1916. He was killed in an accident during practice before a Formula Two race at Hockenheim, Germany.

DRYBURGH

SIR WALTER SCOTT (1771–1832), the poet, novelist and inventor of one fanciful but enormously influential brand of 'Scottishness', is buried here, in the north transept of the abbey. Outside is the grave of FIELD MARSHAL LORD HAIG (1861–1928), hated hero of World War I. His strategy of dogged attrition was ultimately successful in wearing down the resistance of the Kaiser's forces on the Western Front, but it wore quite a hole in the allied armies too.

ETTRICK

The poet JAMES HOGG (1770–1835), the 'Ettrick Shepherd', was born in a cottage here and buried in the churchyard. Genuinely a shepherd, his literary abilities were 'discovered' by Walter Scott, Byron and other leading literary lights, and he became a key figure in Scottish letters. His verse is now largely forgotten, but his fame endures thanks to his remarkable tale of the supernatural, *The Private Memoirs and Confessions of a Justified Sinner* (1824).

Also in the churchyard is the famous local character TIBBIE SHIEL (1783–1878), who kept the inn nearby at St Mary's Loch. A friend of Hogg, who for a time held a sort of rustic literary salon at the inn, she welcomed a stream of distinguished visitors to her lonely hostelry down the years.

MELROSE

ROBERT BRUCE's heart (see Dunfermline, Fife) was buried here, in the abbey, after its trip to the Holy Land. A mummified heart matching its description turned up during excavations in the chapter house in 1921. The chapter house – where the monks gathered for their meetings – seems an odd place for a royal heart to have been buried, but it has been suggested that it may have been placed here for its own protection during the Reformation, when monasteries were being looted and burned, and holy relics were not well regarded.

TEVIOTHEAD

In the churchyard lies HENRY SCOTT RIDDELL (1798–1870), the local minister and the author of popular patriotic songs, including 'Scotland Yet' and 'Oour ain Folk'.

Central

BALQUHIDDER

ROBERT MACGREGOR, 'ROB ROY' (1671–1734) is buried here, beside his wife Mary and his two sons Coll and Robert ('Robin Oig'). A cattle rustler, extortionist and all-purpose brigand, he moved easily from one side to the other during the Jacobite rebellion of 1715. His son Robert, a chip off the old block, was hanged in Edinburgh for killing a MacLaren in a dispute over land (which land Rob Roy had indeed usurped). Mistaking the grave site entirely William Wordsworth was moved to write his deathless lines on Rob Roy a few miles away at the head of Loch Katrine: a grim warning to all grave-spotters.

Dumfries & Galloway

BALMAGHIE, NEAR CASTLE DOUGLAS

SAMUEL RUTHERFORD CROCKETT (1860–1914) was minister here until 1895, when the success of his kaleyard novels (sentimental fictions about poor but contented Scottish folk of a sort which were then enjoying a huge vogue) persuaded him to retire and write full time. He died in France but was returned here for burial in the churchyard.

DUMFRIES

In the northeast corner of St Michael's churchyard is buried ROBERT BURNS (1759–96), with his wife Jean Armour and five of their children. He was brought up in Ayrshire, coming southeast to Dumfries to work for the Excise Office. He had a sticky period when he was investigated for subversion, on account of his publicly expressed support for the French Revolution, but survived to continue an irreproachable career as civil servant. Burns' elevation as national bard began in his lifetime, and his body lay in state in the town hall before being carried to its rest by two regiments with military bands, as well as some 10,000 ordinary members of the public. His grave became a shrine for exiled Scots – and for his fellow poets. William Wordsworth came in 1803:

> I mourned with thousands, but as one
> More deeply grieved, for He was gone
> Whose light I hailed when first it shone,
>   And showed my youth
> How Verse may build a princely throne
>   On humble truth.

Keats came fifteen years later on his first visit to Scotland, by which time Burns had been moved into the present large mausoleum, which wasn't much to the young poet's taste. But then, there wasn't anything much in Scotland that *was* to his taste: 'Keats has been these five hours abusing the Scotch and their country,' reported his friend and travelling companion Charles Armitage Brown: 'He says that the women have large splay feet … and … thanks Providence that he is not related to a Scot, nor any way connected with them.' Well, they were probably just as happy not to be connected with *him*.

Six miles south of Dumfries at Sweetheart Abbey Lady Devorgilla was buried in 1290, together with her husband's heart, which she'd had embalmed after his death twenty-one years earlier.

ECCLEFECHAN

The 'Sage of Chelsea' and the scourge of the materialism and industrialism of his age, THOMAS CARLYLE (1795–1881) was born here at Arched House, which now belongs to the National Trust for Scotland. He described the village under the name of 'Entepfuthl' in his book *Sartor Resartus*. His grave, and that of his parents, can be seen in the churchyard (as, incidentally, can that of Archibald Arnott, who was the doctor to Napoleon on St Helena).

IRONGRAY, NEAR DUMFRIES

In the churchyard is Helen Walker (c. 1760–91), Scott's original for Jeanie Deans in *The Heart of Midlothian*. Scott himself had a memorial erected for her here.

LANGHOLM

Christopher Murray Grieve was buried in the town cemetery. He is better known under his *nom de plume* as HUGH MACDIARMID (1892–1978), the poet and – in his own iconoclastic way – patriot. MacDiarmid himself had chosen for his headstone the phrase 'A disgrace to the community', but he was overruled and given a more respectable epitaph, a famous quotation from his long poem *A Drunk Man Looks at the Thistle*:

> *I'll ha'e nae hauf-way hoose, but aye be whaur*
> *Extremes meet – it's the only way I ken*
> *To dodge the curst conceit o' being richt*
> *That damns the vast majority o' men.*

MOFFAT

The road designer JOHN MCADAM (1756–1836) lived at Dumcrieff House, to the southeast of the town by Moffat Water, though his experiments in road construction, begun in Ayrshire, were continued down in Falmouth where he was responsible for organizing food supplies for the navy. He it was who developed the idea of using broken stone in roadbuilding. He is buried here in the local churchyard.

PARTON

In the ruins of the old chapel in a little cemetery outside the village is the grave of the experimental physicist and electromagnetics pioneer JAMES CLERK MAXWELL (1831–79), who spent his childhood here.

Fife

DUNFERMLINE

KING ROBERT I, THE BRUCE (1274–1329, reigned 1306–29) was buried in the abbey here, but the site of his grave was lost after the Reformation, when the abbey was partly demolished. Workers clearing the site for a new church in the early nineteenth century chanced upon the tomb, with Bruce inside, his skeleton shrouded in gold cloth. Even had there been no other evidence, it would have seemed likely that this was indeed Bruce, but it could clearly be seen where the breastbone had been cut through so that the heart could be removed. (A much-travelled organ, Robert's heart was taken out and embalmed at his own request: always regretting never having been on a crusade, he asked that one of his knights should take his heart with him to the Holy Land. Sir James Douglas obliged (see Douglas, Strathclyde), and the heart duly went off to smite the Saracen. Its tour of duty completed, it was reburied in Melrose Abbey.) The present tombstone dates from 1889.

THE MISERABLE MONARCH

So holy was SAINT MARGARET, QUEEN OF SCOTLAND (c. 1046–93, reigned 1070–93), her confessor and biographer reports approvingly, that throughout her entire life she was never once known to laugh. A stone marks the site of the Miserable Monarch's shrine at Dunfermline Abbey, but she hasn't been there for quite some time, having been removed for safe keeping at the time of the Reformation and never returned. Not that she seems to have been that safe in exile: her head wound up at the Jesuits' Scottish College at Douai, France, only to disappear during the Revolution, while the remainder, acquired by Philip II for the collection of holy relics he was accumulating at his vast palace-cum-mausoleum outside Madrid, the Escorial, is a mere shadow of its former self. An attempt to find Margaret in 1991 yielded only her teeth. The first time, no doubt, she ever showed them in a smile.

LOWER LARGO

In the churchyard here is the admiral SIR ANDREW WOOD (1455–1539). He had won a famous naval victory over the English.

Grampian

ARBUTHNOTT, NEAR STONEHAVEN

After his tragically early death, the author James Leslie Mitchell, better known as LEWIS GRASSIC GIBBON (1901–35), was buried here, just down the hill from the croft at Bloomfield where he spent much of his childhood and set *Sunset Song*, the first novel of his great trilogy *A Scots Quair* (1932–4). His parents out of sympathy with his writerly ambitions, Grassic Gibbon spent an unhappy time in Glasgow, unsuccessfully attempting to make it as a journalist, before he found a precarious vocation as a novelist. With his friend Hugh MacDiarmid (see Langholm, Dumfries & Galloway) he sought to establish a literature that would be truly Scots, representing the nation of Scotland rather than the northerly English county of 'Scotshire'.

LONGSIDE

The Episcopalian minister here for over sixty years, the poet JOHN SKINNER (1721–1807) is buried in the churchyard. His witty, energetic Scots poetry and songs strongly influenced the writing of his friend Robert Burns.

LOSSIEMOUTH

Just south of the town, in the churchyard at Spynie, lie the ashes of socialist activist MARGARET MACDONALD (1870–1911); she would be joined some decades later by her husband, JAMES RAMSAY MACDONALD (1866–1937), the local boy, born out of wedlock, who made good as leader of the Labour Party and, indeed, the first Labour prime minister. Margaret would perhaps have turned in her urn when, in the economic crisis of the early 1930s, her husband did the responsible thing/dirty deed and cut a deal with Baldwin to form a 'National Government' whose plans included reducing unemployment benefit. He certainly managed to antagonize most of his party. Lewis Grassic Gibbon (see Arbuthnott, above) wrote witheringly of 'that philosophy of socialism which Ramsay MacDonald was wont to exfoliate in the days before, glancing downwards and backwards, he caught sight of the seemly shape his calves occupied inside the silk stockings of Court dress'. Reviled by most of his party, Ramsay MacDonald doesn't seem to have worried, but relaxed instead into a comfortable old age of Uncle-Tomism and Homespun Highland Wisdom.

Highland and Orkney Islands

DINGWALL

In the cemetery here lies NEIL GUNN (1891–1973), who lived in the neighbourhood for most of his life, and made it the setting for many of his haunting novels of rural Scottish life.

DURNESS

A tombstone in the churchyard reads:

Here doth lye the bodie
Of John Flyne, who did die
By a stroke from a sky-rocket,
Which hit him in the eye-socket.

GLENCOE

A monument on the hill at the north end of the village commemorates around forty MacDonalds, killed 13 February 1692 by Campbell soldiers billeted here. The massacre was in punishment for the MacDonalds' tardiness in swearing allegiance to William III (though they had in fact taken the oath, despite dragging their feet a bit). They were put to the sword in the village, or fled into the mountains around, where they died of exposure. CHIEF MACIAN was murdered, and is buried on the island of Eilean Munde, in Loch Leven, where there's another monument. Not for the last time, an official inquiry condemned the outrage, without actually bringing any of the perpetrators to book.

GLENFINNAN, LOCH SHIEL

St Finnan's Isle, in the Loch, was for centuries the burial ground for the clan MacDonald, who built a chapel there in the sixteenth century.

INVERNESS

The disaster of Culloden in 1745 effectively put an end to the Young Pretender's pretensions. The dead were buried on the spot: 1200 clansmen and, in a separate 'Field of the English', seventy-six of the Duke of Cumberland's men – actually mostly Scots. In flight for his life, Prince Charlie

was lucky to escape (see Kilmuir, Skye, Western Isles). He returned to the continent and grew old – not especially gracefully, by all accounts.

MAINLAND, ORKNEY ISLANDS

In Harray churchyard, his grave marked by a standing stone over six feet high, lies comic novelist ERIC LINKLATER (1899–1974). This famous Orcadian was actually born and brought up in South Wales, but his father was the real thing, and Linklater himself identified strongly with the islands all his life.

SANDAIG

The ashes of *Ring of Bright Water* man GAVIN MAXWELL (1914–69) were buried here, by the remains of the cottage where he'd once lived with his famous otters.

Lothian

DALMENY

In a vault in the Rosebery's private aisle (practically an annexe of the church, behind the organ loft), rests Archibald Philip Primrose, the EARL OF ROSEBERY (1847–1929), the might-have-been prime minister. He actually was prime minister briefly in 1894–5, but nobody noticed. Winston Churchill summed up his career:

At first they said 'He will come.' Then for years 'If only he could come.' And finally, long after he had renounced politics for ever, 'If only he would come back.'

The three remarkable things about the otherwise unremarkable Rosebery are that he married the stupendously wealthy heiress Hannah Rothschild in 1878, that he became prime minister, albeit briefly, and that he owned not one but three Derby winners. Claud Cockburn summed up his achievement:

> *By marrying a Rothschild, being a Prime Minister and winning the Derby, he demonstrated that it was possible to improve one's financial status and run the Empire without neglecting the study of form.*

Oh yes, there was a fourth remarkable thing about Rosebery: feeling his end near at hand, he sent a servant out to buy a gramophone, and gave his staff instructions that when it seemed he was reaching his last moments they should put on a record of the Eton Boat Song to send him fittingly to his rest.

EDINBURGH

OLD CALTON BURIAL GROUND, WATERLOO PLACE: DAVID HUME (1711–76) is here, the distinguished atheist commemorated by a big non-religious monument. Non-belief wasn't so widespread in the eighteenth century, and Hume's had given him a certain notoriety. His final illness and death intrigued the public: would the great atheist embrace the consolations of religion at the eleventh hour? Their disappointment when he didn't was to some extent tempered by their admiration for the 'philosophical' calm he showed, but there was still considerable resentment of his irreligion, and his family had to have his grave guarded for a time after his burial for fear of desecration. Among his friends, Hume's resolute refusal to kow-tow to the cosmos caused some concern. James Boswell was tormented by the thought that such a good man as Hume should be damned on account of his atheism. He relaxed only after dreaming that he'd 'discovered' a secret journal in which the philosopher made clear his closet Christianity. Even though he woke up and found it wasn't true, this dream seems to have allayed his fears for his friend. This is the kind of thing that gets religious belief a bad name.

There's a big monument here too to Abraham Lincoln, who is shown freeing a slave: it marks the graves of five Scotsmen killed in the American Civil War. WILLIAM BLACKWOOD (1776–1834), the founder of *Blackwood's Magazine*, a literary and political magazine famous through the nineteenth century (and published as late as 1976) is also here.

CANONGATE: Here in the churchyard lies ADAM SMITH (1723–90), the proto-Thatcherite father of modern economics, author of *Inquiry into the Nature and the Causes of the Wealth of Nations* (1776).

ROBERT FERGUSSON (1750–74) was the poet who perhaps more than any other revealed for Burns the possibility of a contemporary Scots poetry. His health – mental and physical – shattered by the struggle to endure a working life as a clerk and to reconcile the tensions in his own mind over a religious vocation he was never sufficiently sure of to pursue but felt guilty for neglecting, he ended up in bedlam, where he took his own life. His grave remained unmarked when Burns came to Edinburgh; though in debt himself, Burns paid for a stone to be erected and wrote him an epitaph:

No sculptured marble here, nor pompous lay,
No storied Urn, nor animated Bust;
This simple Stone directs Pale Scotia's way
To pour her Sorrows o'er her poet's Dust.

Burns was busy in this churchyard, also erecting a stone with the inscription 'Clarinda' for a woman he was in love with, MRS AGNES MACLEHOSE (1759–1841), who was married (though separated from her lawyer husband) with two children. To her he'd written passionate letters, and various songs, including:

Had we never lov'd sae kindly
Had we never lov'd sae blindly
Never met – or never parted
We had ne'er been broken-hearted ...

The correspondence continued through Burns' marriage with Jean Armour, though the poet remained a faithful husband to the grave (see Dumfries).

Another literary inmate is MARY BRUNTON (1778–1818), the Orkney-born writer, author of such novels as *Self-Control* (1810–11) and *Discipline* (1814), which combine romantic flavour with respectable morality, an appropriate mixture in a writer who in life eloped to marry a minister.

Beneath the wall of the church lies DAVID RIZZIO (c. 1533–66), the Italian singer, secretary and favourite of Mary, Queen of Scots, murdered (stabbed fifty-six times, lest there should be any doubt) in front of the Queen by her husband Darnley and his men. Darnley himself seems to have come to a bad end; the following year a house he was staying in was mysteriously blown up in the night, Darnley and a servant being found dead, apparently strangled, not far away. (He's buried in Holyrood Abbey, see below.)

BUCCLEUCH CEMETERY: In the tiny cemetery here on Buccleuch Street is the grave of ALISON RUTHERFORD (1713–94), the literary hostess and poet who wrote the famous lament 'The Flowers of the Forest'. (The plaque on the graveyard's outer wall gives her married name, Mrs Cockburn.) It was in Buccleuch too that DEACON WILLIAM BRODIE was buried after his execution in 1788. By day an eminently respectable, sober cabinetmaker and guild official (hence the title 'Deacon'), by night Brodie used the keys his customers provided him with to pursue a career as a burglar, raising the money he needed to feed a compulsive gambling habit. It was Brodie's story that gave Stevenson the idea for his 1886 novel *The Strange Case of Dr Jekyll and Mr Hyde*. Also here is CHARLES DARWIN (1758–78), forebear of the more famous author of *The Origin of Species* (who is, of course, in Westminster Abbey). Who knows to what heights of achievement this promising man might not have ascended had he escaped this untimely end as a medical student: he cut his finger while dissecting a baby's brain and died of the resulting infection.

DEAN CEMETERY: Here the sons of Alexander Nasmyth (see St Cuthbert's, below) have their impressive tomb. They seem to have inherited their father's talents and interests, PATRICK NASMYTH (1787–1831) becoming a landscape painter of note, JAMES NASMYTH (1808–90), though himself no mean artist, winning his real fame as an engineer. His steam-hammer – designed in a matter of half an hour in response to a request from Isambard Kingdom Brunel (see Kensal Green, West London) – revolutionized heavy engineering work: able to summon up many times the strength of the strongest blacksmith, it was sensitive enough to crack an egg in a wineglass without breaking the glass. A later arrival is ELSIE INGLIS (1864–1917), the suffragette who braved official condescension and downright obstruction to found the Scottish Women's Hospitals, which brought medical attention to thousands of soldiers suffering in the horrors of the Great War, from Serbia to the Somme. Though she herself worked heroically in appalling conditions on the Eastern Front, her death seems to have been the result of a cancer which would have taken her anyway.

GREYFRIARS CHURCHYARD: Among the earlier inmates of Greyfriars is the historian and heretic GEORGE BUCHANAN (1506–82), the Protestant poet laureate to the Catholic Queen Mary.

One dark night in 1638, it's said, the Covenanters gathered here to sign their agreement to resist the English rites being prescribed by Charles I. 'No King but Christ!' cried the Presbyterian Scots. Resting the parchment upon a flat gravestone, the rich and poor signed together, many writing in their own blood. Forty years on Greyfriars would witness the unhappy conclusion of the story. In 1679, twelve hundred Covenanters, defeated at Bothwell Bridge, were brought back to Edinburgh and held prisoner here for five months, kept in the open with little in the way of food. Some were eventually released, some were transported, and some ended their days here, whether through natural causes or execution. A hundred or so were buried in a long pit, near the Martyrs' Monument.

Less deserving of our sympathy, perhaps, is JOHN PORTEOUS (d. 1736), the Captain of the Town Guard who gave his name to one of the eighteenth century's most violent bouts of rioting. His overreaction to a minor disturbance at a public execution led to his men killing six people. He was tried and found guilty, but the authorities granted him a reprieve, whereupon an angry mob forced their way into the High Street Guardhouse, dragged him out and lynched him. A gentler fame altogether is that of the poet ALLAN RAMSAY (c. 1685–1758), who was born in Leadhills, Strathclyde, and who was the author in 1725 of *The Gentle Shepherd* – a Scots pastoral comedy which in 1728 was made into a ballad opera. Ramsay was also an artistic entrepreneur, the founder of a theatre and subscription library and generally a beacon of the Edinburgh cultural life of his time. There's a verse on his memorial slab in the church wall:

> *Tho' here you're buried, worthy ALLAN,*
> *We'll ne'er forget you, canty Callan,*
> *For while your Soul lives in the Sky,*
> *Your GENTLE SHEPHERD NE'ER can die.*

Brave words, but it's a while since *The Gentle Shepherd* really packed them in at the box-office.

HENRY MACKENZIE (1745–1831), the lawyer and Man of Feeling, is here too: an increased interest in eighteenth-century writing has in recent years boosted the status of his unashamedly 'sentimental' novels from the completely forgotten to the hopelessly marginal. Much less accomplished, but much more famous, is the doggerel laureate WILLIAM MCGONAGALL (1825–1902). He is somewhere about here, though his grave is unmarked, the authorities having obdurately refused to come through with a state funeral. McGonagall's appallingly inept verse commemorations of the Tay Bridge Disaster and other important events of his age have won him a place in literary history – if only as a dire warning to would-be poets. Also unmarked is the grave of the mathematician and scientist JAMES GREGORY (1638–75), who invented a reflecting telescope before Newton. The architect, brewer and entrepreneur WILLIAM ADAM (1689–1748) is here in an imposing mausoleum built for the family by his sons Robert, James and William.

These great men and these crucial historic moments are all very well: the real reason anyone outside Edinburgh has heard of Greyfriars is that bloody dog. Owned by PC Jock Grey (1813–58) the faithful Skye terrier, Bobby, kept vigil on his owner's grave for fourteen years, before he died himself and was buried beside his master.

HIGH KIRK OF ST GILES: A monument in the south aisle is the nearest most of us are likely to get to the grave of ROBERT LOUIS STEVENSON (1850–94). He is buried in Samoa, where he stayed during his last years, finding life in paradise anything but idyllic. Those actually buried here include JAMES GRAHAM, MARQUESS OF MONTROSE (1612–50), near whose tomb is a copy of the National Covenant (see Greyfriars, above), of which he was one of the first signatories. After leading the Covenanters in defence of Presbyterianism for four years, Montrose went over to Charles I, and harried the Covenanters in Scotland to great effect before being defeated and forced into exile in 1645. In 1650 he returned, and resumed his guerrilla operations at the head of a rag-tag-and-bobtail army of Highlanders, until he was betrayed by a follower, led in ignominy to Edinburgh and paraded through the city to the Grassmarket, where he was hanged from a gibbet. His head was displayed on a spike on the Tolbooth while his body was buried among the criminals outside the city boundary. (The old town prison, the Tolbooth, stood next to St Giles' until it was finally pulled down in 1817. The 'Heart of Midlothian', an appropriately shaped pattern in the cobbles not far from the main door of the High Kirk, marks where its entrance used to be, and would itself for a time be a place of execution.) In 1661 Montrose was reassembled and interred with great ceremony in a lavish tomb in the High Kirk, his epitaph being taken from lines which Montrose had written on the window of his cell the night before his execution:

> Let them bestow on every airth a limb;
> Then open all my veins, that I may swim
> To thee, my Maker! in that crimson lake;
> Then place my parboiled head upon a stake,
> Scatter my ashes, strew them in the air
> Lord, since thou knowest where all these atoms are
> I'm hopeful Thou'lt recover once my dust,
> And confident Thou'lt raise me with the Just.

Almost directly opposite Montrose off the north aisle is the tomb of his old enemy, the leader of the Covenanter camp ARCHIBALD CAMPBELL, MARQUESS OF ARGYLL (1598–1661). In 1650, with Cromwell in the ascendant south of the border and himself and his Covenanters in control in Scotland, he had watched complacently from a window in Moray House (now a College of Education) as Montrose was led up the Canongate to his death. Eleven years later, it would be his turn. He was beheaded in the High Street, his head exhibited on the Tolbooth.

JOHN KNOX AND THE MONSTROUS REGIMENT

Most of the land between St Giles' and Cowgate in Edinburgh constituted, in medieval times, the town cemetery. Traces were uncovered in subsequent building work, and the bones were sometimes moved to Greyfriars (which had started life as an overspill for St Giles' burial ground) and sometimes simply built over. Hence JOHN KNOX (c. 1514–72), minister of St Giles', the famous Protestant firebrand and the misogynistic sounder in 1558 of the *First Blast of the Trumpet Against the Monstrous Regiment of Women*, is believed to lie beneath parking space number 44, behind the statue of Charles II. (There's supposed to be some sort of commemorative tablet, but at the time of going to press there's just a plain, pinkish concrete slab that wouldn't be out of place in someone's suburban patio.)

HOLYROOD ABBEY: Various Scottish royalty rest here, including DAVID II (d. 1370) and JAMES II (d. 1460). HENRY STEWART, LORD DARNLEY (1546–67), the husband of Mary, Queen of Scots is also among those present. The murdered Rizzio is thought to have been buried here at first, before he was moved up the road to Canongate (see above).

ST CUTHBERT'S: JOHN NAPIER (1550–1617), who experimented valiantly with the use of manures but whose chief title to fame rests in his invention of logarithms, is buried here at St Cuthbert's on Princes Street. A Celtic cross marks the grave of ALEXANDER NASMYTH (1758–1840), artist and engineer. He painted landscapes and portraits (including that of Burns) and, in his quieter moments, designed steamboats. (On top of all this, he fathered an important Edinburgh family, for whom see Dean Cemetery.) The novelist SUSAN FERRIER (1782–1854) also lies in St Cuthbert's churchyard. Most critics would feel that she's not as interesting a writer as THOMAS DE QUINCEY (1785–1859) – who was, in fairness, as interesting a character as you're ever likely to meet. In the preface to his *Confessions of an English Opium Eater* (1821), De Quincey notes the feelings of shame he's had to come to terms with before feeling able to come clean about his habit:

> *Guilt and misery shrink, by a natural instinct, from public notice: they court privacy and solitude: and, even in their choice of a grave will sometimes sequester themselves from the general population of the churchyard, as if declining to claim fellowship with the great family of man...*

Given that he managed to overcome this fear of public notice and publish his *Confessions*, however, it's not so surprising to find him buried here – set back a little, it's true, on the slope above the church, but in a perfectly open situation and surrounded by respectable Edinburgeois.

HADDINGTON

In the ruined choir of St Mary's Church is the tomb of JANE WELSH CARLYLE (1801–66), wife of the cantankerous Sage of Chelsea (see Ecclefechan, Dumfries & Galloway), with whom she seems to have found life demanding but on the whole rewarding. A poet of sorts, she is most famous now for her letters, which provide a sharp, acerbic account of her circle and her time.

LASSWADE

In the graveyard of the ruined church was buried the poet, historian, inventor (of weapons and scientific instruments) and doughty unionist campaigner WILLIAM DRUMMOND (1585–1649). His death was reputedly a result of his grief at the execution of England's Charles I, three years earlier. That's an awful lot of grief, and very slow in taking effect.

WHITTINGEHAME, NEAR DUNBAR

Whittingehame was the birthplace of the Conservative leader ARTHUR JAMES BALFOUR (1848–1930), who is buried in the Balfour family plot in the churchyard. Prime minister from 1902 to 1905, he resigned from the leadership in 1911 after a series of electoral defeats, and was kicked upstairs to the Lords. It was there, in 1917, that he made his greatest contribution to history, giving Palestine simultaneously to the Jews and to the Arabs.

Strathclyde

AUCHINLECK

The most famous hanger-on in English Literature, JAMES BOSWELL (1740–95) is buried here, in the local church. His father, a judge, built Auchinleck House, three miles to the west of here by the banks of the Lugar. Thanks to the Life of Johnson Boswell tends to be associated with London. In fact he spent most of his life in Scotland, feeling like an exile in his own country, pining for London – for the stimulating social life (and the seamy sexual one) it could offer.

BUTE

At Rothesay on Bute is the tomb of JOHN STUART, LORD BUTE (1713–92) who as prime minister managed to bring the Seven Years' War to an end with the Peace of Paris, then quit while he was ahead, resigning after less than a year in office. In retirement he lived near Christchurch, on the Dorset coast, but he had always taken pride in his family's island ancestry, and when he died (the shock from a minor fall on a cliff near his home leading to more severe complications which carried him off a few months later), he was brought to Bute for burial.

CARDROSS

The novelist TOBIAS SMOLLETT (1721–71) was born near here at Dalquhurn, but left as a young man, heading south first to Glasgow and then on to London, seeking his fortune as a writer. In 1768 he went even further south, settling in Leghorn (Livorno), where he died, and where he is buried in the English cemetery.

DOUGLAS

At St Bride's Church are buried several members of the Douglas family, including SIR JAMES DOUGLAS, who was killed by the Moors in Spain in 1330, while en route to the Holy Land with Robert Bruce's heart (see Dunfermline, Fife). The Fifth Earl of Douglas, Archibald 'Bell the Cat', was given his nickname after he alone of Scotland's angry nobility had the courage to brave royal wrath and kill, in 1482, the hated Robert Cochrane, the low-born favourite of James III.

GLASGOW

NECROPOLIS: On a spectacular hilltop site behind the Catholic Cathedral is the city's first cemetery designed on scientific principles, first proposed by city historian Dr John Strang, and designed by John Bryce. An influx of impoverished immigrants from Ireland and the Highlands, living and dying (at a rate of around 5,000 a year) in overcrowded, disease-ridden slums, had stretched the city's churchyards to breaking point, and the wealthier classes were becoming concerned not merely about the social implications of being buried in such company but about the possible consequences for their bereaved relations when they came to visit their graves. The Necropolis set out to 'afford a much wanted accommodation to the higher classes [and] convert an unproductive property into a general and lucrative source of profit'. It's also a place of considerable atmosphere and interest.

It's ironic that such a great cemetery, for all its spacious vistas and fine sculptuary, contains so few interrees of lasting national importance. Fame has always been handed out very grudgingly to those 'in trade', and the reputations of the great merchants and industrialists who built Glasgow have for the most part proved ephemeral. The nearest thing to a famous name here is probably WILLIAM MILLER (1810–72), the author of 'Wee Willie Winkie', and even he only has a monument here: he's actually buried in an unmarked grave at Tollcross, in the city's East End. The tomb of actor-manager JOHN HENRY ALEXANDER (d. 1852) is of interest, taking the form of a sculpted stage complete with curtains and footlights. Alexander had been broken by the disaster at his Theatre Royal in 1849: a false alarm of fire caused a panicked exodus in which sixty-five people were trampled to death. He never really recovered, and died three years later.

WILLIAM MOTHERWELL (1797–1835), the poet and ballad-collector, compiled *Minstrelsy, Ancient and Modern* (1819), wrote *Poetical Remains* (1848) and collaborated with James Hogg on a new edition of Burns (1835). There isn't much left of his memorial thanks to the weather and vandals. The dramatist JAMES SHERIDAN KNOWLES (1784–1862) enjoyed both popular and critical success in his day ('the first tragic writer of his time', said William Hazlitt), but his work is pretty much forgotten now. The same goes for MICHAEL SCOTT (1789–1835), the author of engaging stories such as *Tom Cringle's Log*, which did for the Caribbean (where he'd worked for a time as an estate manager) something of what Somerville and Ross (see Castletownshend, Cork) were to do for Ireland.

COVENANTERS' MEMORIAL: The old memorial was at the top of the High Street; that was renewed a couple of times before being moved to Castle Street, where it was set in the side of a cinema. When the cinema was demolished, it was set in an arch of the new motorway nearby. The inscription reads:

> *Here lye Martyrs thre*
> *of Memory,*
> *Who for the Covenants did die;*
> *And witness is,*
> *'Gainst all these nations perjury.*
> *Against the Covenanted cause*
> *of Christ, their Royal King;*

The British rulers made such laws,
Declar'd twas Satan's reign.
As Britain lyes in guilt you see,
'Tis asked, o reader! art thou free?

The grocer SIR THOMAS LIPTON (1850–1931) was buried in the Southern Necropolis, Caledonia Road.

In the Western Necropolis, Maryhill, is the grave of SIR WILLIAM SMITH (1854–1914), who in 1883 founded the Boys' Brigade from among the pupils of the North Woodside Mission's Sunday School. Its aim 'The Advancement of Christ's Kingdom among Boys and the Promotion of habits of Reverence, Discipline, Self Respect and all that tends towards a true Christian Manliness'. Another evangelist, who would never lose his Christian beliefs even though he would find fame preaching a more secular gospel, was JAMES KEIR HARDIE (1856–1915), one of the founders of the Labour Party and, from 1900 until his death, its first MP, representing the South Wales constituency of Merthyr Tydfil. He was born just to the southwest of Glasgow in the Strathclyde village of Legbrannoch, near Holytown. He caught pneumonia on a visit to Glasgow and died soon afterwards. A big turnout of his socialist comrades listened in mounting indignation as the clergyman officiating at his funeral, an old friend from Hardie's pre-socialist Christian missionary days, rambled on about those times, without so much as a hint of the later vocation that had made him one of the great heroes of the British left.

JOHN 'JOCK' STEIN (1922–85) was cremated at Linn Park. As manager between 1965 and 1978, Stein took Celtic FC to ten league titles and, in 1967, the European Cup, making them the first British holders. From 1978–82 Stein went on to manage Scotland's national team.

'CITY CEMETERY'

Spain's Luis Cernuda was among the greatest poets of the twentieth century. Glasgow was just one stage among many in the dismal odyssey of exile his life became after Franco's triumph. Between 1939 and 1943 he worked as a lector at the University, coaching undergraduates and loathing every minute. Commuting in to work each day from his lodgings he would see a graveyard from the train. In its dreariness it spoke to something deep within him, and he described it in one of his most famous poems (without, unfortunately, leaving us a clue to which 'City Cemetery' he was immortalizing):

> ... Not a leaf, not a bird. The stone and nothing
>   else. The earth.
> Is hell like this? Here there is pain without
>   forgetting,
> With noise and misery, long and hopeless cold.
> Here the silent sleep of death does not exist:
> Life still stirs among these graves, like a prostitute
> Plying her trade beneath the motionless night.
>
> When darkness falls from the cloudy sky
> And the smoke from the factories settles
> In grey dust, voices come from the pub,
> And then a passing train
> Whips up long echoes like an angry trump.
>
> It's not the Judgement yet, anonymous dead.
> Calm yourselves, sleep; sleep if you can.
> Maybe God too has forgotten you.

GREENOCK

You'll have to take the plaque's word for it that JOHN GALT (1779–1839) is buried here, in the Old Cemetery, Inverkip Street, since the graveyard isn't normally open to the public. His father a sea-captain, Galt had spent his youth here, the family having moved from Irvine, further down the Firth of Clyde, when he was ten. As a young man he went to London and pursued careers in business and letters with equal enthusiasm and pretty well equal erraticness. It would, finally, be as a writer that he made his mark, even though much of his work vanished on publication into instant obscurity. His business ventures (including a grandiose attempt to organize the settlement and development of Ontario) were all without exception failures, but some at least of his writing – notably the Ayrshire regional novels such as *Annals of the Parish* (1821) and *The Provost* (1822) – did endure, to be rediscovered with pleasure by modern readers.

HAMILTON

The mausoleum of DOUGLAS ALEXANDER, 10TH DUKE OF HAMILTON (1767–1852) was said to have cost £40,000 to construct and was intended to be the eighth wonder of the world. The duke, who believed he was the true heir to the Scottish throne and wanted an appropriately imposing resting place, had himself buried in the black marble sarcophagus of an Egyptian princess, for which alone he had paid £11,000. In 1927 the mausoleum was demolished and the Duke's remains removed to Bent Cemetery. The sarcophagus was examined by experts, and proved to have belonged not to a princess but to a court jester.

IONA

St Oran's Cemetery is the oldest Christian cemetery in Scotland. The small island of Iona was the bridgehead of the Irish monks who, led by St Columba, or Colmcille (521–97), first set out to convert Pictish Scotland, establishing a monastery here in 563. According to one tradition, Columba is buried here, which seems appropriate enough, but Irish tradition prefers to believe that he's buried with Patrick and Brigid in Downpatrick, Down. No fewer than forty-eight Scottish kings (not to mention some from Ireland and Norway) are thought to have been buried here. DUNCAN I (1001–40, reigned 1034–40) was famously murdered by another supposed Ionian inmate, MACBETH (c. 1005–57, reigned 1040–57). The chapel here was built in 1080 by Queen Margaret, it's said. These ancients were recently joined by the Labour Party leader JOHN SMITH (1938–94).

KILMARNOCK

In a corner of the Howard Park, a tablet marks the mass grave dug during the cholera epidemic of 1832.

RHU

In the churchyard here is the grave of engineer HENRY BELL (1767–1830), who first had the idea of using steam power for navigational purposes. In 1812 he successfully launched the 30-ton steamboat *Comet* on the Clyde, and for the next eight years it plied regularly between Greenock and Glasgow, providing Europe's first ever passenger steamboat service.

Tayside

ARBROATH

KING WILLIAM THE LION (1143–1214), the founder of the abbey in 1176, was buried here before the high altar.

DUNDEE

Howff Cemetery was given to the city in 1564 by Mary, Queen of Scots. The land had belonged to Greyfriars Friary before that was dissolved; it was outside the currently populated area, so seemed a healthy location. Up to 1776 it was used as a meeting place for trade and craft guilds as well as a burial ground, and many of the monuments bear interesting tradesmen's symbols. Notable inmates include JAMES CHALMERS (1782–1853), the Dundee bookseller and newspaper proprietor who invented the adhesive postage stamp and thus saved the new penny post system from collapse.

DUNKELD

Little Dunkeld, or Inver, across the river from Dunkeld proper, was the birth and burial place of the legendary fiddler NIEL GOW (1727–1807), composer and performer of reels and Strathspeys.

FORTINGALL

A cairn at the east end of the village marks the ground where plague victims were buried in the seventh and fourteenth centuries.

GASK, NEAR PERTH

No obvious traces remain, but in the chapel near the ruined Old House is the grave of secret songwriter CAROLINA OLIPHANT, BARONESS NAIRNE (1766–1845). The author of 'Caller Herrin'', 'The Hundred Pipers', 'Bonnie Charlie's Now Awa'', 'Will Ye No Come Back Again', and many, many more, her true identity was not revealed until after her death.

KIRRIEMUIR

SIR JAMES BARRIE (1860–1937) is buried here, in the New Church Cemetery. Born in Kirriemuir at 9 Brechin Road, now a Barrie museum, he referred to the town as 'Thrums' in his novels. Barrie's old age was marred by the heartbreak he felt over the death in 1921 of his ward Michael Llewelyn Davies – one of a family of young boys he'd befriended in a London park and adopted after the deaths of their parents. Michael's loss (he drowned in an Oxford bathing pool with a friend in what was suspected to have been a suicide pact, and was buried in London, in St John's churchyard, Hampstead) proved a crushing blow. He had already lost Michael's elder brother George, supposed to have been the original for Peter Pan, on the Western Front in 1915. Barrie could on occasion find some philosophical consolation, once jotting in his notebook:

> One who died is only a little ahead of procession all moving that way. When we round the corner we'll see him again. We have only lost him for a moment because we fell behind, stopping to tie a shoe-lace.

But for the best part of two decades grief was Barrie's more or less constant companion.

PERTH

Born locally, EUPHEMIA 'EFFIE' MILLAIS (née Gray, 1828–97) had the most famous pubic hair in history, the shocking discovery of this departure from the Greek classical norm, according to legend, having blighted the honeymoon and brief married life of critic and idealist John Ruskin. Ruskin's friend the Pre-Raphaelite painter John Everett Millais proved more worldly, however: the couple subsequently married and lived very happily together. Effie is buried here, in the Kinnoul graveyard, while her husband was given a St Paul's burial in London. Ruskin went single to his Coniston, Cumbria, grave.

Western Isles

BARRA

By the ruined church of St Barr at Eoligarry lies SIR COMPTON MACKENZIE (1883–1972), who lived on the island between 1934 and 1953 and set his 1947 novel *Whisky Galore* here. A larger-than-life character, Compton Mackenzie found time in between writing over a hundred books to serve as a spymaster in the Aegean during the First World War and to be tried afterwards for offences against the Official Secrets Act, to found and run *Gramophone* magazine, and to promote his own distinctively whimsical brand of Scottish nationalism. His funeral was an appropriately colourful affair: the piper who'd played the lament, an old friend of Compton Mackenzie's, keeled over and died as the service ended. 'There was a dramatic quality in that graveside death,' observes his biographer Andro Linklater, perhaps a little over-enthusiastically, 'which those familiar with Monty's life immediately recognised. It belonged to a more romantic age when a knight might share his sovereign's fate or a harper fall by his chieftain's side. In dying thus poignantly, Calum Johnston made heroic both his own end and the burial of the man he admired.'

KILMUIR, SKYE

In the churchyard here, her grave marked with a Celtic cross, lies FLORA MACDONALD (1722–90), wrapped in a sheet used by Bonnie Prince Charlie. In 1746 Flora brought the Young Pretender, disguised as her maid, from Benbecula to nearby Monkstadt House, when he was on the run after his defeat at Culloden. She was imprisoned in the Tower of London, but released the following year in the general amnesty. She emigrated to North Carolina in 1774, but returned home five years later. No longer quite such a young pretender, and extremely embittered, Charles Edward Stuart (1720–88) died in Rome and was buried in St Peter's. ◆

4

Wales

Ashes to Ashes

Dr William Price of Llantrisant, Mid Glamorgan, was by any standards a confirmed eccentric. Not only was he a vociferous supporter of the charter for people's democracy, which demanded a vote for every adult male, regardless of class or education; he also believed that he was a descendant of the Druids. When he was eighty-three, the young girl he had moved into his house bore him a child. Never one for modesty, Price called his son and heir Iesu Grist. Sadly, Iesu died in infancy, and it was now that Price pulled off what was perhaps his most egregious eccentricity and shouldered his way into funerary history. Taking the dead child to a nearby hilltop at Caerlan Field, he proceeded to cremate him. When they saw what was happening the local people were incensed. A crowd gathered, and Price was saved from lynching only by the intervention of the local constables. He was committed to the 1884 Cardiff Assizes and stood trial. To everybody's astonishment he was acquitted. He had, in effect, made cremation legal. Ten years later he himself died: he too was cremated at Caerlan Field, where a tablet has been placed in his memory by the Cremation Society.

Living as we do in a godless age in which even Christians understand the idea of bodily resurrection in a more figurative sense than they used to, the old fear of cremation has become difficult to understand. Not too long ago, however, the possession of all relevant limbs and bodily organs – albeit perhaps the worse for wear after centuries in the earth – was assumed to be a necessary precondition for resurrection on the Day of Judgement. It would be as an act of defiance against this view that the atheists, freethinkers and radicals who first had themselves cremated would take the stand that they did. Cremation stood for self-conscious modernity, for freedom from superstition. No longer a shocking gesture, cremation still seems distinctly 'modern', appealing as it does to the particular values of our age. Thanks to our obsession with efficiency and hygiene, cremation for many is the preferred option. Burial is about festering in a dank, dirty hole in the ground, where bugs creep and worms crawl and where the body gradually disintegrates year in, year out in slow, disgusting decay. Cremation, by contrast, is fast, fully automated and final.

It is also liberating. The new individualists don't want their bodies arranged according to the dictates of the Church in parish churchyards, or lined up by the state in uniform, regimented municipal cemeteries. Cremation offers the possibility of a privatized, personalized end. You can have your ashes buried with a parent or loved one, or scattered just about anywhere you like. In doing that you can in an important sense take control of what you are, and how you wish to be regarded. Where once your funeral and your gravestone defined you (your family's loving inscription far less eloquent in summing you up than the magnificence or otherwise of your gravestone), now you can define yourself. The ashes of engineer Roy Hughes, for instance, were recently placed in a tunnel deep beneath the streets of Liverpool: a devoted railwayman all his life, he had long envisioned – and finally designed – the central loop line that bound Merseyside's various suburban lines into a single continuous system. Now there's a corner of that system that is forever Roy Hughes.

The possibilities are endless. If you've lived all week for Saturday home games you can have your ashes scattered at the stadium: why go for hallowed ground when you can have hallowed turf? If you've lived most intensely walking with a lover or spouse – or just walking the dog – at some favourite beauty spot, no problem: you can have your ashes sprinkled there. Fell-walker Alfred Wainwright now bedecks a favourite mountaintop (see Buttermere, Cumbria), while birth-control campaigner Marie Stopes had herself tipped off a favourite cliff (see Portland Bill, Dorset). Anthony Blunt has his ashes scattered on the slopes of Martinsell hill (see Marlborough, Wiltshire) to commemorate not the sophisticated art historian, or the devious spy, but the ingenuous nature boy who went for country walks here with his brothers. Cremation is prized nowadays because it seems to streamline the business of death, to make everything simpler and more efficient. More efficient it may be, but simpler it certainly isn't: though they may not be set in stone any more, the rituals and symbolism of death are as complex as ever, and carry just as much force. The difference is that, where once it was the integrity of the corporeal body which had to be protected at all costs, now it's a less tangible – but equally sacrosanct – matter of personal identity.

Clwyd

COLWYN BAY

BERTRAND RUSSELL (1872–1970) lived near here at Plas Penryhn, on Portmeirion peninsula, and was cremated at the town crematorium. He'd insisted that there be no ceremony whatever, and no procession 'whether organized or spontaneous': his ashes were simply to be scattered. There's a memorial plaque to him in the chapel at Trinity College, Cambridge.

LLANGOLLEN

LADY ELEANOR BUTLER (1745–1829) and MISS SARAH PONSONBY (1755–1831) came from Ireland in 1779, having effectively eloped, and settled here at the house of Plas Newydd, where they lived together till they died – the former in 1829, the latter two years later. As the 'Ladies of Llangollen' they acquired fame for their strange cohabitation and their mannish attire, and many, including such illustrious personages as the Duke of Wellington, Sir Walter Scott and William Wordsworth, made the pilgrimage to see them. They had the exterior of the house bedecked with carvings by local craftsmen and the custom was for visitors to bring them a piece of wood-carving as a present; Wordsworth, it's said, brought a sonnet instead, but this wasn't well received. They're buried in the churchyard, along with their maid and friend Mary Caryll.

LLANSILIN

By the southern wall of the church is the grave of the Welsh-language Cavalier poet HUW MORUS (1622–1709).

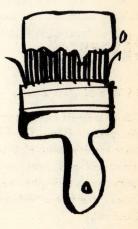

MOLD

Born at Penegoes, near Machynlleth, the landscape painter and portraitist RICHARD WILSON (1714–82) ended his days here, in the churchyard.

TREMEIRCHION

In the church here is the tomb of Hester Piozzi. Née Salusbury, Hester is best known as Dr Johnson's friend and correspondent MRS THRALE (1741–1821), the hostess to many of the gatherings at which, as recorded by Boswell, Dr Johnson spoke so wisely and well. The friendship foundered when, after the death of Mr Thrale, a respectable brewer, Hester married the Italian singer Gabriel Mario Piozzi, a match of which the learned doctor strongly disapproved.

WREXHAM

In the church of St Giles lies ELIHU YALE (1649–1721). His father, from a prominent local family, having emigrated in 1637, Yale was born in Boston, Massachusetts, but moved back to Britain at the age of four. As the East India Company's colonial administrator in Madras, he sent books and goods to Newhaven, Connecticut. They were then sold, the money raised being used to endow the university which bears his name. His tomb was restored by the university in 1874; the epitaph reads:

> *Born in America, in Europe bred,*
> *In Africa travelled and in Asia wed,*
> *Where long he lived and thrived; in London dead.*
> *Much good, some ill he did; so hope's all even,*
> *And that his soul through mercy's gone to heaven.*
> *You that survive and read his tale take care*
> *For this most certain exit to prepare.*
> *When blest in peace, the actions of the just*
> *Smell sweet and blossom in the silent dust.*

Dyfed

CARMARTHEN

In the church, along with various local dignitaries, lies SIR RICHARD STEELE (1672–1729), poet, playwright, essayist and (co-)founder with Joseph Addison of *Tatler* and *Spectator* magazines. He died here of a paralytic stroke, having some years previously arranged a burial in Westminster Abbey for his locally born wife. Steele's vault was reopened in 1876, when his skeleton was found to be wearing 'a peruke tied with a black bow'. There's no excuse for letting standards slip, even in death.

FISHGUARD

Carreg Gwasted Point, two and a half miles west of the town, was the scene in 1797 of the last ever invasion of Britain, when a French expeditionary force made its landing here. The intended destination had been Bristol, but bad weather necessitated the force's landing here. Jemima Nicholas, who is buried in Fishguard churchyard, captured several of the would-be invaders single-handed, armed only with a pitchfork.

LAUGHARNE

DYLAN THOMAS (1914–53), who lived here in the Boat House, Cliff Walk, was actually in New York when he went into that good night, but he was brought back here for burial. He's in the churchyard, his grave marked by a plain wooden cross. He always denied that Laugharne was the model for Llareggub, the setting for his most famous work, *Under Milk Wood*.

LLANDYFAELOG

In the churchyard lies the early Methodist leader PETER WILLIAMS (1723–96); his 1770 edition of the Bible was the first to be printed in Wales.

ST DAVID'S

In the cathedral incongruously placed in what can by any stretch of the imagination only be described as a village, Welsh patron ST DAVID (d. c. 601) is supposed to have been buried. Some bones found in a hidden recess behind the high altar during modern restorations could indeed be all that remains of his corporeal form.

The great chronicler and travel-writer GIRALDUS CAMBRENSIS (Girald de Barri, c. 1146–c. 1223) was based here for much of his life. He was elected bishop, but the appointment is thought to have been blocked by the English, fearing his nationalist, perhaps secessionist, ambitions for the Welsh Church. He was laid to rest in the cathedral – perhaps (though nobody really knows) in the south choir aisle. Here too was buried EDMUND TUDOR (c. 1430–56), who as father of Henry VII, first of the Tudor monarchs (see Westminster Abbey, London), has a good deal to answer for one way and another.

STRATA FLORIDA

A yew tree in the graveyard of the ruined Cistercian abbey is traditionally held to mark the grave of the fourteenth-century bard DAFYDD AP GWILYM. A lyric poet whose work combined earthiness and a love of nature with a sophisticated feel for the Welsh and continental literary traditions, he is generally considered to be the pre-eminent figure in Welsh poetry.

TALIESIN

A mile to the east of the village is an ancient tomb, said to be that of the sixth-century bard TALIESIN. It is by no means certain that Taliesin is buried here, of course; indeed there's some doubt as to whether he existed at all, the verse that has been ascribed to him having been most likely the work of a number of unknown poets.

Gwent

MATHERN, NEAR CHEPSTOW

In the chancel of the church by the north wall, as the slab says:

> *Here lyeth intombed the Body of Theoderick king of Morganuck or Glamorgan, commonly called St Thewdrick, and accounted a Martyr because he was slain in battle against the Saxons, being then Pagans, and in defence of the Christian Religion. The Battle was fought at Tintern, where he Obtained a Great Victory, he Died here being in his way homeward. Three Days after the Battle, having taken Order with Maurice his son who succeeded him in the Kingdom that in the same place he should happen to Decease a church should be built and his body buried in ye same, which was accordingly performed in the year 600.*

Repair work in 1881 uncovered a stone coffin — perhaps that of the King.

Gwynedd

BARDSEY ISLAND

No fewer than 20,000 saints are said to have been buried on this tiny island, which was a centre for Christianity from the sixth century, when St Cadfan founded the Abbey of St Mary. The sheer volume of sanctity here is supposed to have stemmed from the dark times of the seventh century, when Christianity was being driven out of England by Saxon invaders – then still pagans. No memorials to these saints have endured, but their bones are unearthed from time to time.

LLANFAIR

Beneath the communion table in the church lies ELLIS WYNNE (1671–1734), a preacher and writer in Welsh. His most enduring work *Y Bardd Cwsg* (The Sleeping Poet) is actually a version of a work by the Spanish writer Quevedo.

LLANYSTUMDWY

Though actually born in Manchester, DAVID LLOYD GEORGE, First Earl of Dwyfor (1863–1945) was to all intents and purposes a local boy. Left alone on the death of his father, his mother brought the year-old David and his older sister to live here with their uncle, a shoemaker. Prime minister during the First World War, Lloyd George spent a tempestuous half-century in the Commons (and thanks to his notorious womanizing had quite a complicated life outside it). His oratorical style wasn't universally approved. 'Mr Lloyd George...spoke for a hundred and seventeen minutes,' novelist Arnold Bennett reported on one occasion, 'in which period he was detected only once in the use of an argument.' He's buried on the bank of the River Dwyfor, his grave topped with a boulder taken from the river bed and inscribed with just his initials and dates.

PENMYNYDD, ANGLESEY

In St Gredifael's Church are various early Tudors, including Henry VII's great-grand-uncle GRONW FYCHAN, with whom the family's rise to power is believed to have begun in the fourteenth century.

Mid Glamorgan

ABERDARE

In the graveyard of the church of St John lies, or rather stands, David Williams (d. 1789). He insisted on being buried upright, so that he would be ready to answer the summons of the trump at the Last Judgement.

ABERFAN

The cemetery here has a memorial to 116 children and 28 adults killed in the disaster of 21 October 1966, when mining waste from a tip above the town poured down the hillside to engulf houses and the village school.

Powys

ABBEYCWMHIR

Practically nothing survives of what was once the biggest abbey in Wales, but you can just about make out where the high altar was, and there a thorn tree is said to mark the spot where the headless body of LLEWELYN, the last prince of an independent Wales, was buried secretly after he was killed by Edward I's men in 1282. His head was taken to London and exhibited on a spike in Cheapside.

CARNO

Designer and entrepreneur LAURA ASHLEY (1925–85) was buried in the churchyard here. She died after falling downstairs at her home.

LLANSANTFFRAED

In the churchyard beside the River Usk lies the local doctor and poet, HENRY VAUGHAN (c. 1621–95). In an age when most writers don't seem to have felt any strong regional identification, Vaughan was clear about the strength of his loyalty to his native Brecon. He referred to himself as a 'Silurist', from the ancient tribe, the Silures, who had once ruled the area, and in one poem he addressed the River Usk by its old name, declaring that he pursued fame for its benefit rather than his own:

> Isca, whensoever those shades I see
> And thy loved arbours must no more know me,
> When I am laid to rest hard by thy streams

And my sun sets where first it sprung its beams,
I'll leave behind me such a large, clear light
As shall redeem thee from oblivious night.

The poet would himself languish in oblivious night till
taken up by those interested in devotional verse in the
Victorian era, and then afterwards, in the twentieth
century, by literary critics interested in what had come to
be known as the 'Metaphysical Poetry' of the seventeenth
century.

BY THE RIVER USK

**Visiting the grave of seventeenth-century poet Henry
Vaughan in Llansantffraed, Siegfried Sassoon described
the scene:**

Above the voiceful windings of a river
An old green slab of simply graven stone
Shuns notice, overshadowed by a yew.
Here Vaughan lies dead, whose name flows on for
ever
Through pastures of the spirit washed with dew
And starlit with eternities unknown.
Here sleeps the Silurist; the loved physician;
The face that left no portraiture behind;
The skull that housed white angels and had vision
Of daybreak through the gateways of the mind.
   Here faith and mercy, wisdom and humility
   (Whose influence shall prevail for evermore)
   Shine. And this lowly grave tells Heaven's
    tranquillity.
   And here stand I, a suppliant at the door.

357

LLANWNOG

In the church is the tomb of JOHN CEIRIOG HUGHES (1832–87), most famous of the Welsh lyric poets. When he wasn't writing poetry he was stationmaster at Llanidloes and later manager of the Van Railway.

MONTGOMERY

The 'Robber's Grave' in St Nicholas' churchyard belongs to JOHN DAVIES, who was hanged in 1821 for highway robbery. He died protesting his innocence, however: in proof of this, he claimed, no grass would grow on his grave for a generation. So, apparently, it turned out.

NEWTOWN

In Old St Mary's churchyard by the river, beside the ruins of the church, is the grave of the socialist entrepreneur ROBERT OWEN (1771–1858). He was born in Newtown, though he's usually associated with New Lanark, Strathclyde, where in 1800 he began his great experiment in co-operative living and working. Owen managed to run his cotton-mill there profitably while still giving his hands the best in housing, healthcare and education. Other industrialists were duly impressed, though few in practice sought to emulate his methods. Radical commentators had mixed feelings: Owen's role might well be that of a benevolent despot, it was felt, but he was still very much the despot. It was always his mill, and what he said went.

South Glamorgan

FLAT HOLM ISLAND

The knights who murdered Thomas à Becket at Canterbury are supposd to have been buried on this island five miles off Penarth, though there doesn't seem to be any real evidence for this.

FLEMINGSTON

IOLO MORGANWG (Edward Williams, 1746–1826) died here and was buried in the churchyard. A stonemason and later a land surveyor by trade, he was also a self-taught poet and historian – and an accomplished forger. His taste for adding to and amending original Welsh manuscripts hasn't endeared him to his scholarly posterity, though all acknowledge his considerable gifts. The Gorsedd ritual which he devised as an approximation of an ancient Druidic ceremony has now been incorporated into the procedure of the National Eisteddfod.

West Glamorgan

ABERAVON

In the graveyard of the church of St Mary is martyr of the labour movement DIC PENDERYN (Richard Lewis), hanged for the part he was falsely alleged to have played in the

Merthyr Riots of 1831. He ended up being buried here in the middle of the night, after being refused interment in Cardiff, Llantrisant and Bridgend.

OYSTERMOUTH, BISHOPSTON

The prudish THOMAS BOWDLER (1754–1825), compiler of the notorious *Family Shakespeare*, is buried in the churchyard here. It's less well known that he borrowed a bowdlerized version of Gibbon too. ◆

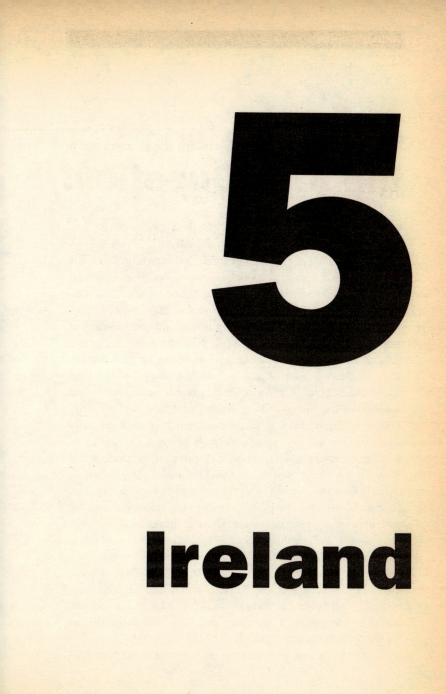

5

Ireland

Quicklime and the Irish Question

When is a grave not a grave? Deny the dead a proper grave and in some sense you obliterate their very identity. Hence, in the seventeenth and eighteenth centuries, those murderers for whom it was felt that 'hanging was too good' were given an extra turn of the retributive screw after their deaths when they were sent off, by order of the court, to the dissecting table.

Something of the same thinking lay behind the later use of quicklime in burying those executed by the Law. A greyish, strongly alkaline powder of calcium oxide, quicklime is fiercely corrosive, eating away at any organic material it comes into contact with. Heaped into a coffinless grave it wraps itself round the body within like (as Oscar Wilde put it, not too fancifully) a 'sheet of flame'. Now that cremation has become a generally acceptable option and people willingly consign themselves to the flames rather than envisage the prospect of undergoing natural decay in the ground, the idea of quicklime has lost much of its power to shock: after all, it only does slowly and chemically what is done in the crematorium. Looked at another way, indeed, it merely does quickly and inorganically what is done slowly and organically in the ground. In the past, when Christians still looked forward to the resurrection of the body and physical integrity was thus a matter of some importance, that wasn't how it seemed. There was a world of difference. Natural decay broke the body down, admittedly, but quicklime, like dissection, made it somehow cease to exist altogether, to vanish as though it had never been.

It is not surprising then that the state should use this method in dealing with its executed enemies. When the Easter Rising of 1916 was eventually put down and its ringleaders captured, they obviously had to be punished and it was decreed that they should be shot. The British commanding officer in Dublin, General Maxwell, scheduled 112 executions in all but was stopped after fifteen, prime minister Herbert Asquith having decided that enough was enough. After their execution by firing squad in a stone-breaking yard at Kilmainham prison, the bodies of Patrick Pearse, James Connolly, John MacBride, Joseph Plunkett and eleven other leading conspirators were taken to Arbour Hill Barracks and buried in quicklime there. This was more than a final bit of vindictiveness on the part of the government: flung in a limepit in an anonymous Arbour Hill yard, the rebels wouldn't have graves at all; it would be as if they, and their rebellion, had never happened. The families of the dead did ask that the bodies be returned so that they might be given a decent burial. Again, Asquith's instincts seem to have been humane. He was, however, talked out of it by Maxwell, who argued that 'Irish sentimentality will turn these graves into martyrs' shrines to which annual procession, etc, will be made which will cause constant irritation in this country.' Which is, interestingly enough, almost exactly what Pearse had said a year earlier beside the grave of O'Donovan Rossa (see Glasnevin, Dublin): 'They have left us the graves of our Fenian dead, and while Ireland has these graves Ireland unfree shall never be at peace.' General and rebel were of one mind, therefore, about the power of the grave as symbol and focus of resistance.

The problem for Maxwell was that if the existence of a grave was undesirable, the lack of one wasn't necessarily any better. For if a gravestone can be a shrine and a rallying point, it's also a good way of nailing a body down. The fate of Connolly, Pearse and their comrades set off a mood of resentment and rebellion in the Irish population which they had conspicuously failed to arouse when alive. Written a century earlier, Robert Emmet's 'Lines on Arbour Hill' proved prophetic:

> *No rising column marks this spot,*
> *Where many a victim lies,*
> *But oh the blood which here has streamed,*
> *To heaven for justice cries.*

Graveless as they were, the men of 1916 represented an enormous item of national unfinished business.

Antrim

BELFAST

ST ANNE'S CATHEDRAL: In the magnificent marbled nave of the cathedral on Donegall Street is the tomb of SIR EDWARD CARSON (1854–1935), who promised civil war if the government's Home Rule Bill went through: 'Ulster will fight, and Ulster will be right,' he roared. People have a one-dimensional view of Ulster Unionism. In addition to Carson the founder of the UVF there was a cuddly Carson who supported women's suffrage and opposed the death penalty. There was even Carson the wit: when placed in charge of the Admiralty on the formation of the coalition of 1916, he observed waggishly, 'My only great qualification for being put in charge of the Navy is that I am very much at sea.' Then too there was Carson the barrister: in 1895, as a young QC, he had defended the Marquess of Queensberry against the misguided libel suit brought by Oscar Wilde, which Carson and Queensberry were able to turn into a trial of Wilde himself for homosexuality. Queensberry was acquitted, and Wilde was ruined.

STORMONT CASTLE: Strictly speaking across the county line in Down is Stormont Castle. Here, in an enclosed plot east of the parliament building, is the tomb of JAMES CRAIG, FIRST VISCOUNT CRAIGAVON (1871–1940), and Lady Craigavon. A militant opponent of the Home Rule Bills proposed by Gladstone and Asquith, he was one of the founders of 'Northern Ireland', and its first prime minister. 'Ours is a Protestant Government and I am an Orangeman,' he said, just in case there should be any doubt. In 1929 he abolished proportional representation in the province, worried that the electorate might make 'mistakes'.

Armagh

ARMAGH

BRIAN BORU (c. 941–1014), King of Munster who went on to make himself King of all Ireland, was buried with great ceremony in what is now the Anglican Cathedral.

LURGAN

Here, in the graveyard of Shankill Church, lies Margorie McCall: 'lived once, buried twice', according to her gravestone. By tradition, she 'died' around the 1850s and was duly interred. Once darkness had fallen, graverobbers after the rings the corpse was known to be wearing stole into the churchyard and dug the coffin up again. Opening it, the resurrectionists realized they'd resurrected more than they'd bargained for when the dead woman stepped out – now apparently fully recovered from her coma. Margorie went straight home (her mother getting almost as much of a shock as the graverobbers when she heard her daughter's distinctive knock on the door) and picked up her life where she'd left off, going on to have children and live out her natural span in the usual way. In the fullness of time she died again and was reburied: this time for keeps.

Clare

FEAKLE

In an unmarked grave somewhere in the churchyard lies the Gaelic poet BRIAN MERRIMAN (1747–1805). The illegitimate son of a country gentleman, Merriman was a native of Clare and lived for many years in Feakle, working as a schoolteacher and farmer, before moving to Limerick where he remained until his death. The action of his great burlesque epic *The Midnight Court* (1780; this translation by Thomas Kinsella) unfolded a few miles up the road from Feakle, near Lough Graney. There the narrator falls asleep one afternoon and finds himself at a remarkable trial at which a tribunal of women, headed by a formidable matriarch, hears the cases against husbands and wives argued

back and forth by witnesses in hilarious and highly indelicate
terms. In the end, unsurprisingly, the men are judged to have
failed their women – in life in general and in bed in
particular. Turning on the astonished narrator, like Merriman
himself an unmarried man, the matriarch declares that he is
to be the first miscreant punished under a new ruling:

> We enact hereby as a law for women:
> a man twenty-one and not yoked to a mate,
> to be forcibly dragged by the head, without pity
> and tied to this tree beside this tomb.
> There strip him bare of jacket and vest
> and flay with a rope his back and his waist.
> All such persons brimming with years
> who basely conceal their under-spike
> letting go to waste, with joy toward none,
> clout of their balls and vigour of limb
> – hoarding their maleness, with women available
> hanging unplucked on the branches above –
> lascivious ladies, dark with lust,
> I leave it to you to handle their pains!
> Invent ordeals of fire and nails,
> spend womanly thoughts and brains upon it,
> assemble your counsels all together
> and I'll sanction you for the use of force...

Fortunately, before the penalty can be exacted, the terrified
narrator wakes up in a cold sweat. The shortage of young
men which made able-bodied bachelorhood a crime and
which condemned lusty girls to wed doddery old fools is
treated with joyous comedy in *The Midnight Court*, but
beneath the raunchy humour the poem hints at the tragedy
of a dispossessed nation depleted by emigration, its men

forced into exile, to seek a livelihood in America or to serve
in the armies of Britain and Europe.

Cork

BLACKROCK

In the graveyard of St Michael's Church of Ireland church is
the mathematician GEORGE BOOLE (1815–64) who until his
death (from the pneumonia which developed after he was
caught out in a sudden shower) had taught at the University
of Cork. He'd been awarded a chair there despite the fact
that, a cobbler's son from Lincoln, he had no degree and was
largely self-taught. He had none the less managed to do
pioneering work in logic and, of course, develop 'Boolean
Algebra'.

CASTLETOWNSHEND

Side by side in the graveyard of the Church of Ireland church
of St Barrahane lie the cousins EDITH SOMERVILLE
(1858–1949) and Violet Martin (1862–1915) – better known
by her nom-de-plume MARTIN ROSS – who collaborated on
the twee and rather patronizing but hugely successful
Experiences of an Irish R.M., about the winning ways of the
Irish peasantry as exhibited before the bench of an Anglo-
Irish resident magistrate. Somerville lived in the village, at
Drishane House. Her burial degenerated into farce, when
the place she'd requested next to Martin proved to be
solid rock, completely defeating the gravediggers' spades. A

neighbour sent in search of dynamite eventually managed to beg some from a nearby Garda barracks, but the blast broke the cross on Martin's grave, and it had to be restored.

CORK

The English composer SIR ARNOLD BAX (1883–1953) died here and is buried in St Finbarr's cemetery. A confirmed celtophile, Bax also wrote stories under the name Dermot O'Byrne.

FARAHY

The big house, Bowen's Court, was demolished in 1960 and the church is no longer used, but the graveyard is still there, with the graves of the Bowen family, including the novelist ELIZABETH BOWEN (1899–1973), perhaps the last representative of a vanished tradition of distinctly Anglo-Irish literature.

Donegal

STRANORLAR

In the Protestant churchyard here is the grave of ISAAC BUTT (1813–79), a barrister and founder of the Irish Home Rule movement. A man of considerable culture, he published a translation of Virgil's *Georgics*, but he scandalized respectable opinion in the 1860s by defending the Fenian prisoners in court.

Down

DOWNPATRICK

According to an ancient tradition, the churchyard here boasts no fewer than three top saints – PATRICK (c. 390–c. 461), BRIGID (d. c. 525) and COLMCILLE (c. 521–97; but see also Iona, Strathclyde) – in one grave, which is now marked with a monolith of Mourne granite.

Dublin

DUBLIN

ST PATRICK'S CATHEDRAL: The tomb of JONATHAN SWIFT (1667–1745), Dean of St Patrick's and 'English' literature's most bitter, scathing – and entertaining – satirist, is here. By his own orders 'deeply cut and strongly gilded', the Latin epitaph he composed for himself is inscribed on a tablet placed in the wall seven feet above the grave. The inscription was later translated by Yeats:

> *Swift has sailed into his rest;*
> *Savage indignation there*
> *Cannot lacerate his breast.*
> *Imitate him if you dare,*
> *World-besotted traveller, he*
> *Served human liberty.*

A recent biographer, David Nokes, notes that in this epitaph Swift is, for all his clerical cloth, 'as always, silent on the prospects of another world'.

ST ANN'S CHURCH: Liverpool-born poet FELICIA HEMANS (1793–1835), the perpetrator of the immortal poem 'The Boy Stood on the Burning Deck', lived just up from St Ann's on Dawson Street. Her own verses on her monument give a fair idea of her poetic style:

> Calm on the bosom of thy God
> Fair spirit! rest thee now.
> E'en while on earth thy foot-steps trod
> His seal was on thy brow.
> Dust to its narrow house beneath
> Soul to its place on high.
> They that have seen thy look in death
> No more may fear to die.

ST WERBURGH'S CHURCH, WERBURGH ST: In one of twenty-seven vaults in the crypt here is the tomb of LORD EDWARD FITZGERALD (1763–98), cashiered from the army after joining in a toast to the abolition of hereditary titles during a visit to revolutionary Paris, where he stayed as a guest of Tom Paine. One of Wolfe Tone's United Irishmen, he died of wounds sustained while resisting arrest.

KILMAINHAM: Its elegant façade thrown into sharp relief by the intimidating bulk of the neighbouring prison, what was founded in 1688 as the Royal Hospital – Dublin's equivalent of London's Chelsea Hospital – now houses the collection of the Irish Museum of Modern Art instead of grizzled British army veterans. Many old soldiers remain, however, awaiting the reveille of the Last Day. A complex of three burial grounds was associated with the hospital: one for officers, one for squaddies and the third, Bully's Acre, a free cemetery that naturally became popular with the city's poor. There was rioting when in 1764 the hospital, worried about overcrowding, attempted to close access. The headless body of rebel ROBERT EMMET (1778–1803) was brought here after his execution and buried with his follower Felix Rourke, but it was secretly moved soon after, nobody really knows where. Emmet had a thing or two to say about death and burial, notably in his famous speech from the dock at his trial:

> I have but a few more words to say... I am going to my cold and silent grave – my lamp of life is nearly extinguished – my race is run – the grave opens to receive me, and I sink into its bosom. I have but one request to make at my departure from this world, it is – the charity of its silence. Let no man write my epitaph; for as no man who knows my motives dare now vindicate them, let not prejudice or ignorance asperse them. Let them rest in obscurity and peace. Let my memory be left in oblivion, my tomb remain uninscribed, until other times and other men can do justice to my character. When my country takes her place among the nations of the earth, then, and not till then, let my epitaph be written.

They'll have to find him first: when Emmet considers Ireland truly has taken her place among the nations of the earth, perhaps he'll vouchsafe just where it is he wants that epitaph to be placed?

Bully's Acre was closed in 1832, the cholera epidemic of that year having left it dangerously overfilled.

THE LEGEND OF ROBERT EMMET

Coming in 1803, just a few years after the suppression of the United Irishmen's Rising, Robert Emmet's insurrection-ette was history repeating itself, the second time as farce. Since the Irish love a loser even more than the English do, Emmet acquired mythical status, Tom Moore's famous poem capturing the somewhat sugary potency of his legend:

> Oh breathe not his name, let it sleep in the shade,
> Where cold and unhonour'd his relics are laid;
> Sad, silent, and dark, be the tears that we shed,
> As the night-dew that falls on the grass o'er his
>   head!
> But the night-dew that falls, though in silence it
>   weeps,
> Shall brighten with verdure the grave where he
>   sleeps,
> And the tear that we shed, though in secret it rolls,
> Shall long keep his memory green in our souls.

GLASNEVIN CEMETERY: Like the great municipal cemeteries of Britain, Dublin's biggest public cemetery, on Finglas Road, was founded in the mid-nineteenth century. From the first it was open to all, but since Protestants traditionally preferred the more exclusive Mount Jerome, it tends to be associated with Catholics. Glasnevin was immortalized in literature by James Joyce's *Ulysses* (1922), in which Leopold Bloom comes here for the burial of Paddy Dignam. Like many before him, Bloom is struck by the sheer volume of activity at Glasnevin: 'must be twenty or thirty funerals every day,' he muses. Joyce himself – like his wife, Nora Barnacle – was buried in Zurich. Moves to have him brought back in time for the 1982 centenary of his birth were not successful. It's not clear in any case what he would have thought of the idea. He did after all choose a life, if not of silence, at least of exile and punning: it's hard to see him – even after forty years in the cold Swiss ground – submitting tamely to a reverent, dignitary's burial in his home city. In the absence of the son, you can at least see the parents: Mary Jane Murray and John Stanislaus Joyce are both buried here.

Many more famous Irish people have gathered about their heads what Yeats rather quaintly called the 'Glasnevin coverlet', including several of the heroes of Irish Nationalism, starting with DANIEL O'CONNELL (1775–1847), whose funeral was the first of the great occasions of mass mourning in which Ireland would come to specialize. The London *Times* didn't, presumably, feel his loss quite so deeply, having once even felt the need to break into verse to describe him as:

> *Scum condensed of Irish bog,*
> *Ruffian, coward, demagogue,*
> *Boundless liar, base detractor,*
> *Nurse of murders, treason's factor.*

The Liberator was buried minus his heart (which at his request was sent to Rome in a silver urn) beneath a grand monument. But perhaps the biggest outpouring of national mourning would be for CHARLES STEWART PARNELL (1846–91), brought back to Ireland after his death in exile in Brighton. Parnell's funeral procession numbered 30,000, was watched by 130,000 spectators, and took the whole day to wend its way across Dublin to Glasnevin. Wreaths proclaimed that the Chief had been 'murdered by priests', the mourners' grief perhaps heightened by the shameful awareness that they'd allowed themselves to be manipulated by the British, who had indeed exploited Irish sanctimoniousness to devastating effect. Parnell had attempted to promote the cause of Home Rule, but a discomfited London managed to foster the idea that, as the parish priest of Roundwood, Wicklow, put it for the ready comprehension of his rustic flock: 'Parnellism is a simple love of adultery and all those who profess Parnellism profess to love and admire adultery.' It was early evening by the time the burial took place: the young Maud Gonne, who was there in the crowd, would later tell Yeats that she had seen a shooting star fall just as the coffin was lowered into the ground. It sounds fanciful, and nobody else among the many thousands present seems to have noticed it. According to historian Robert Kee, however, the astronomical records confirm her claim. Shared with his mother Delia, whose Fenian activities had so shocked her son as a grave young Cambridge undergraduate, Parnell's grave has since 1940 been surmounted by a granite boulder brought from his native Wicklow, and inscribed simply 'Parnell'. The woman who 'brought him down', Kitty O'Shea (Katharine Parnell, in fact, since she had married him three months before he died) didn't fare so well, getting a regular grave in the town cemetery at Littlehampton, West Sussex, where she was living at the time of her death.

The Fenian leader JOHN O'LEARY (1830–1907) is buried at Glasnevin, the interment more famous than the man thanks to Yeats' poem 'September 1913', whose refrain runs: 'Romantic Ireland's dead and gone,/It's with O'Leary in the grave.' What's actually with O'Leary in the grave is his protégé, the writer and patriot JAMES STEPHENS

(1880–1950), buried beside his mentor and friend. Another Fenian whose burial arguably counted for more than his life was GEREMIAH O'DONOVAN ROSSA (1831–1915), at whose burial Patrick Pearse gave the unforgettable speech that set the stage for his rising of the following year (and stressed once again the centrality of the grave in the Irish mythic order):

> *Life springs from death and from the graves of patriot men and women spring living nations. The Defenders of this Realm have worked well in secret and in the open. They think that they have purchased half of us and intimidated the other half. They think that they have foreseen everything, they think they have provided against everything; but the fools, the fools, they have left us our Fenian dead, and while Ireland holds these graves Ireland unfree shall never be at peace.*

Pearse's fervour for blood-sacrifice is notorious, though in his personal life, it's said, he was a gentle man, and so squeamish he could hardly endure the sight of a cut finger.

Another rebel snuggling down beneath the Glasnevin coverlet is MICHAEL COLLINS (1890–1922), who outraged Republican feelings by first supporting the 1921 treaty settling for a North-less Free State and then becoming president of its provisional government. In 1920, amid the non-stop troubles of the war against the British, he'd asked in a letter, 'When will it all end? When can a man get down to a book in peace?' He was never to catch up on his reading, being killed two years later in an ambush by diehard Republicans (only the most determined conspiracy theorists really believe they were British agents), his signature of the treaty having represented, as he'd realized himself at the time, the signing of his own death warrant. His limestone cross monument was, apparently, all that President de Valera would allow. Dev had always been jealous of Collins, says his biographer Tim Pat Coogan, and he was afraid of being embarrassed or upstaged by some more elaborate memorial with a potentially inflammatory inscription. Collins' supporter over the 1921 treaty, the Sinn Fein founder ARTHUR GRIFFITH (1871–1922), is also buried here.

A late arrival among the dead of 1922 is ERSKINE CHILDERS (1870–1922). Best known to British readers for his classic adventure novel *The Riddle of the Sands* (1903), Childers, who came from an Anglo-Irish background, served in British intelligence for some years. He got a bit overexcited later in life, though, and, as Winston Churchill put it, 'espoused the Irish cause with even more than Irish irreconcilability'. The Free State government didn't look too kindly on his romantic ardour, and condemned him to death – which was only encouraging him in his mood of martyrdom. 'It seems perfectly simple and inevitable,' he thrilled in a letter to his wife from Death Row, 'like lying down after a long day's work.' He was killed by a firing squad and his body thrown into a grave at Beggar's Bush, then two years later, when tempers had cooled and nerves calmed a little, given a proper burial here among the heroes.

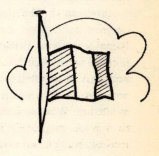

Where's Maud gone? MAUD GONNE MACBRIDE

(1865–1953), the unrequiting love of W.B. Yeats (and one of the relatively few Irish rebels to have been born in Aldershot), is here in Glasnevin, as is COUNTESS CONSTANCE MARKIEWICZ (1868–1927), another of the fiery women of Irish Republicanism. The Liverpool-born Republican and Labour leader JIM LARKIN (1876–1947) was also buried here. The government turned a blind eye while playwright, personality and sometime volunteer BRENDAN BEHAN (1923–64), was being buried here by the IRA with full military honours.

The following year the remains of SIR ROGER CASEMENT (1864–1916) were abruptly returned by the new Wilson government in London, half a century after his execution for treason at Pentonville. Given that his body had been buried in quicklime at Pentonville after his execution, there wasn't too much left of him: it was even suggested that his remains might have become mingled with those of the notorious serial murderer, Crippen, executed around the same time. Such as they were, however, they were buried in a plot which had been kept in readiness to receive Casement, but which nobody had really been expecting to use. Casement was arrested on the Kerry coast after being landed by a German submarine: he'd been trying to organize co-operation between Britain's enemies in Ireland and Germany. A controversial figure in the Republican movement, there's still been no absolutely definitive proof as to whether the notorious diary, which indicates the hero's homosexuality, is the real thing or, as many in Ireland have always insisted, a British forgery. (Recent tests seem to confirm its authenticity. The motive for the forgery has never in any case been as clear-cut as many nationalists have assumed: if a 'genuine' verdict confirms the unthinkable thought that an Irish patriot might have been homosexual, it authenticates other less convenient things in the diary too, such as Casement's testimony on British-backed atrocities in Africa.)

EAMON DE VALERA (1882–1975) was not to be denied his place among Ireland's fallen heroes. The President of Sinn Fein and then founder of Fianna Fáil, Dev bitterly opposed the Free State's very formation but then clung limpet-like to power for much of its subsequent history, being Taoiseach for most of the 1940s and 1950s and then President from 1959 to 1973.

Glasnevin also provides an ignominious last resting place for sensitive plant GERARD MANLEY HOPKINS (1844–89), who regarded his time in Ireland, whither he was sent by his Jesuit masters to drill unwilling farmboys in Classics at the Catholic University, as a dreary exile among the barbarians. 'Tomorrow I shall have been three years in Ireland, three hard wearying years,' he wrote to his friend Robert Bridges in 1887. 'In those I have done God's will (in the main) and many many examination papers.' He's buried in an unmarked grave, just to the left of the entrance of the Jesuit plot.

MOUNT JEROME: Despite his Catholicism, Gerard Manley Hopkins might have felt a little more at home among the better sort in the Ascendancy cemetery of Mount Jerome than in Glasnevin. Distinguished denizens include SIR WILLIAM ROWAN HAMILTON (1805–65), who could speak thirteen different languages by the age of nine, and won Trinity College's Chair in Astronomy (and the position of Irish Astronomer Royal) when he was still an undergraduate. He was probably really boring. Be that as it may, his radical work in the field of algebra was to prove of enormous importance. He it was who invented the notion of quaternions, and with them a new algebraic approach to three-dimensional geometry. As Samuel Butler put it:

In mathematics he was greater
Than Tycho Brahe or Erra Pater
For he by geometric scale
Could take the size of pots of ale.

The novelist JOSEPH SHERIDAN LE FANU (1814–73) is also here. Great grand-nephew of the dramatist Richard Brinsley Sheridan (who's in Westminster Abbey), he specialized in occult mysteries and chillers. GEORGE RUSSELL, 'AE' (1867–1909), poet, painter, journalist and mystic, is here too, as is playwright JOHN MILLINGTON SYNGE (1871–1935), whose *The Playboy of the Western World* provoked rioting at its first performance at the Abbey Theatre in 1907 with its outrageous suggestion that Irish peasants might take in an avowed murderer. The artist JACK B. YEATS (1871–1957) was buried here. Unfortunately, it was decided not to use the epitaph he'd written for himself some years earlier:

Under no stones
Nor slates
Lies Jack B.
Yeats.
No heaped up rocks.
Just a collection box,
And we thought a Nation's folly
Would like to be jolly
And bury in state
This singular Yeat.
But they were not so inclined
Therefore if you've a mind
To slide a copper in the slot
'Twill help to sod the plot.

Well, W.B. Yeats couldn't paint. His grave is, of course, at Drumcliffe, Sligo. Their father John Butler Yeats, another eminent artist, died in New York and is buried up in the Adirondacks, at Chestertown.

Born in Ayr, but a resident of Dublin for three decades, JOHN BOYD DUNLOP (1840–1921), the inventor in 1888 of the pneumatic tyre, is buried in Deansgrange, as, beneath a vast tombstone of white marble topped by a bronze bust, is tenor JOHN McCORMACK (1884–1945), who abandoned a successful international career in opera for what turned out to be a no less successful career as singer of Irish ballads. A few days after his death, a mysterious note in McCormack's hand was found, which seemed to suggest that the singer had had some premonition of a death which had actually come quite suddenly after an attack of pneumonia:

> I have lived again the days and nights of my long career. I dreamed at night of operas and concerts in which I had my share of success.
>
> Now like the old Irish minstrels, I have hung up my harp – for my songs are all sung.

His own harp hung up, the Cork-born short story writer FRANK O'CONNOR (1903–66) was also buried here, albeit rather less ostentatiously.

Just to the northeast of Dublin, in St Finstan's graveyard, Sutton, is writer PADRAIC COLUM (1882–1972), immortalized by James Joyce as 'Patrick What-do-you-Colum', with his wife Mary, also a writer.

PORTMARNOCK

His own being over, *This Is Your Life* presenter EAMONN ANDREWS (1922–87) took up residence here, in Balfinnan Cemetery.

Galway

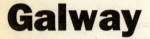

GALWAY

In the city's Bohermore Cemetery is the grave of WILLIAM
JOYCE (c. 1906–46). Known as 'Lord Haw-Haw' on account
of the plummy tones of his wartime broadcasts from Berlin,
Joyce's origins were actually pretty obscure, his connection
with Galway fairly tenuous. Born in Brooklyn, New York,
to an Irish father and an English mother, he came with them
to Ireland in 1914, but the family stayed only eight years
before moving on to England. In 1933, Joyce joined
Mosley's British Union of Fascists, but he was expelled in
1937 and founded his own British National Socialist Party,
giving unequivocal backing to Hitler. Joyce went to
Germany just before war broke out. He was arrested while
trying to escape in 1945, and hanged at Wandsworth. His
remains were moved here in 1976.

One of the luminaries of the Celtic Twilight, the co-
founder with Yeats and Synge of Dublin's famous Abbey
Theatre, the dramatist and folklorist Isabella Augusta, LADY
GREGORY (1852–1932) is here too, with her sister Arabella.
A proud aristocrat, she'd found herself out of sympathy with
the New Ireland and had left her Coole Park, Sligo home,
the scene of important literary and political gatherings in
years gone by, to live with Arabella in Galway.

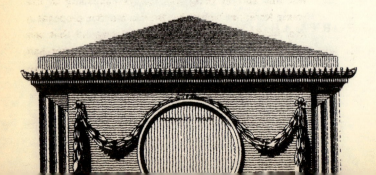

RAIN ON RAHOON

A little way outside the town of Galway in the little cemetery at Rahoon lies Michael Bodkin, an early sweetheart of Nora Barnacle, Mrs James Joyce, and traditionally believed to be the original for Michael Furey in the story 'The Dead'. The night before Nora's departure for Dublin in 1900, in heavy rain, the twenty-year-old Bodkin, a TB sufferer, had left his sickbed to serenade her, dying of exposure as a result. Not surprisingly, such sublimity in love left Joyce feeling rather inadequate. He commemorated the event also in the poem 'She Weeps Over Rahoon':

> Rain on Rahoon falls softly, softly falling,
> Where my dark lover lies.
> Sad is his voice that calls me, sadly calling,
> At grey moonrise.
>
> Love, hear thou
> How soft, how sad his voice is ever calling,
> Ever unanswered, and the dark rain falling,
> Then as now.
>
> Dark too our hearts, O Love, shall lie and cold
> As his sad heart has lain
> Under the moongrey nettles, the black mould
> And muttering rain.

But this sort of thing was always happening to the young Nora: her biographer Brenda Maddox proposes a rival for the Michael Furey role, pointing out that one Michael Feeney, a sixteen-year-old schoolteacher, had died of pneumonia in very similar circumstances three years earlier, when Nora was nearly thirteen.

Kerry

MUCKROSS

Just to the north of the village are the ruins of Killegy Church. The churchyard is dominated by the tombs of the local Herberts of Muckross, but the modern visitor is more likely to be interested in a man who was briefly one of their employees, RUDOLF ERICH RASPE (1737–94), who is also buried here. The Hanover-born geologist would have been surprised if he'd known he was destined to lie beneath such a very western sky, and appalled if he'd known he was going to owe his place in posterity to the book *Baron Munchausen's Narrative of his Marvellous Travels and Campaigns in Russia*, which he published anonymously in 1785, not feeling that writing fiction was a fit occupation for a scientist. A geologist of undoubted ability and impressive energy, Raspe poured all the money he had into the quixotic attempt to develop and test a grand geological theory of everything he had come up with. When he had nothing left, he pawned antique coins and medals belonging to his German employer the Landgrave of Hesse-Kassel, of whose collections he'd been given the curatorship. A bad move. Inevitably, he was found out, and he had to leave Germany in something of a hurry. He worked for a time in England and Scotland before washing up here, where he'd been given a job managing the copper mines on the Muckross Estate. He died a year after his arrival.

Nearby, to the west of the village, is Muckross Abbey. Two great Irish bards are buried here. EOGHAN RUADH Ó SÚILLEABHÁIN, or Owen Roe O'Sullivan (1748–84), was murdered by servants of a Colonel Cronin, who had taken violent exception to one of O'Sullivan's irreverent satires.

Don't worry if you hear muffled shouting underfoot: you're just walking on the grave of the great lyric poet AODHAGÁN Ó RATHAILLE, or O'Rahilly (1670–1726). 'I shall not cry for help until I am placed in a closed coffin,' he announced in his last poem. A fiercely proud, patriotic man, O'Rahilly felt nothing but contempt for the incoming planters taking over Ireland in his day. They were worthless barbarians all, he considered.

Kildare

BODENSTOWN

In the graveyard of the Church of Ireland church lies THEOBALD WOLFE TONE (1763–98), the leader of the United Irishmen's Rising of 1798. Captured by the British, he attempted suicide on the morning he was supposed to be hanged, 12 November 1798. 'I find I am but a bad anatomist,' he's said to have whispered to the doctor who attended him after it turned out he'd painstakingly sawed through his windpipe instead of cutting his jugular vein. He did eventually die of these wounds, but not until several days after his execution had been scheduled. Never did a hero make such a thoroughgoing hash of his death as Tone – and never does it seem to have mattered less. His grave is Irish Nationalism's holiest shrine, with annual pilgrimages on the Sunday after his birthday, 20 June. Different groups, from the army of the Irish Republic to the Irish Republican Army, process to the grave – in strict rota to avoid embarrassment or worse – and honour it according to their own distinctive traditions.

OUGHTERARD

In a vault beside the ruins of an ancient hilltop round tower lies the original genius ARTHUR GUINNESS (1725–1803). After the success of the local brewery he started in Lexslip in the 1750s, he seriously considered setting up in Wales, before finally plumping for Dublin in 1759. He didn't buy the St James' Gate site outright, but took a 9,000-year lease, which means there's only 8,800 years' drinking-up time to go. There was some dispute at first over water rights at the site, the city corporation claiming he wasn't entitled to use the water there. The sheriff's men came round, but Guinness saw them off with a pickaxe, and they haven't been back since.

Londonderry

DERRY

In Derry City Cemetery lies MRS C.F. ALEXANDER (1818–95), author of such hit hymns as 'All things bright and beautiful', 'Once in royal David's city' and 'There is a green hill far away'. Her husband WILLIAM ALEXANDER (1824–1911), Bishop of Derry and ultimately Primate of All Ireland, was buried beside her.

Louth

DROGHEDA

In the north transept of St Peter's Church is the head of ST OLIVER PLUNKETT (1625–81) who more or less clandestinely served as Archbishop of Armagh, till he was arrested and taken to London to stand trial on trumped-up charges stemming from the trumped-up 'Popish Plot' of 1678. He was executed at Tyburn in 1681, the last Catholic to be martyred there. There wasn't too much left of him by the time the executioners had finished, but apart from this head there are some other relics in England, at Downside Abbey in Somerset and in St-Giles-in-the-Fields, London. Plunkett's canonization in 1975 was a major event for Catholic Ireland, the much-vaunted Land of Saints and Scholars not in fact having produced another saint in 750 years. (The last had been St Laurence O'Toole (1128–80), who died in France and was buried there at Eu; he was canonized in 1225.)

Mayo

BALLYNAKILL

Here halfway between Moyard and Cleggan is OLIVER ST JOHN GOGARTY (1878–1957), a poet and later a politician, but most famous simply as a (sometimes oppressively) larger-than-life personality and raconteur, in which capacity he would serve as the original for Buck Mulligan in Joyce's *Ulysses*. His house at Renvyle was burned out in 1923 by the IRA, who had taken exception to his public support for the Free State Treaty.

CASTLEBAR

What's left of the ancestral home of the Moore family, Catholic landowners, is a few miles south of here on the shores of Lough Carra. Beneath a cairn on Castle Island, the ashes of the family's most distinguished son, the artist, novelist and critic GEORGE MOORE (1852–1933), are buried. Cremated in London, where he had lived for most of his adult life, his ashes were brought back to Ireland in an urn he'd had copied from a bronze-age urn in a Dublin museum. The local people weren't wild about either Moore's studiedly immoral, decadent novels or the exaggerated disdain he liked to express towards the Irish, but it was his family's Free State sympathies in the Civil War that proved the last straw. The house was burned out by the IRA in 1923, and has been a blackened ruin ever since.

CRAUGHWELL

In Killeenan church is the grave of the blind Irish-language poet ANTOINE Ó REACHTABHRA, or Raftery (1784–1835). The last great representative of an ancient tradition, his oral poetry wasn't written down till the end of the nineteenth century, when it was taken up by the folklore movement.

STRAIDE

MICHAEL DAVITT (1846–1906) was born here, but his family was evicted when he was six, and forced to emigrate to Lancashire. There, at the age of eleven, he lost his arm while working in a cotton mill. As a young man he worked clandestinely with the Fenians for a time before coming out into the open to agitate directly against landlordism and its abuses, founding the Land League. There's a plaque and a tall cross on the grave, which is in an atmospheric setting near a ruined friary. (It's not reported where Davitt's arm was buried: he was young and obscure at the time he lost it, and in any case, for all Ireland's relish for funerals, there's never been anything to match the behaviour of Mexican *caudillo* Santa Anna, who staged a full state funeral for his leg in 1838 – the rest of him lived until 1876.)

Monaghan

INNISKEEN

In the churchyard lies locally born poet PATRICK KAVANAGH (1904–67), whose grim 1942 masterpiece *The Great Hunger* paints a disenchanted picture of the Irish rural idyll in all its emotional and sexual deprivations. Two stepping stones from the nearby stream have been lain across the grave (if you get your feet wet, you know who to blame); one is inscribed:

> *There were stepping stones across a stream. Part of my life was there. The happiest part.*

There's also a cross at the head of the grave, with the inscription:

> *And pray for him who walked apart on the hills loving life's miracles.*

A death-mask completes the scene. This adds up to quite a lot of commemoration for a poet who asked, in his 'Lines Written on a Seat on the Grand Canal, Dublin':

> *O commemorate me with no hero-courageous Tomb – just a canal-bank seat for the passer-by.*

In the event he would get this too, his friends placing a
bench at his favourite spot, near the locks at Baggot Street
Bridge.

Roscommon

FRENCHPARK

In the Protestant churchyard, a mile and a half west of the
village crossroads, is the grave of the poet, playwright and
scholar DOUGLAS HYDE (1862–1949), who wrote both in
English and – under the name An Craoibhín Aoibhinn – in
Irish. He was the founder, in 1893, of the Gaelic League, and
from 1938–45 served as the Irish Republic's first president.

KILRONAN

In the cemetery of Kilronan Abbey, by the shores of Lough
Meelagh up by the Sligo border, is buried TOIRDHEALBHACH
Ó CAERBHALLÁIN, or Carolan (1670–1738), the blind
harper, composer and poet, acclaimed by Goldsmith as 'the
Last Irish Bard'. Carolan was born in County Meath but
moved with his family to Connaught, where at the age of
fourteen he was blinded by smallpox. His fame spread across
Ireland and beyond. He loved his drink, though, and it was
thought that this hastened his end. Even at the point of
death, apparently, he called for drink, reports Goldsmith,
whereupon:

> Those who were standing round him, surprised at the
> demand, endeavoured to persuade him to the contrary; but

he persisted, and, when the bowl was brought him,
attempted to drink, but could not; wherefore, giving away
the bowl, he observed, with a smile, that it would be hard
if two such friends as he and the cup should part at least
without kissing, and then expired.

Carolan's wake went on for four days, and was attended by
crowds of people from all over Ireland.

Sligo

DRUMCLIFFE

Under bare Ben Bulben's head
In Drumcliff churchyard Yeats is laid.
An ancestor was rector there
Long years ago, a church stands near,
By the road an ancient cross.
No marble, no conventional phrase;
On limestone quarried near the spot
By his command these words are cut:
  Cast a cold eye
  on life, on death.
  Horseman, pass by!

Pedestrians, however, are allowed to stop and look. It's all
been done as poet, playwright, mystic and, later, statesman
W.B. YEATS (1865–1939) wanted it.

It would be a pity if he weren't here to enjoy it. For ten
years he wasn't, indeed. He died at Roquebrune, near

Monaco, where he'd gone for the sake of his health, and was given what was supposed to be a temporary burial there. It wasn't until 1949 that the Irish Navy brought his remains back to Dublin – and in any case there have been persistent rumours since that they brought the wrong man.

Waterford

WATERFORD

A wealthy merchant who took up the religious life after his wife died in 1789, EDMUND IGNATIUS RICE (1762–1844), founder of the Christian Brothers, a notorious teaching order, has his mausoleum here at Mount Sion. Rice was moved to found his order by the poverty and desperation he saw in Ireland's urban slums. A sort of low-rent Society of Jesus, the Christian Brothers' motto might have been 'Give us the boy, and we'll knock him about a bit, force-feed him basic learning and give you the conventional, conformist and rather unimaginative man.' Sneering aside, the brothers did bring education and opportunity to a large section of the Irish community who could never have hoped for such things before. Expanding their base of operations to the big cities of mainland Britain (subsequently, indeed, beyond), they played a crucial part in the rapid if ruthless creation of a Catholic middle class. ◆

INDEX